BUOYANCY ON THE BAYOU

Buoyancy on the Bayou

Shrimpers Face the Rising Tide of Globalization

Jill Ann Harrison

ILR Press

AN IMPRINT OF
CORNELL UNIVERSITY PRESS
ITHACA AND LONDON

First published 2012 by Cornell University Press
First printing, Cornell Paperbacks, 2012
Printed in the United States of America

Library of Congress Cataloging-in-Publication Data

Harrison, Jill Ann, 1977–
   Buoyancy on the bayou : shrimpers face the rising tide of globalization / Jill Ann Harrison.
       p. cm.
   Includes bibliographical references and index.
   ISBN 978-0-8014-5074-7 (cloth : alk. paper) — ISBN 978-0-8014-7833-8 (pbk. : alk. paper)
   1. Shrimp industry—Louisiana.   2. Shrimpers (Persons)—Louisiana.   3. Shrimp fisheries—Louisiana.   4. Globalization—Economic aspects—Louisiana.   I. Title.

   HD9472.S63U5263 2013
   338.3'72538809763—dc23   2012023311

Cornell University Press strives to use environmentally responsible suppliers and materials to the fullest extent possible in the publishing of its books. Such materials include vegetable-based, low-VOC inks and acid-free papers that are recycled, totally chlorine-free, or partly composed of nonwood fibers. For further information, visit our website at www.cornellpress.cornell.edu.

Cloth printing   10   9   8   7   6   5   4   3   2   1
Paperback printing   10   9   8   7   6   5   4   3   2   1

To Ryan and Henry

CONTENTS

ACKNOWLEDGMENTS

One of the first words I learned during my initial few days of living on the bayou was *lagniappe* (pronounced *lan-yap*). Lagniappe is commonly used to describe that little something extra given out of kindness. Metaphorically, it is the thirteenth roll in a baker's dozen. It is also a word that keeps crossing my mind as I think about the research and writing processes that have resulted in this book. There are numerous individuals who generously provided me with lagniappe, which facilitated this project's completion. I am especially grateful to those current and former shrimp fishers and their families who generously shared with me their thoughts about their livelihoods and provided me with many delicious meals. I am particularly thankful to those whom I call "June and Herbert Batiste" and their family, who provided me with a place to stay and an immeasurable amount of assistance with this project. This book could not have been completed without them. I also thank Reuben Teague for his generous hospitality whenever I'd visit the great city of New Orleans during my research.

Buoyancy on the Bayou is based on research that was initially collected while I was part of the Department of Sociology at the Ohio State University. There I was provided with tremendous assistance from a host of faculty and graduate student colleagues. First and foremost I thank Steven H. Lopez, adviser and friend, whose intellectual and emotional support provides the basis on which this research rests. His mentorship throughout my entire career as a sociologist embodies the definition of lagniappe. I offer heartfelt thanks for the degree of care and acumen that characterized the feedback he provided, both on the drafts he carefully read and through the countless conversations we had along the way. I owe Steve a lifetime of gratitude. I also thank Vincent Roscigno and Linda Lobao who contributed vital insight and encouragement to this project. Many of my colleagues also deserve special recognition. Thank you to Ryan Light, Melanie Hughes, Deniz Yucel, Susan Ortiz, Sherry Mong, Colin Odden, Jason Whitesel, Lori Muccino, Shelley Pacholok, and Dan Tope. Additionally, I offer my gratitude to many of my colleagues at the University of Oregon for their assistance and advice as I worked to complete this book. Thank you to Eileen Otis, J. Shiao, Ellen Scott, Richard York, and Jim Elliot.

Thanks go out to Fran Benson, Kitty Liu, Candace Akins, Karen Hwa, and Margery Tippie at Cornell University Press for a relatively smooth and very pleasant experience throughout the publication process. I am also grateful to James Cook for sharing his insight and some wonderful advice as I worked toward having this research published.

I extend gratitude to my family for the unflagging support they continually provide. My appreciation and love goes out to Thomas and Marilyn Harrison, whose encouragement provides the foundation to all of the roads that have led to my successes, big and small. I am forever indebted to my amazing sister, Becky Harrison, a bright and shining light in my life, and to Amelia Costanzo—both of whom I can always count on for encouragement and fun. I thank Michael and Linda Light for their warmth and love. To my son, Henry, I am eternally thankful; you make my life as joyful as it can possibly be. Finally, I thank my best friend and partner, Ryan Light. As a highly skilled sociologist, the intellectual contributions he made to this project are considerable. But more important, he throws in lagniappe on a daily basis in all that he sets out to do. This is especially true of the enduring patience and thoughtfulness he continuously and unconditionally provides. He somehow always manages to transform my excessive worry and anxiety into calm satisfaction. This is no easy feat. Thank you, Ryan.

Buoyancy on the Bayou

Prologue

In April on the bayou, shrimp fishers arrive at the docks early to prepare their boats for the upcoming May season, the busiest time of the year. But April 2010 would be different. On April 20 the Deepwater Horizon oil rig burst into flames and added yet another tragedy to an area already beset with them. Just as coastal communities of southeastern Louisiana had made it firmly on the road to recovery from the devastation wrought by hurricanes Katrina, Rita, and Ike, the BP oil spill cast a harsh spotlight on the region once again. For nearly three months, oil flowed freely from the damaged rig at an estimated rate of fifty thousand barrels a day until it was finally capped in mid-July. In the end almost five million barrels of oil flowed into the Gulf, making it the largest accidental marine oil spill in the history of the petroleum industry. Many shrimp fishers surely found themselves on the water that spring, but it wasn't to haul in their nets, heavy with shrimp. They sailed their boats into the black, oily water to lay oil-containment boom and to control the fires on the water that had been purposefully set to burn away the black slick. That spring, there was little else they could control.

In the weeks and months that followed the spill, journalists and scholars have raised important questions about the oil spill's impacts on those who depend upon coastal resources to earn a living: oyster harvesters, crabbers, and deep sea fishers. Shrimp fishers capture a great deal of this attention, perhaps because their large, majestic vessels are emblematic of southern Louisiana. Although it is too soon to know the full impact of the spill on the domestic industry, many of the reports on shrimp fishers end with a similar question: Will they be able to overcome the environmental challenges doled out by the spill? Although the spill has certainly made life more difficult for the shrimpers, most people do not realize that they have been struggling to stay afloat for almost a decade now, before both Hurricane Katrina and the Deepwater Horizon oil spill were part of the region's history.

What ultimately plunged the shrimp fishing industry into a state of crisis was not a storm or an accident, or was even related to the delicate ecosystem that provides such a bounty of resources. Rather, it was the result of industrial restructuring that opened the market to a flood of farm-raised foreign shrimp. If we are to truly understand how shrimp fishers will deal with the aftermath of the oil spill, we need to be familiar with the struggles that they were going through *before* the spill happened. This book is about a livelihood imperiled by waves of a different sort, the waves of globalization. It is the story of economic change and shrimpers' resistance to it. While the future remains uncertain, the shrimp fishers' tenacity in the decade-long struggle to remain afloat is not. From their determination and in some cases their loss, we can learn much about the importance of work in providing us with much more than our daily bread.

The story of how I came to be so interested in the working lives of shrimp fishers traces the collapse of the Louisiana shrimp fishing industry and provides a useful context for introducing this case study. As a lifelong, landlocked midwesterner who gets too seasick to go out on boats, my deep passion for understanding the working lives of shrimp fishers may seem a little curious. But there is a fairly strong thread that connects their experience to mine.

It begins with college graduation. Like many recent graduates, I had no idea what I wanted to do next. In the confusion and anxiety that often accompany the uncertainty of possibilities, there was a nagging feeling of wanderlust that I just could not ignore. Up until that point I'd lived in the town where I was raised, and I wanted to go somewhere unfamiliar and do something that pushed me out of my comfort zone, something that would enable me to get a bit dirty before I began a future career. Little did I know just how muddy I would get when I made the decision to join Ameri-Corps, the federal program that provides community service opportunities in exchange for a monetary award to defray educational expenses. Ameri-Corps offers thousands of opportunities in locations all across the country, and I was pretty open regarding what to do and where to go.

As I pored over the possibilities described on the program's website, I was drawn to one in particular, located in a small town in southeastern Louisiana. The job description outlined two primary duties. The first involved educating local students and other community members about the severe coastal erosion problems that Louisiana currently faces. I knew nothing about wetland ecology or the coastal erosion problem, but fortunately for me a familiarity with the region was not a requirement. The job's other duty involved trudging around in the marshes and swamps to plant different varieties of marsh grasses. Marsh grass, as I later found out, helps to hold soil in place and is therefore a valuable defense against the wind and waves that accelerate coastal erosion. The job sounded perfect: it would both take me to an exotic location and allow me to get my hands dirty and my feet wet, quite literally. I applied for the job, and as good fortune would have it, a few months later—in January of 2001—I found myself leaving town and heading toward Louisiana, to a town I refer to in this book as Bayou Crevette.

On the day I pulled into town for what was to be a year-long experience, I was immediately struck by the presence of the shrimping industry, a presence signaled throughout the town. Most visible were the shrimp boats, impressive vessels sitting docked along the bayou that flowed the entire length of the community. Even though it was a chilly winter day, people were out on their boats, working hard to get them in order for the upcoming spring season. Boatbuilding businesses were in evidence, too, permitting passersby a glimpse of boats in progress. I would be tracking this progress later on my daily commute through town. The streets were lined with other sea-related businesses—net shops, hardware stores, and seafood docks—and all of these hummed with activity. In addition to the

sights was the smell, that of the muddy bayou commingling with the distinctive, pungent odor of seafood that is natural to fishing communities.

I had been instructed by the AmeriCorp program's director to go first
to the home of her parents, June and Herbert Batiste, for a welcoming dinner (I use pseudonyms to refer to participants throughout the book). Their
cozy little house, partially hidden by the gigantic live oak tree that took up
much of their front yard, sat less than a hundred yards from the bayou.
Over a delicious gumbo dinner, June described how she and Herbert—
who were at that time in their early seventies—had worked a significant
portion of their lives as shrimpers. They retired from shrimping in the
1980s, after the last of their five children left the area to attend college.
But because they had a half-dozen grandchildren, they wanted to build a
new boat so they could give them the experience of trawling, in the process
teaching them the importance of hard work and passing along a love and
appreciation for the craft that was so intimately connected to their family
history.

Like others I met during that year, the Batistes were intensely proud of
what the shrimp fishing industry had provided their town and their family. Many of our conversations focused on the many adventures they'd had
aboard their beloved wood-hulled boat, aptly named *La Belle Vie* (meaning "the good life"). Their boat was not only the means by which they had
earned a living it was also their vehicle for exploring the world. During
their younger days, June, Herbert, and their five children had sailed the
shrimp boat to many locations in Central and South America, as well as
the Caribbean. June took great delight in telling me the story of how they
sailed *La Belle Vie* up the East Coast to Boston for their daughter's graduation from college. As part of the festivities, they hosted the university's
president for a celebratory meal on board. They prepared the meal in the
La Belle Vie's small galley, using shrimp and crabs that they themselves
had harvested from the inland waters of the Gulf of Mexico near their
home. This story—told and retold to me on multiple occasions—certainly
illustrated and reinforced the pride they took in their livelihood and their
Cajun roots.

It became obvious to me early on in my experience that people in the
town took great pride and enjoyment in preparing meals for others—
especially outsiders. And being an outsider myself, I enjoyed countless

meals cooked by people who were eager to feed the "AmeriCorps kids," as we were known throughout the community (although I was in my early twenties at the time). These delicious meals almost always showcased food that came directly from the rich, natural areas that surrounded the bayou community. The indigenous ingredients included a variety of meats—crab, shrimp, alligator, crawfish, many types of gulf fish—as well as local produce—okra, cushaw, and mirliton. Meals were usually accompanied by the story of how the ingredients were obtained. If whoever prepared the meal had not caught or harvested them themselves, then they had usually been given them by somebody who had—a friend, relative, or neighbor. Some of my hosts loved to boast about how—unlike those of us up North—they never had to buy seafood, adding—rather sanctimoniously—that they would not want to eat that frozen stuff anyway.

Fresh shrimp was almost always incorporated into these home-cooked meals, and as a result I heard a great deal about the shrimping industry. Older folks told me stories about shrimping before they had motorized boats, and about how they had quit school—sometimes at age eleven or twelve—to learn the craft from their parents or grandparents. Younger people filled me in on current practices as they described the trip that harvested the shrimp for our current meal. A few of my AmeriCorps co-workers got to enjoy the experience of shrimp fishing firsthand; regrettably, my strong susceptibility to seasickness prevented me from enjoying it myself. But in any event, local pride in the shrimp industry was highly apparent, and multiple times throughout the year shrimp was celebrated in the form of shrimp and seafood festivals, shrimp boils, and seafood cook-offs. Every day it seemed that people wanted to talk about their families, their work, and their community. Little did I know then that this generosity was my first lesson in ethnography and that these stories would eventually occupy over ten years of my life.

After I planted thousands of marsh grass plugs, and talked to hundreds of school kids about environmental issues, the year-long program came to a successful end. AmeriCorps on the bayou was a perfect antidote to my post-college case of wanderlust. Renewed from months of crawling around in the thick, odiferous mud of the wetlands, I decided to begin my "real life" in graduate school back in the Midwest. But surrounded by books and articles in my small, shared windowless office, I could not forget about the bayou. I often found myself yearning to go back, to breathe in the moist air of the wetlands, to soak up the sounds of the fiddle and accordion, and to eat the delicious Cajun food that, like so much of regional cuisine, can only truly be found in its place of origin. As a result, through the years I made several trips back to the bayou.

The first trip I made back to Bayou Crevette was in 2003 to visit some friends. During that trip, I certainly got my fill of the thick and hearty food and swamp air, but I could not help but notice the palpable feeling of uneasiness and concern that lingered when I asked how folks had fared with the latest shrimping season. This anxiety and pessimism had simply not existed during my AmeriCorps year, when fisher folk and deckhands alike had gloated about the shrimp (and cash) they were hauling in. But this time people described how dockside prices had abruptly fallen and told of the rumors swirling around that the depressed prices would be permanent. Prices had plummeted in the past, they told me, but this time was different—this time they feared they would not rebound. Surely, I thought, they must be exaggerating, as just two short years ago the industry had been vibrant and very much alive. I was hesitant to believe what I heard, although I was saddened just the same.

The severity of the decline crystallized when I visited June and Herbert. After only one full season of fishing on their brand-new boat, they were already expressing great regret over having built it. They were struggling to keep up with all of their expenses, even though the bulk of the labor was done by one of their sons and their grandchildren, who worked only for the bounty of their catch and the richness of experience as payment. I left the bayou feeling troubled and concerned, and when I went back to Ohio and the grind of graduate school, I continued to keep tabs on the state of the industry.

Two years later, in 2005, Hurricane Katrina ravaged the Gulf Coast. Within a month of its devastation, I went back to the bayou, this time to offer my services to those who needed help with recovery. Fortunately, Bayou Crevette had been spared the level of flooding and destruction experienced by New Orleans and other coastal communities. It had lost one of its prominent seafood docks (later rebuilt), and the storm debris in the Gulf caused damage to nets and made fishing difficult, but by and large the community's industry dodged the lion's share of Katrina's wrath. But hurricanes aside, the industry was still caught firmly in the grip of a downward spiral. People continued to worry about the plummeting dockside shrimp prices, but this time their worries were compounded by the sharp increases in overhead costs, especially fuel costs, which had spiked sharply in the middle of the decade. High fuel costs subsequently pushed up the prices of other necessities, like ice, groceries, and supplies. It was plainly evident from the widespread worry and dismay expressed by shrimpers and nonshrimpers alike that the industry's future was even grimmer than a couple of years before.

In addition, there were other, more visible changes in the shrimping situation that went beyond verbal worry and dismay. Most noticeable was the substantial number of boats that lay docked along the bayou adorned with "for sale" signs. The increase in the number of these signs became the topic of a joke that I heard (time and again) from shrimpers: "It's gotten so bad that everyone has decided to change the name of their boat to the same thing, *The For Sale*." Unfortunately, among the renamed boats was June and Herbert's almost-new, blue-hulled vessel, used for only two shrimp seasons. Other discernible changes included the closing of businesses—net shops, ice sheds, and seafood docks. The boatbuilding business was also reeling, as people were no longer willing to bet on the industry's future with brand-new boats.

To put it simply, the shrimping industry did not have the same presence in the community as it had only four years earlier, when I pulled into town for the first time.

I went back to Ohio feeling worried for June and Herbert's family and the others whose livelihoods were threatened. I was dismayed and confused over what had happened. Why had the industry tanked so sharply in such a short amount of time? This was especially perplexing given the growing popularity of shrimp over the past several decades. Shrimp has become less of a luxury food and more of a staple in the American diet. It was once something people splurged on for celebration, but now it is now possible to feast on "endless" piles of shrimp at all-you-can-eat buffets or even at fast food restaurants. The demand for shrimp among American consumers has been relatively strong and so, I thought, shrimp fishers should be doing better—not worse—than they had in the past. What was the problem?

After doing a little preliminary research, the predicament became abundantly clear. Shrimp fishers were now facing the same problem that those working in the steel mills during the 1970s: cheap imports. The waves of globalization had finally crashed into the shores of the U.S. commercial shrimp fishing industry.

As I dug around for more information, I found out that around the late 1990s, the technology for growing shrimp in hatcheries had been greatly improved. As a result, countries that exported shrimp—China, Thailand, Vietnam, and Ecuador to name the largest—were able to ramp up production. Although the technology for cultivating shrimp in ponds began to expand as far back as 1980, these endeavors had been plagued for years by crop failures and disease outbreaks (Belton and Little 2008). However, by the end of the century most of these problems had been remedied. As a result, the United States experienced a dramatic increase in the importation rate of foreign, farm-raised shrimp.

While this may be good news for the shrimp-loving American consumer, who is now able to indulge in low-priced all-you-can-eat shrimp fests at the local Red Lobster, the news has not been so favorable for domestic shrimp producers. As more imports poured in, dockside prices for U.S. shrimpers plummeted sharply and quickly. Similar to what had happened to the U.S. steel industry, shrimp fishers now had to struggle to effectively compete against low-wage producers overseas. The sharp rise in overhead costs—especially fuel—had made it even more difficult for shrimp fishers to turn a profit. I was both fascinated and saddened by what was happening on the bayou, particularly by how the shrimpers were dealing with the prospect—and the actual incidence—of leaving their industry behind.

My interest in the collapse of the shrimping industry is in no way haphazard but is easily traced back to my own experience with occupational decline. I was born and raised in Youngstown, Ohio, a rust belt town that experienced great hardship when the steel industry completely collapsed in the early 1980s. My father was one of the tens of thousands of steelworkers there who lost a livelihood with the industry's ruin, and although I was just a little girl, I experienced firsthand many of the negative effects of deindustrialization. In addition to the financial problems created by unemployment, my father's anxiety and tension regarding the inability to find reliable work took a toll on his self-worth. As a young child I watched as the once-quiet neighborhood I grew up in quickly transformed into the crime-ridden and poverty-stricken area that it remains today. And I watched as my parents became more and more worried about how we were going to make ends meet. As I became a little older and more aware of things like class differences, I realized that my family's struggles were hardly an isolated event. I learned from friends and relatives that our struggles were being experienced in other houses in our neighborhood and those in other parts of the city.

Given this deeply personal experience, I wondered if occupational decline would have the same effects on the bayou as it did in Youngstown. Many questions began to emerge: What, exactly, was happening to the once-vibrant Louisiana shrimping industry? How were shrimp fishers responding to the collapse of an industry that is not only important to their economic survivalbut is also linked tightly to their heritage and cultural identities? And how might the community be changed by occupational decline? These questions continued to nag at me, despite being nearly a thousand miles away, and eventually my desire for answers led me back down to the swamps and marshes of the bayou. And with June and Herbert graciously allowing me to stay with them while I conducted my field research, I spent the summers of 2006 and 2007 traipsing around the community, trying to locate and talk to as many current and former shrimp fishers as possible. Fortunately, most of the shrimp fishers I encountered generously permitted me access to their working lives, often inviting me into their homes or onboard their boats (that sat docked as we chatted). Their stories are presented here.

This book is about shrimp fishers from one coastal community in southeastern Louisiana. But more generally, it is about how individuals respond to large-scale economic change and industrial restructuring, largely a consequence of the forces of globalization. Throughout the book, I draw from the rich ethnographic data I collected to show how local actors respond to economic challenges. And while focusing on the responses of the shrimpers to the collapse of their industry is culturally worthy in itself, there is value that goes well beyond it. While most studies of industrial decline focus on communities where few jobs are available after an industry leaves, my case study shows that even though alternative employment opportunities exist, some forgo those opportunities to try to fulfill what they perceive as their cultural calling. Others reluctantly leave this identity behind. From the shrimp fishers' experiences with industrial decline, we stand to gain a greater understanding of the importance of the work that we do in shaping our social lives and our understanding of the world around us.

1

SETTING SAIL

What We Can Learn from Louisiana Shrimp Fishers

If you have ever purchased wild-caught American shrimp, there's a good chance that it was caught by a Louisiana shrimp fisher. Louisiana is a major player in the U.S. seafood industry. Nearly one-third of the nation's seafood comes directly from Louisiana's estuaries, wetlands, and coastal areas.[1] But if the seafood industry is a crowning feature for Louisiana, shrimp is its largest jewel. Of the entire Gulf of Mexico region (Alabama, Western Florida, Louisiana, Mississippi, and Texas) that supplies the overwhelming majority of domestic shrimp—nearly 85 percent in 2006—Louisiana was the leading producer, contributing almost half of the region's shrimp landings.[2]

Fortunately for Louisiana shrimp fishers, Americans love shrimp, making it the most-consumed seafood product in the United States today.[3] Served at the most elite restaurants, it can also be purchased at many fast food restaurants. But shrimp hasn't always enjoyed this kind of mass appeal. When the Louisiana shrimp fishing industry began in the late nineteenth century, shrimp was far from the popular staple that it is today. In fact, in large part because of its insect-like quality, shrimp was largely shunned by elite populations and was a food that mostly poor people ate. Marketed mainly to Chinese immigrants, it was also a common staple for the recently arrived Acadian exiles who settled the inhospitable coastal wetlands area of southern Louisiana. Americans, especially wealthy Americans, did not eat shrimp, even though it was available in the marketplace.[4]

The shrimp that was sold back then was not the fresh (or freshly frozen) product that we find in the seafood section of grocery stores today. Instead it came sun dried and salted or water packed in a can like today's sardines (a fish that is still sometimes associated with poor people and roustabouts in the same way shrimp used to be). Most shrimp was shipped to either China or to the American West, where a growing Chinese immigrant population created great demand for it.

As the final product differed from what we know today, so did the process through which it was harvested and sold. Shrimp was not caught by independent shrimp fishers who owned their own vessels, nor did the industry resemble anything close to what was depicted in the popular film *Forrest Gump* (a film that continues to shape the public's perception of shrimp fishers), with fleets of majestic shrimp boats bobbing gently along as clouds of sea gulls hover close above. Back in the early days, there were no motorized boats that dragged trawl nets across the ocean floor or pulled skimmer nets atop the shallow surface of the Gulf waters. Rather, shrimp was manually harvested by haul seines—large, weighted nets that encircled the shrimp—that were pulled by hand or by sailboat. Those who worked the nets, called *seiners*, were not owner-operators of their own nets or sailboats; instead they were low-wage workers who labored for companies, usually owned by the processors who packed and shipped the shrimp, who cared little about providing them with decent wages or working conditions.[5]

The Louisiana shrimp industry as we know it today was born out of conditions consistent with the processes of industrialization, whereby waged laborers supplied a specific commodity to distant and international markets. A series of technological advances that began at the start of the twentieth century profoundly transformed the industrial structure of shrimp fishing. The development of motorized boats and nets made it easier for fishers to trawl a larger area for a longer period of time, and refrigeration and shipping technologies permitted the shrimp to be shipped in a fresh state that many found more appealing than canned or dried. These important industrial changes had repercussions not only for those directly involved in shrimp production but for the nation as a whole. The meanings attached to the consumption of shrimp suddenly underwent a significant transformation. Initially a food for the poor and oppressed, it became a luxury product that only the wealthy could afford to consume on a regular basis. For the nonwealthy who could not afford shrimp's high cost, it came to symbolize a celebration, a special occasion worthy of splurge. And shrimp held its reputation as a delicacy for most of the twentieth century.

Up until around the year 2001, business hummed along as usual for shrimp fishers. There were good years and bad years—years when haul totals or prices would fall or rise—but generally catching shrimp provided what fishers described to me time and again as "an honest living." Hard work translated into economic success, and shrimp fishers prided themselves on their relatively light debt loads and ability to make it without relying on government subsidies. Fishing provided shrimpers with enough money to pay cash for necessities and luxury items as well—new trucks, fishing gear, and vacations (usually hunting trips). Debts were kept to a minimum, and on the rare occasions when fishers needed to buy things on credit, they were quick to pay them off. But shortly after the turn of the new century, Louisiana shrimp fishers were unexpectedly confronted with one of the most devastating floods they had ever been up against. This flood, however, was not the kind that results from broken levees or unseasonably high amounts of rainfall. Instead, it was the result of what some have called the "pink tsunami": the extraordinary increase in the amount of farm-raised foreign imports into the U.S. seafood market. Ever since then, shrimpers have struggled to get by.

For shrimp-loving consumers, imports have made the product much more affordable, and as a result shrimp has undergone yet another image makeover: from luxury food to kitchen staple. Because of imports, we can now purchase shrimp at the drive-through window of some fast food restaurants for less than the cost of a cup of Starbucks coffee. Although we might assume differently, the increase in demand has not been a boon for domestic shrimp fishers. Even working at full capacity, they can only supply what they catch from the sea. As consumer demand has increased, domestic shrimp's market share has held steady, estimated at around 10 percent over the past several decades. The problem for shrimpers is that the flood of imports resulted in a quick and dramatic plunge of dock-side prices. Domestic producers relying upon wild-caught methods of pro-duction currently face enormous difficulties in staying afloat. For many shrimp fishers, the difficulties have been too much to bear, and they have chosen to leave the water permanently.

The hand dealt to shrimp fishers—their struggle to survive in an indus-try being taken over by foreign imports—is in many ways similar to that previously dealt to millions of industrial laborers in the 1970s and 1980s. The process of decline in the manufacturing sector—particularly steel, auto, textiles, and apparel—is generally referred to as *deindustrialization*. Deindustrialization is a process that has been around for quite some time, but the factors that contribute to it have shifted over the decades. The earli-est research on deindustrialization and economic dislocation—that is, un-employment that results from layoffs or plant closings—attributed them to firms' abilities to produce more with fewer workers vis-à-vis job-cutting technological advancements.[6] But since the 1980s, most researchers have at least partly associated them with intensifying economic globalization processes that enable firms to outsource production to low-wage regions of the world.[7] Globalization is a widely deployed concept in social scientific research, and as such it has been the subject of debate since it burst onto the academic scene. The abundance of research on the causes, character, and consequences of economic globalization reflects its complexity as a concept and the difficulties involved in encapsulating its core essence. Defining it, therefore, is always a tricky endeavor, but my understanding of economic globalization follows the lead of the political sociologists David Brady, Jason Beckfield, and Wei Zhao, who define it "as international economic exchange and the flow of goods, services, people, information, and capital across national boundaries."[8]

Economic globalization is driven by several key mechanisms, most no-tably improvements in transportation and communication technologies that make doing business more efficient. Some globalization scholars have shown that intensifying globalization processes—usually measured by looking at international trade and investment—facilitate the movement of production to developing countries and thus contribute at least partially to deindustrialization in the manufacturing sector.[9] As economies become more globalized, foreign competition puts pressure on firms to remain competitive. One solution has been to relocate production to countries where operational costs are held down by extremely low wages and lax regulations. To put it simply, it is no longer cost effective to manufacture or purchase domestically produced goods.

The shift toward a global economy has fundamentally changed the livelihoods of many American workers in the manufacturing sector, but it has also affected extractive industries such as farming, mining, and logging.[10] Plant closings, permanent layoffs, and the selling off of the family farm have all been unfortunate outcomes for workers affected by this process. Globalization and deindustrialization have left in their wake a host of personal and social problems for individuals, families, and communities. When companies pack up and leave town, they not only leave behind crumbling infrastructure, they also abandon entire communities. Displaced workers are of course the most immediately affected, as they suffer the direct loss of income and the stress and anxiety that come along with the uncertainty of what is next for them. But the process does not end with the shutting of factory doors or the receiving of layoff notices. It is a protracted process that causes suffering indirectly for others as well: the small business owners dependent upon customers who have extra money to spend; home owners whose houses plummet in value as people move away and their houses fall into disrepair; and children who attend deteriorating schools that are deprived of income provided by a shrinking base of taxpayers. The importance of work and industry goes well beyond the bank accounts and 401(k)s of those who take home paychecks. Work provides the backdrop against which entire communities and the people within them thrive. The sociologists Roger Friedland and A. F. Robertson eloquently captured the multidimensionality of the concept of work when they stated:

> Work provides identities as much as it provides bread for the table; participation in commodity and labor markets is as much an expression of who you are as what you want. Although economists typically assume that work is a disutility to be traded off against leisure or income, it actually contains other kinds of utility, ranging from the expression of an identity (I am a metal worker), to relative performance (I am a good metal worker), social value (it is good to be a metal worker—or—it is good to work), gender (it is good for a man to be a metal worker), or prestige (it is better to be a metal worker than a salesperson).[11]

This book is about the plight of a specific group of workers recently impacted by globalization processes and the ensuing collapse of a domestic industry: Louisiana shrimp fishers in a small bayou community. But on a broader level, it is a study of how workers make sense of the uncertainties and risk that accompany our continually shifting, restructuring industrial world. By exploring on a deeper level how they respond to industrial decline, I bring to the surface a more comprehensive understanding of the consequences of the processes of globalization for those living in smaller communities with long-standing cultural distinctiveness. I bring Friedland and Robertson's conceptualization of work with me through this analysis, because it crystallizes beautifully the sentiments shared with me by shrimp fishers and other community members I encountered through my research. Because people identify themselves in large part through occupation and work, changes in work processes alter personal identity and the meanings that people bring to their lives. Throughout the book, I provide a nuanced understanding of the degree to which livelihoods defined by local cultures and traditions survive in an era in which there are clearly identifiable economic and social changes stemming from the processes of globalization.

This study is part of a rich tradition of research on the dynamic relationship between occupational decline, community, and culture. Previous work on this topic has brought to light the growing significance of cities and communities as sites of globalization processes through which a restructuring of political, economic, and cultural arrangements occurs that reflects the shift toward a global system of production.[12] Other relevant research examines how global forces have more generally impinged upon the structure of work processes and local cultures.[13] I contribute to this important work in at least two ways. First, by treating the reformulation of occupational and cultural identities as a course of action linked to changes in traditional work practices, I stress the importance of broader historical, economic, and spatial contexts to local actors' meaning-making processes, that is, how it is that they make sense of their social worlds and their places within it. I also investigate how members of a small community confront the processes of globalization in order to preserve what they can of traditional ways of life. My analysis highlights the agency—or the capacity to act—that people have with regard to how they reorganize economic and social lives in a way that connects to a deeply ingrained cultural identity. Globalization is not merely an imposing condition for communities but is an ongoing process shaped by interaction that accounts for cultural practices across time and place. This consideration of globalization as a highly nuanced process diverges from and challenges the more traditional academic treatment of globalization as a monumentally imposing force resulting primarily in top-down changes.[14]

From Wageworker to Captain: The Evolution and Structure of the Present-Day Shrimp Fishing Industry

In order to fully comprehend shrimp fishers' responses to the crisis, it is helpful to have a basic understanding of the structure and function of the present-day industry. Most shrimp fishers are owner-operators of their vessels, but as mentioned previously, it wasn't always this way. Shrimp fishers at the turn of the last century were typically low-wage seiners working for companies that provided few if any workplace protections. A series of technological advances beginning around the 1920s created the conditions that brought shrimp fishers from their position of waged underlings to serving as captains of their own ships, quite literally. The first of these technological advances was the introduction of the otter trawl net that occurred in the late 1910s.[15] An otter trawl is a conical, bag-shaped net that is dragged behind a gasoline- or diesel-powered boat. Soon thereafter the skimmer—or butterfly—net was developed. Skimmer nets are attached to the bow of the boat and can be lowered perpendicularly on either side (giving the boat a butterfly-like appearance) to skim the shallow surface of the water, where shrimp are especially abundant at night.[16] The development of the shrimp trawling vessel was beneficial because it reduced the labor power necessary to harvest shrimp that haul seines required.

Other important advances include improvements in refrigeration, shipping, and transportation technologies. Trawl boats equipped with ice could travel farther distances for longer periods of time, dramatically increasing the volume of shrimp landings. Refrigeration technologies also permitted shrimp processors to shift their production away from canned and dried products—which could better sustain the hot, humid climate of south Louisiana—and toward fresh and frozen shrimp that were much more appealing to American consumers. As a result, shrimp and seafood gained significantly in popularity among U.S. consumers. But despite its growing popularity, in comparison to meat—beef, pork, and poultry—it was still a relatively scarce product. In the 1940s industrialized agricultural techniques resulted in unprecedented rates of meat production, making various types of meat more affordable. But unlike cattle, chicken, or pig farmers, shrimp fishers are subject to the seasonal harvest of a limited capacity commodity. Because of this, seafood supplies could not outstrip demand, and shrimp along with other seafood products (such as oysters and lobsters) came to be considered a luxury food. Shrimp prices reflected its newly found status as a delicacy and quickly spiked: in the decade between 1940 and 1950, shrimp prices increased by over three times in real terms.[17]

Together, the decreased labor requirements that trawl boats facilitated and the rise in dockside prices due to increased demand created the conditions for the owner-operatorship of boats that characterizes the industry today. In addition to owning their own boats, some shrimp fishers pooled their resources to purchase and operate ice boats that delivered ice to the boats so they could stay out longer and catch more shrimp. Out of these developments, shrimp fishers gained considerable independence from the shrimp processors that had previously employed them. But while no longer beholden to the companies for waged employment, they were not—and generally never have been—fully independent from processors. As the geographer Brian Marks explains, by the mid-twentieth century

> a pattern of local market power in the fishery began to emerge of nominally independent, owner-operating shrimpers, free to sell to any of a variety of middlemen but often tied to particular buyers by a variety of financial and personal ties. These dealers sold to processors that had oligopolistic power to determine the prices those shrimp buyers could pay (while themselves subject to pressures on prices from buyers for national markets they could not control). The basic framework of this system remains in place to the present.[18]

Throughout most of the postwar era, Louisiana shrimp fishers enjoyed relative stability in average dockside prices. Production and prices peaked in the late 1970s, largely as the result of a boatbuilding boom spurred on by an increase in federal loan guarantees, but they declined slightly over the 1980s. The 1990s were a period of economic growth in the United States that enabled consumers to spend more money on such luxury food items as shrimp.[19] Indeed, the trawlers I spoke with described the 1990s as among the best years that the shrimp fishery had ever experienced. While imports began to creep incrementally into the market at higher and higher rates throughout the late 1980s and early 1990s, demand growth offset the increase in volume, and dockside prices stabilized from their fall through the 1980s. Shrimp fishers enjoyed the prosperity of favorable market conditions, and even as late as 2001, some—like June and Herbert Batiste—bet on the continued viability of the industry and made investments in new boats. These decisions were made in complete unawareness that only a few years later a glut of farm-raised imported shrimp would ride the waves of the pink tsunami, crash ashore, and force the industry into a sharp and perhaps permanent decline.

The Industrial Structure of Louisiana Shrimp Fishing

How do shrimp that spawn so far out in the Gulf of Mexico come to land on our plates? A general comprehension of the fishery's industrial structure is useful for the purpose of this project for several reasons. For starters, a working knowledge facilitates a greater understanding of exactly why the domestic shrimp fishery has recently fallen into a sharp decline, and why shrimp fishers are sometimes forced to leave the industry or suffer the consequences of staying afloat. Furthermore, gaining basic insight into the industrial structure enables us to better understand the potential solutions that some shrimp fishers have put forth as a way to remain viable despite the decline. Finally, throughout my research it became clear that shrimp fishers often refer to shrimp processors and dock owners in an adversarial context. The industrial structure of the modern-day shrimp fishery forces most shrimp fishers to rely on processors and/or dock owners to purchase their products, making the fishers subject to the prices offered. What is more, when we recall how the fishers started out in the industry subjected to poor working conditions and low wages set by processors, we see that the history of the shrimp fishing industry is marked with that adversarial relationship, the legacy of which continues today.

Figure 1 depicts the general structure of the contemporary shrimp fishing industry. The Louisiana shrimp industry is divided into four distinct sectors, and participants are identified by the function they perform: production, handling/wholesaling, processing, and retailing.[20] Shrimp fishers, who typically own and operate the boats and nets used to harvest shrimp,

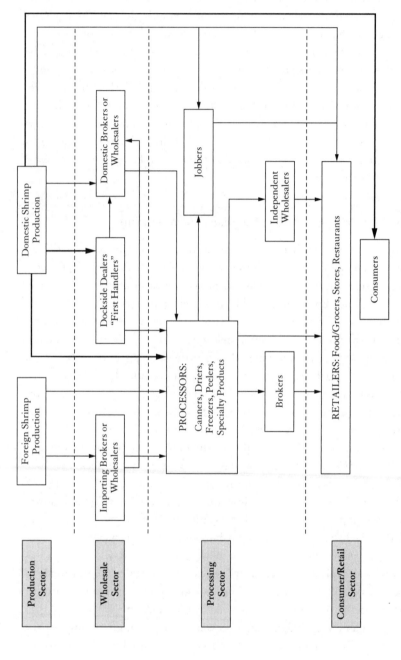

Figure 1. Structure of the Louisiana shrimp fishing industry.
Source: Diop 1999.

are located within the production sector as domestic shrimp producers. A small percentage of Louisiana's domestic shrimp is supplied by shrimp fishers in other states (mainly Texas and Alabama), but Louisiana shrimp comprises most of the domestic supply. The other component of the production sector consists of foreign producers who supply shrimp products that are produced and harvested in foreign countries and shipped to the United States. Some of the imported shrimp are wild caught by foreign shrimp trawlers, but the bulk of the imported supply is comprised of shrimp raised and harvested on aquacultural shrimp farms. Over the past decade the volume of imported shrimp in the U.S. market has risen sharply. This increase in imported shrimp is a significant factor in the collapse of the domestic shrimp fishery and will be discussed in greater detail later in the chapter.

The next sector of the shrimp industry is comprised of the "first handlers," or wholesalers, who are engaged in the handling of the shrimp landings. Dockside dealers (or seafood docks) are located within this sector. Dealers mainly purchase shrimp directly from the fishers, but they often offer other services to shrimpers, such as selling ice or renting dock space so the shrimpers can tie their boats up nearer to the gulf. Some dockside dealers also engage in importing shrimp from other countries to sell to processors.[21] Although some shrimp fishers bypass the docks and sell directly to the consumer, most of the shrimp fishers that I spoke with continued to sell their shrimp to a seafood dock. At the time of research, there were three primary seafood docks located in Bayou Crevette. One of those later closed as a result of the import crisis (but before the BP oil spill disaster).

The third sector is made up of shrimp processors. Shrimp processors are typically firms that buy shrimp from the first handlers (the docks) and process it into consumer products. Depending on specific demands, processors (or the "jobbers" that they contract the work out to) typically peel and devein, can, dry, bread, or freeze the shrimp. From there the shrimp is typically sold to brokers or independent wholesalers, who in turn sell directly to the consumers in the retail sector.

Because of the volume of shrimp that Louisiana produces, the shrimp industry is a highly valuable resource to the state. It alone represents about 85 percent of the total value of the state's edible fishery production.[22] The shrimp industry as a whole—the harvesting, handling, processing, distribution, and retailing of shrimp—contributes significantly to the state economy. At the end of the twentieth century, it was estimated that the industry contributed nearly $2 billion to the state economy and supplied approximately 22,000 full-time jobs.[23] At the local level, the industry's importance is even more apparent. In Terrebonne Parish, one of the state's largest shrimp-producing parishes, the shrimp industry supplied over 3,100 jobs and generated around $52.07 million in salaries and wages.[24]

The Import Crisis

In 2001 dockside prices tumbled precipitously. To illustrate this trend, dockside prices for Northern Gulf of Mexico (including Louisiana) 36/40 count[25] headless shrimp went from $4.15/lb at the beginning of the May 2001 season to $3.10 that November. The following May headless 36/40s sold for $2.60/lb and then fell to $2.18/lb by the end of the season in November.[26] This drop in dockside prices was unprecedented and much unexpected, and since 2001 prices have continued to remain low, as depicted in Figure 2.[27]

Several key factors play into the collapse of dockside prices. First, in 2001 the U.S. economy began to falter, and as a result domestic demand for shrimp flattened out. At the same time, shrimp imports continued to

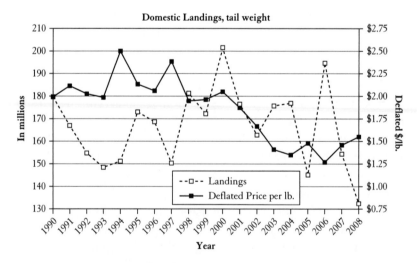

Figure 2. Deflated ex-vessel value expressed in real per-pound prices, 1990–2008.
Source: Haby, Rickard, and Falconer 2010.

pour into the U.S. market at increasing rates.[28] For multiple reasons, the United States is the most attractive market for shrimp exporters, far more so than the European Union or Japan, the other major markets for imports. Around 2000 the economies of EU countries and Japan were much more economically weak relative to the United States and thus unable to absorb any extra shrimp.[29] Additionally, unlike Europe and Japan, the United States had no significant tariffs or quantitative restrictions on imported shrimp. Both the lack of tariffs and the strength of the U.S. dollar relative to other currencies provided incentives for importers to dump their products on U.S. shores.[30]

But perhaps more significantly, the dramatic downturn the industry suffered is best explained by another factor: the sudden overabundance of farm-raised shrimp. Shrimp aquaculture has existed for hundreds of years in various forms, but present-day shrimp farming practices were developed in Taiwan in the 1970s and then quickly diffused to parts of Southeast Asia and South America.[31] Despite the availability of aquacultural technologies, most imports entering the U.S. market prior to the 1990s were harvested in the same way as in the present-day Gulf, through trawling. If shrimp farming is such an old method for harvesting shrimp, why did it take so long for farmed shrimp to dominate the import market and eventually collapse dockside prices?

The answer to this question in many ways parallels the story of the growth of the modern-day agro-food system in the United States. In the postwar era, the American diet began to include a great deal more of grain-fed livestock, especially poultry, beef, and pork. The swift increase in meat consumption wasn't because Americans suddenly and collectively decided that they liked those meats enough to incorporate them into almost every meal. On the contrary, the American diet became more meat-centric as a result of changes in productive technologies and the governmental policies that led to huge surpluses for meat and grain producers. The creation of the agrichemical industry (which included corporations such as Monsanto and Archers Daniels Midland [ADM]) provided new means for farmers to minimize some of the risks historically associated with farming: crop failures due to pests, poor soil quality, or livestock diseases.

As a result of these and other technologies (such as the creation and use of hybrid seeds), more produce and livestock could be grown on the same amount of land, a system of production known as *intensive agriculture*. The turn toward intensive agriculture resulted in huge surpluses in grain and corn. These surpluses drove prices down and led to insecurities among producers. Governmental policies enacted to deal with problems created by surpluses have certainly favored larger farms, and smaller farmers faced pressures to turn toward more intensive means of growing food—or as food journalist Michael Pollan puts it, "to get big or get out."[32] As a result, many family farmers have been forced out of business. Industrialized farming has now become the norm.

The development and growth of the shrimp farming industry closely parallels this history of industrialized farming. In the 1950s demand for shrimp far surpassed what domestic producers could supply on their own. To meet demand, shrimp imports began to gain a significant share of the U.S. market. As mentioned earlier, most of that imported shrimp was harvested through the same seasonally based trawling methods used by most domestic producers today. With domestic and foreign trawlers working at full capacity and demand for shrimp continuing to grow,[33] in the 1970s foreign producers began to seek out other methods of harvesting shrimp to meet this demand and turned to aquaculture as a possible solution.

The earliest shrimp farming enterprises were typically quite small and produced enough shrimp to meet the needs of families or small communities. But as the global demand for shrimp escalated, shrimp farming took a sharp and decisive turn toward a model of intensive production (that is, increasing the volume of shrimp produced in a designated area). Foreign producers thus followed the path taken by the industrialized grain and livestock farmers in the postwar United States. Funded in large part by the same U.S.-based agribusinesses that spurred intensive agriculture—ConAgra, Armour, ADM, and Ralston Purina among them—foreign producers cleared more land for shrimp farms and ratcheted up the concentration of shrimp grown in ponds.[34] Intensive aquaculture, like factory farming, has been targeted by critics for the host of problems that results from increasing concentrations of shrimp.[35] These problems are what account for the decades-long gap between the rise of intensive shrimp farming and the arrival of the pink tsunami on the shores of the United States. For nearly thirty years, shrimp farms were plagued by many forms of disease that kept them from producing shrimp healthy enough for export. Just like cows or pigs, shrimp raised in close proximity in industrialized shrimp farms—akin to saltwater feedlots—are highly susceptible to disease, in large part because they are forced to live in high concentrations of their own waste. Poor management by shrimp farmers has only exacerbated the problems. For example, on some Thai shrimp farms, chicken coops have been constructed over or nearby the shrimp ponds, so that the shrimp and fish can be fed by the chicken manure falling from above. This kind of unsanitary practice is what often results in a disease outbreak that can wipe out an entire crop.[36]

Disease outbreaks impelled shrimp farmers to figure out cost-efficient ways to control disease and improve the quality of their crops. While they had been experimenting for decades, it wasn't until the late 1990s that they achieved considerable success. To a small extent, diseases were reduced as a result of basic improvements in aquacultural practices, but most of the reduction was due to the use of antibiotics and other chemicals. The health of the shrimp improved, but there was no guarantee of the same for the humans who consumed it. Many of the chemicals used by shrimp farmers have been proven unsafe for human consumption. In 2001 food inspectors at the European Union detected the presence of chloramphenicol—a powerful antibiotic particularly harmful to humans and banned in most countries, including the United States and Canada—in shipments of shrimp from Thailand, India, China, Vietnam, and Indonesia and rejected the shrimp.[37]

Some of this rejected shrimp found its way into the U.S. market, where food safety regulations are not as stringent and where the chances of detection are much smaller. In 2006 only 1.34 percent of imported shrimp were given a sensory examination (looking at it, smelling it), and only 0.59 percent were inspected more thoroughly in a lab.[38] In fact, the dumping of the rejected shrimp accounts for a part of the sharp spike in shrimp imports, depicted in Figure 3. Despite the bans on shrimp tainted with chloramphenicol and other chemicals, they are still being used by many large industrial shrimp farms today. A 2003 survey of Thai shrimp farmers found that 74 percent reported using antibiotics on their shrimp.[39]

There are other reasons beyond the use of harmful chemicals that the shrimp farming industry has been a major source of controversy. Environmentalists have pointed toward the devastation of coastal wetlands and mangrove habitats that have resulted from the spread of industrial shrimp farms. In addition to a host of other ecological benefits, mangroves are essential to the prevention of coastal erosion. Like the marsh grasses

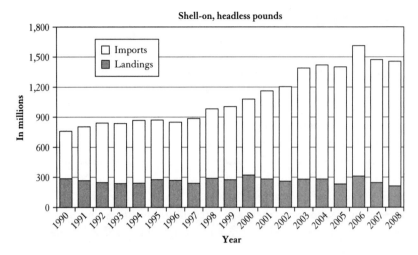

Figure 3. The contribution domestic landings and imports make to the
U.S. shrimp market, 1990–2008.
Source: Data from Haby, Rickard, and Falconer 2010.

planted along the banks of bayous, their root systems help to hold valuable sediments in place.[40] Wetland biologists estimate that in the past twenty years 35 percent of the world's mangrove forests have vanished, largely as a result of extensive shrimp farming.[41] In their book *Shrimp: The Endless Quest for Pink Gold,* nature writer Jack Rudloe and biologist Anne Rudloe point out the extent to which shrimp farms are responsible for mangrove destruction: "Eventually, many farm ponds became so disease-ridden that they had to be abandoned. When ponds were no longer viable, the shrimp farmers moved on, and in the same fashion as slash-and-burn farmers, they plowed up new mangroves to make new ponds, destroying still more fisheries."[42] Other researchers have highlighted how the struggle over land rights and access to mangroves has led to violence among residents who are dislocated from their homes for the purpose of constructing shrimp ponds.[43]

Despite these valid environmental concerns, one thing remains certain: imported farm-raised shrimp, however controversial or questionable, has taken over the market and appears to be here to stay. Between 1997 and 2001, annual exports of shrimp from all hundred or so countries that export to the United States grew by an average of 53.6 million pounds per year.[44] A sizeable majority of the shrimp, 49.3 million pounds, came from

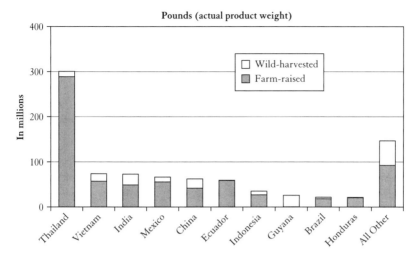

Figure 4. Import volumes from both the top ten and the remaining
shrimp-exporting countries delineated by production method, 2001.
Source: Data from Haby, Rickard, and Falconer 2010.

the ten largest exporting countries, shown in Figure 4. In 2001 Thailand
was clearly the largest exporter of shrimp to the United States. Since then,
Vietnam and China have substantially increased their production.[45] As
Figure 4 demonstrates, most of the imported shrimp is farm raised as op-
posed to wild harvested.

Today domestic producers only supply around 10 percent of the shrimp
in the U.S. market. Most demand—over a billion pounds a year—is met
through farm-raised imports.[46] Why do domestic fishers contribute so few
shrimp to the market? Quite simply, shrimp trawlers lack the productive
capability to meet increased consumer demand. Even working at full capacity, they can only produce what is available to them in the sea. So why
don't domestic producers take a hint from foreign producers and increase
their volume through farm-raising shrimp throughout the year? The answer is simple: climate. Although shrimp farms can be found in many locations across the country, they are usually very small ventures, as the United
States lacks the warm and balmy climates necessary to harvest multiple
crops a year. Turning toward shrimp farming is thus not an option for
domestic producers seeking to maintain viability in the shrimp industry.
Shrimp fishers wishing to remain competitive must therefore rely on less

efficient, more uncertain, and seasonal means of production. Before they even hit the water, they already are fighting an uphill battle of remaining competitive in the face of farm-raised imports. This battle bears the classic hallmark of modern-day deindustrialization.

Shrimp fishers are hardly the first group of workers forced to compete in a market flooded with cheaper imports. Deindustrialization is a long-standing process, but it grew more visible in the 1970s when steel and textile mills and auto assembly plants began to shut their doors, leaving workers out in the cold and communities to suffer the ravages of unemployment and economic uncertainty. A rich and extensive body of research undertaken by social scientists documents the consequences of deindustrialization for individuals, families, and communities. The bulk of this research focuses on the negative economic impacts for those affected by unemployment or its prospects. Plant closings and mass layoffs set off an unfortunate domino effect that often results in a sharp decline in the living standards and health and well-being of both individuals and their communities. People who have been permanently laid off as a result of downsizings or plant closings face a host of economic hardships as they struggle to make ends meet. For example, the ensuing stress caused by income loss puts tremendous strain on mental and physical health and personal relationships.[47] If couples can afford to, they divorce; those who can't afford the cost of legal separation may do so emotionally and live with the tensions.[48] At a time when people most need medical help or such social services as therapy or relationship counseling, the loss of health care benefits creates barriers to affordable access.

Communities as a whole also suffer from the ravages of economic dislocation. Cities such as Flint and Detroit, Michigan, and Youngstown, Ohio, are poster cities for the negative ramifications of deindustrialization. Even today these cities continue to struggle, decades after the auto and steel industries collapsed. At their worst, many deindustrialized communities experience severe population losses as people leave the community in search of other, more stable forms of employment. Those who are left behind have less income to spend on their homes and in local economies. Neighborhoods fill with vacant and neglected houses, sending property values on a downward spiral.[49] The ripple effects of mass economic dislocation force many businesses to close, diminishing employment opportunities for those needing work and contributing to unemployment statistics. The resulting loss of tax revenues can prevent communities from keeping up with routine maintenance and repairs, and as infrastructure crumbles, so do schools and hospitals and the overall quality of education and health care.[50] Many deindustrialized communities also suffered a spike in criminal activity as desperate individuals turn to illegal activity to make ends meet or to fuel drug addictions, another unfortunate side effect of unemployment. These continue to be realities against which residents who stay must struggle on a day-to-day basis.

Deindustrialization is not only a research interest of mine, it is also an intensely personal one, as I came of age in Youngstown, Ohio, during its darkest days. Although I was just a little girl when my dad lost his job at the steel mill, I can remember in vivid detail the struggles we went through as a family. I remember the shame my dad expressed when he had to use food stamps to buy our groceries, and my mother's embarrassment over her need to ask the priest at our church to forgive the tuition she owed so that my sister and I could continue to attend the Catholic school where we were enrolled. They fought and quarreled over who would have to ask their parents for the next loan so they could pay the bills. I also remember how our neighborhood was all of a sudden no longer a safe place to play. By the time I was ten years old, I witnessed a number of criminal acts, including a couple of gunfights and the mugging of a woman who lived on the next block. I also remember vividly the day when our eighty-year-old female neighbor was raped and robbed in her house during the middle of the day. A band of neighborhood men ran through the streets with their guns drawn to search for the perpetrator. After that day, we were no longer allowed to stray from where my parents could closely watch us.

Like so many others, our family moved to the suburbs before I went to high school, but through the years I would occasionally drive by my childhood home. It was painful to see the house falling more and more into disrepair, and the last time I drove by, not more than a year ago, I was shocked to find a vacant lot where my home once stood. I later found out that the house had burnt down, the cause of which was unknown, but it had been vacant for several years. There are still people who live in that neighborhood, children who will never know their neighborhood as the vibrant and safe place that it was when smoke rose from the chimneys of thriving mills.

On the bayou, once again witness to a community that I knew fairly well falling into industrial decline, I was worried. Would shrimp fishers on the bayou suffer the same fate as those living in rust belt communities who are still reeling from the loss of industry a quarter century later? The answer to this is probably not. There is a significant difference between the communities of Bayou Crevette and Youngstown, Ohio: Bayou Crevette is located near the oil industry, which supplies numerous skilled, well-paying jobs. Seventeen percent of Louisiana's workforce is employed in oil or oil-related jobs, many of which require skills transferable from shrimping, such as welding, repairing diesel engines, or captaining a tugboat or supply boat for offshore oil rigs. Shrimpers, therefore, aren't necessarily doomed to the same unfortunate fate of unemployed steel and auto workers, or of the family farmers in small rural communities who sell off their farms. In all likelihood, ex-trawlers will find their way into jobs that provide as good—if not better—a standard of living (the average annual oil-industry salary is around $95,000).[51]

We might be tempted to deem them as lucky survivors of industrial decline, or maybe even as victors, who not only escaped from the ravages of industrial decline but came out of it in even better shape. But would this be an accurate depiction? Is there really nothing lost in the transition from one job to the next? Is it safe to even assume that shrimpers would jump ship for higher ground when given the opportunity? Is work "as much an expression of who you are as what you want," as Friedland and Robertson suggest? These are the primary questions that have driven this research project. Over the past decade, a great deal of attention has been directed toward understanding the problems and pressures facing the domestic shrimp fishing industry more generally, but there has been little systematic research to examine the economic, cultural, and social impacts of such drastic changes for those most directly affected: the shrimp fishers, their families, and their communities. From the many conversations I held with folks who were both directly and indirectly affected by the import crisis, we stand to gain an understanding that fills the gaps in our knowledge.

Back to the Bayou

In order to determine exactly how shrimp fishers have weathered the waves of industrial decline, I traveled back to the bayou and spent six months there over a two-year period. The research conducted over this time provides the empirical foundations upon which the remainder of this book is based.[52] During this time, I tracked down and interviewed as many current and ex-shrimpers as possible in order to figure out how they were coping with and making sense of the import crisis and to ascertain what their future plans included. After three rounds of data collection in the field, I had interviewed fifty-four people total. I went into the field armed with academic assumptions gleaned from what I had read about deindustrialization and globalization (as well as from my own experience with it). In most scholarly and journalistic accounts of economic dislocation, the lack of viable alternative employment opportunities is always depicted as the means through which individuals and communities suffer when plants close or permanent layoffs occur. If other, comparable jobs are available for people in need of work, then we might expect many of the negative consequences to be minimized as workers settle into new jobs. I thus assumed that because shrimp fishers were fortunate to live in a region where there were more certain and well-paying jobs available, they would either be preparing to leave the industry or fighting to save it by way of collective action. Much to my surprise, the shrimp fishers' accounts of their lives post–import crisis did not match my expectations. In all, there were three primary ways that shrimp fishers had responded.

First, some shrimp fishers had stuck it out. These "persisters" comprise twenty-two, or well over a third, of the participants in my study. Although I expected there to be some period of mourning over leaving behind an industry so tightly connected to personal identity, I did not entertain the possibility that any of the fishers would outright reject the opportunity to make more money by taking other employment. Why would anyone choose to stay on board a sinking ship when higher ground is within jumping distance? This is especially puzzling given that they readily acknowledged that they could make better money if they sold their boats and took other employment. In other words, they knew that they did not have to suffer but chose to stick it out anyway. Moreover, they did so without hope that future conditions would improve.

As I went boat to boat to talk to fishers about their lives, it became clear that these individuals were highly dedicated to their craft. They loved what they did. The work is hard, dirty, and very smelly, but they were fond of what they did *because* of these features and not despite them. They lit up when they told me about the craft's connection to family history (as many of them were third- and fourth-generation), about how proud they were to carry the banner of their ancestry. But I also heard stories of hardship, about how financial struggles had tarnished the pride they took in what they do. They told me about the personal struggles they've had since the industry collapsed, how marital relationships had been strained by the difficulty of making it on the water now. Some people admitted to being depressed. And—most surprisingly—they also told me that they had no plans on leaving, even though they knew that they could.

Not all shrimp fishers chose to stay in the industry and struggle against the forces pushing them out. Some decided to leave the industry for other jobs. These individuals were more difficult to locate because once one leaves fishing, there are plenty of places to go to find employment. Most of these jobs were directly related to the oil industry (such as offshore worker or boat captain) or in one of its many supporting industries, such as welding, captaining tugboats, mechanical repair, or industry-related retail (selling marine equipment or heavy machinery, for example). By and large, these jobs paid very well and offered the security of benefits and pension packages. What is more, the jobs were obtained with seemingly very little disruption to the fishers' lives. Ex-fishers already possessed the technical skills often required for work as tugboat captains, welders, or mechanics, eliminating the need to obtain the education or credentials often involved with changing careers. And because of their geographic proximity to the oil industry, they did not have to uproot their families to new regions or communities for employment.

Although most of my research participants were what I term "exiters" and "persisters," there was a small group of fishers who did not fit well with either of these responses. This intrepid few refused to leave the industry but had also chosen to change their practices in order to avoid having to rely on the low dockside prices offered by shrimp buyers and processors. In this way they found a strategy for cutting out the middleman and selling their product directly to the consumer. Throughout the book I call these individuals "adaptive innovators."

The adaptive innovation here involved several steps, the first of these a technological upgrade. Traditionally, freshly caught shrimp are thrown into a hatch on the boat that is filled with ice, where they remain until they can be unloaded for sale at the docks. Innovators installed industrial-size freezers in place of the ice holes that freeze the shrimp the instant they are caught. These freezers allow shrimpers to bypass the dockside purchasers (who offer a low price) and sell the frozen product directly to the consumer. Because the shrimp are frozen so quickly after (and sometimes during) the live state, they become a higher-quality product, individual quick frozen (IQF) shrimp, which yield a higher price on the market. Another step the innovators took involved the use of alternative methods to market their products, selling them directly to the consumer through the Internet as well as through contacts they made with retailers, such as grocery store chains, in the community. Further, innovators took advantage of farmer's markets as an opportunity to sell their shrimp.

In the end, I found that some had stayed put, others had left, and a few had changed to adapt to the shifting economic conditions. But why did some leave while others decided to stay? And how were others able to adapt? Individual motivation for action is a fundamental social scientific question. Are people primarily motivated to act for rational or economic reasons, or are nonrational or emotional, subjective reasons what inspire them to social action? Many scholars choose clear sides in this debate, while others attempt to explain the connection between the two.

From Exit, Voice, and Loyalty to Identity, Loss, and Innovation

Albert O. Hirschman's famous book *Exit, Voice, and Loyalty: Responses to Decline in Firms, Organizations, and States* represents an early attempt to bridge the gap that lies between these two broad explanations of social action. His model has since been used in a wide variety of research areas, from consumer behavior to romantic relationships,[53] and it has provided an especially important context for research on issues related to work and employment.[54] Hirschman constructed his theory with the explicit purpose of predicting how individuals—such as shrimp fishers—will respond when confronted with a deterioration of organizational conditions. He argues that those facing such a predicament have two primary forms of recourse: to *exit* for better alternatives, or to stay and use *voice* to advocate for improvements. His third concept, *loyalty*, is introduced as a way to understand what motivates some to cut their losses while others stay in and fight with the hope of restoring conditions to what they were before decline. Loyalty thus represents his attempt to acknowledge how nonmaterial considerations are tied into individual action.

Hirschman's framework appears well suited to understanding the three trajectories of shrimpers for several reasons. First, unlike many dominant theories of deindustrialization and globalization—which typically depict actors as unmoored ships battered by the waves of economic forces—he places agency at the center of his analysis, thereby taking actors' decisions seriously. Next, he focuses on actors' responses to deteriorating conditions, something that Louisiana trawlers have been facing for over a decade. Last, through his concept of loyalty, Hirschman acknowledges the role that noneconomic factors play in decision-making processes. Indeed, the shrimp fishers' responses were somewhat suggestive of his model: some exited while others stayed, and most were clearly loyal to the craft. But when put to greater scrutiny, there are several significant ways that his model fails to adequately account for the personal stories the shrimpers described.

Hirschman's model presumes that individuals who face economic decline will exit for better opportunities if and when they are available. But he also acknowledges that sometimes there are reasons why individuals may delay or forgo exit altogether. He argues that if actors believe that speaking out or protesting against declining conditions may lead to improvements, they may stick it out at least temporarily, an action Hirschman conceptualizes as *voice*. Applying Hirschman's model to shrimp fishers, we might assume that persisting shrimpers have not exited because they believe that their situation will eventually improve and that they are capable of bringing about improvements by advocating for them through voice efforts. But those I spoke with have not used voice in this way. While they made the deliberate choice to forgo better employment alternatives, they were generally *not* optimistic that the industry would recover. What is more, up to that point they had not been making any serious effort toward saving their industry. While voice may often be an important tool for people facing decline, in many situations it may not be entirely usable. The decline of occupations in response to new global supply chains is an area where voice is not likely to make a difference. This is especially true of the shrimp import crisis, as the trawlers, recognizing the necessity of importing shrimp to fill consumer demand, knew that it was unrealistic to try to stem the flow of cheaper, farmed shrimp. Given this, it is unsurprising that the shrimp fishers failed to consider social movement activity—such as strikes or protests—as a viable option for reversing industrial decline.[55]

After voice, actors in Hirschman's model have two options: exit or loyalty. Those who choose neither exit nor voice are depicted as passively loyal, hopeful that things will improve in the future. But a large number of shrimpers refused to leave behind their deteriorating way of life, despite the availability employment alternatives, and do not fit this characterization. They understood that they could exit and that doing so would be financially beneficial. What is more, they stayed without the optimistic expectations that industrial conditions would improve in the future. In a sense, they had chosen to go down with the ship. Why would they choose to suffer if they did not have to? The short answer to this is that they judged their ways of life associated with their occupational identity and way of life to be worth the suffering.

Next, Hirschman views exit as a solution to decline, as a form of agency firmly rooted in a calculation of economic costs and benefits. He presumes that people will take the path to better economic opportunities when they are available and thus considers the transition from one organization to another as a fairly smooth and clean process. Ex-fishers appeared to follow this logic. Most admitted that they were better off financially in their lives as ex-trawlers. But even given their elevated financial statuses, they did not view themselves as victors over industrial decline. As they shared their experiences with selling off their boats and calling it quits, it was obvious that they had gone through a significant degree of heartbreak and loss. For many the transition was far from smooth, and some even regretted leaving their lives as fishers, even though they had profited from that decision. The narratives of these fishers point toward the noneconomic costs of exit. Although Hirschman does recognize that exit may carry noneconomic costs, these costs have been underexplored. The stories shared by ex-shrimpers regarding their experiences with leaving fishing for good provide an excellent opportunity to examine these noneconomic costs. They reveal to us just what is lost when deeply meaningful traditional occupational identities are abandoned. Former shrimpers *are* better off financially, but most experience exit as a personal tragedy that comes with great loss.

After voice and exit, loyalty is the only other possible form of agency available to actors in Hirschman's model. However, the experience of the small group of shrimpers I call "adaptive innovators" shows that Hirschman's conception of agency is too narrow. This group has successfully adapted to the logic of the market in ways that allow them to remain viable producers while simultaneously preserving the meaningful occupational and cultural activities associated with their way of life. By using the Internet to find new and lucrative markets for their high-quality catch, as well as taking advantage of shipping and transportation technologies, these local actors are not only fighting against global forces, they are *using* globalization in judo-like fashion to advance their own agenda. Indeed, changing to adapt is an option that may not always be available to those facing industrial decline. But adaptive innovation is an important form of agency in many organizational settings.

Despite its limitations, Hirschman's theory remains a classic approach to understanding responses to economic change. Because it offers a partial account for many of the transitions that shrimp fishers on Bayou Crevette describe, it is a useful starting point for building an understanding of economic change on the bayou. However, many of the complex emotional and cultural responses to industrial decline remain lost in Hirschman's framework. In order to dig a little deeper into the way that people respond to industrial decline, I reconstruct Hirschman to incorporate a more nuanced understanding of how structural economic forces combine with noneconomic, culturally based factors—emotional attachments, idealized values, meaningful occupational identities, and so on—to produce unique outcomes. In place of exit, voice, and loyalty, perhaps a better way to think about people's choices in situations where they're confronted by occupational decline in a rapidly changing world is through the concepts of identity, loss, and innovation. By reconstructing Hirschman's model, I emphasize the centrality of culturally based considerations to the threat of economic hardship and other consequences of industrial decline.

Identity, Loss, and Innovation

Persisting shrimp fishers are a compelling group because they have chosen to forgo opportunities for economic gain in order to stay the course as fishers. They are indeed loyal to their way of life, but their loyalty is not passive, resigned, or hopeful. It is fiercely, even tragically, purposeful as they struggle to navigate upstream against the logic of the market. But how can we best understand their high levels of devotion to their way of life? While each individual I spoke with shared his or her unique story, there were several strong patterns that wove throughout their narratives, namely the

importance of work, family, and environment to the creation and maintenance of identity. These patterns make perfectly good sense when exam-
ined against the backdrop of the fishers' identification with Cajun ethnicity.

Bayou Crevette is located in the region known as Acadiana. A majority of the people here trace their ancestry back to French settlers who
were expelled from the former Canadian province of Acadia by British
colonizers in the late 1700s.[56] All of the fishers I spoke with—current and
former—identified themselves as Cajun. Most Americans are at least
somewhat familiar with Cajun culture, mostly through the distinctive cuisine and music. Like the food (which, contrary to popular belief, is not
always spicy), the Cajun culture is rich in traditions, many of which persist
today, despite the centuries-long presence of Cajuns in American society.[57]
Some of these customs and core values were evident through the way that
the shrimp fishers described their insistence upon carrying on the legacy
of shrimping or their regret upon having left it behind. They drew upon
their cultural resources as they made their decisions to stay or not stay in
the industry and subsequently with how they have made sense of the outcomes. Although the Cajun culture is rich and diverse, the shrimp fishers'
frequent references to work, family, and environment indicate just how
key these elements are to the creation and maintenance of Cajun culture.

Time and again I heard from these tenacious individuals heartbreaking stories of mounting hardships that involved not only their finances but
also their personal relationships and their feelings of self-worth. By for-
going better-paying and less risky employment opportunities, they chose
to instead preserve their self-identities, which are tightly bound to their
work as shrimp fishers. Their actions speak to the important function
that work plays in the construction and maintenance of identity. Sociologists of work and occupations have long demonstrated the importance of
work spaces as arenas of identity formation.[58] Local labor conditions can
greatly influence our understandings of the world around us. The nature
of the tasks we perform (skilled or unskilled), mechanisms of social control (autonomous or authoritarian), and terms of employment (salaried or
contingent employee) all contribute to self-definitions to varying degrees.
The identities of Louisiana shrimp fishers are tightly bound up with the
work that they perform. Since the settlement of the Acadians in Louisiana,
fishing has been important to the Cajuns' survival, both economically and
physically. The work is hard and dirty and requires a high level of skill

that can only be learned by doing. Because fishers are captains of their own ships, they are typically highly independent and value the autonomy that their way of life provides and are reluctant to leave it behind. Fishers I spoke with cited resilience, tenacity, and self-reliance—all features they associate with "being Cajun"—as characteristics that enabled them to stick it out thus far and for as long as they could.

Shrimp fishing is a cultural pursuit tightly linked to family structure, and as such it is typically an intergenerational pursuit—where knowledge and skills are passed from one generation to the next. Most fishers grew up on trawl boats, and from a young age they both contributed to the family business and learned from their parents and grandparents what it takes to be a fisher. Most shrimp fishers understand the pursuit as their cultural calling, as part of their genealogical destiny. This notion is emblematized in the oft-cited phrase "it's in my blood," which shrimp fishers use to describe why they stay with it. Their descriptions of themselves and their working lives closely match what has been written about Cajun cultural identity by specialists in the field. The sociologists Anthony Margavio and Craig Forsyth studied the link between shrimp fishing and Cajun ethnic identity and wrote that

> being self-employed in [economic pursuits based on extraction from environment] allows Cajuns to set their own work schedules. They can work when they want to or when they need to. For a Cajun the business of life is not business; it is living. Cajuns genuinely enjoy these activities and the family life these pursuits sustain. . . . Very often, they connected shrimping with freedom—not the freedom of contemporary American individualism, but the freedom to be with family. . . . They enjoy catching, cooking, and eating the bounty nature has so richly supplied them. And the enjoyment is doubled because it is shared by kin. This is the core of Cajun culture.[59]

As indicated in the above quote, shrimp fishers also hold a deep connection to and identification with the landscape in which they both live and work. Indeed, the rich ecosystem of southern Louisiana has fundamentally shaped the community's economic structure since its development. The bayous and marshes supplied by the Mississippi river contain a bounty of fish, shrimp, crabs, and oysters that could be caught both for consumption and for the market. The forest and marshlands provide an abundance of animal life to trap for food and for the fur trade. Forests also supplied the trees that have been used to build homes and boats, and also for market exchange. The distinctive and valuable ecosystem provides the important backdrop for where fishers work and play, and they often referenced the importance of being out on the water to why they refused to leave shrimp fishing behind. The fishers took great pride in their ability to "live off the land," as they put it so many times.[60]

To leave behind a way of life one views as a cultural calling requires a great deal of identity work, work in which the persisting fishers were reluctant to engage. Their experiences draw attention to the significance of work to the construction and maintenance of identity, and the way that it is tightly bound with family history and the landscape in which one lives. Only through careful examination of how shrimp fishers make sense of their choices and their outcomes can we fully understand how identity functions in the face of dramatic change. While some have chosen to persist as fishers, others opted to leave that way of life behind for better-paying, more certain employment alternatives. In doing so, they have avoided many of the problems deindustrialization scholars have outlined, especially with regard to economic uncertainty. But when I dug a bit deeper into the transition process and its outcomes, I found that, by and large, ex-fishers did not express the high level of satisfaction that one might expect from individuals who recently dodged the bullet of chronic un(der) employment. Quite the opposite, they shared very painful stories about how hard it was to make the decision to leave the industry behind. Many of these stories included admissions of depression, anguish, and, for some, regret over the loss of a central part of their identities. The types of losses they experienced are more difficult to quantify than other types of losses associated with economic restructuring: income, home value, the vibrancy of civic life. Nonetheless, their losses were important to them, impacting them in profound ways, and at times the magnitude of loss was expressed through deep emotional displays. During conversation with them, a few male shrimp fishers were moved to tears as they described the painful process of selling off their boats. Given the hypermasculine nature of shrimp fishing on the bayou, it was at these times that it became abundantly clear to me just how painful the loss of fishing was for these men.

The work of shrimp fishing is more than a job, and through the fishers' losses we stand to gain a clearer understanding about "the other kinds of utility" to which Friedland and Robertson's conceptualization refers. Shrimp fishing is imbued with cultural significance. For many it was the central element of their personal identity, and those who were forced to walk away from that life sometimes experienced personal struggles as they grappled with their new lives as ex-fishers. Their accounts of how they came to leave the industry and how they have fared since provide us with the valuable opportunity to examine what is lost when workers leave behind a livelihood many considered to be their life's calling.

A small group of fishers chose not to exit but also refused to carry on and struggle in the way that most current fishers were doing. By finding ways to remain viable in a declining industry, these innovators avoided exit without the need to appeal to higher authorities for change through voice, change that typically occurs *from above*. In that sense, their actions represent change occurring *from below*. Of course, not all individuals facing industrial decline have the opportunity to adjust their practices to a better fit with new economic realities. The qualities of the commercial shrimp fishing industry—where shrimpers are small commodity producers akin to being owner-operators of their own productive facility—provide shrimpers with a unique opportunity to adapt. Nevertheless, through an in-depth analysis of their responses to decline, we are pressed to think a bit more about other options that exist beyond exit, persisting, or protest activity.

The case of adaptive innovators thus provides an occasion to explore how actors can creatively use agency to respond to threats brought upon them by globalization and industrial decline. Their narratives demonstrate how they have drawn upon cultural resources—the intersection of work, family, and environment—to figure out a way to stay in the industry *and* be successful. Interestingly, innovating shrimpers are using the tools of globalization that threaten to significantly shrink their industry— namely, improvements in shipping and communication technologies—in order to successfully remain afloat. By using the Internet to find new and lucrative markets for their high-quality catch, as well as taking advantage of transportation technologies, these local actors resist the global forces pushing them out of the industry. Through a detailed assessment of how local actors react when their livelihoods are threatened by deindustrialization and globalization, I find that the outcomes are not always straightforward. Globalization may pose significant challenges to maintaining meaningful occupational identities while at the same time creating new and unexpected opportunities for preserving and extending traditional ways of life.

The Plan of the Book

The remainder of this book draws out conceptually and empirically the perspective set forth above. Chapter 2 focuses on current fishers and highlights how their loyalty to their way of life is grounded in a rich, Cajun cultural history and constructed with great respect to family structures and the resource-rich landscape that provides the backdrop to their everyday lives. Chapter 3 shifts the focus to those who left the industry behind and examines what is lost when meaningful occupational identities are traded for others. Chapter 4 presents the adaptive innovators and their efforts to preserve both their occupational identities and economic well-being through finding creative solutions to the problems caused by the import crisis. In the final chapter, I discuss the potential implications of the BP oil spill for the continuation of the shrimp fishing industry. While the degree to which the oil spill will impact the fishing industry is yet unknown, it has not affected *how* the fishers arrive at the fundamental decisions that they make in response to change. They go through a careful calculation of costs and benefits—both monetary and cultural—as they grapple with what their next move will be, but no matter the impetus for change, the outcomes remain the same: persisting is toil, exit is tragedy, and innovation is risky and unpredictable.

2

Identity

The Struggle to Stay Afloat

I never had so many heartaches in my life. Never so many heartaches in my
life, like trawling is. If there's a hundred things about trawling, probably
80 to 90 percent stabs you through the heart like a vampire with a stick. . . .
But when you can win that one or two or three times, it pumps you up!
It's the greatest thing you will ever see. It's an addiction. I love it."

Glen (persister)

Glen was a third-generation shrimp fisher who began trawling with
his father and older brothers when he was just six years old. He was
legendary in the town, known for his loud, booming voice and colorful,
frank way of talking. Just about every current and ex-shrimper I spoke
with recommended him as somebody who would give me a rich understanding of the state of the industry. "Glen will tell you like it is, he don't
hold back nothing. You'll be entertained if nothing else, yeah," remarked
one trawler.

I arranged to meet Glen in the sprawling field that sat across the road
from his modest shotgun house. As I pulled into the long gravel driveway
that sat next to the lot, he was just finishing up mowing on his giant tractor.
His seven-year-old son sat in his lap, hands on the wheel and a big smile on
his face. Glen, who was in his early forties at the time, had a body type to
match what folks said about his personality: big and hulking, with strong-
looking hands and sun-baked skin. Before the formal interview began, he
insisted that he give me a tour around his property, a sprawling lot that

stretched back over five acres and ended at a shaded canal. The placid, duckweed-covered canal was clearly the crowning jewel of the property to Glen. Hidden behind a natural levee, tall grass, and cypress and tupelo trees, the canal brimmed with wildlife: fish in wide variety, alligators, crabs, frogs, and nutria rats (a problematic nonnative rodent). He boasted proudly that he and his son regularly caught their nightly meals from this canal, including the catfish that he would make for dinner later that night. Thankfully, I was included.

Like most of the other community members I met, Glen was intensely proud of his Cajun heritage. When I asked him to describe what it means to be Cajun, he stated, "We can literally live off the land. Who else can say that?" Self-sufficiency and independence were the most common elements in how the Cajuns I spoke with described their heritage. After only a short time of knowing him, two things became clearly evident. First, his big personality indeed matched what I had been told by others. He did speak with a loud, booming voice, but it was his candid way of talking that set him apart. His choice of words frequently included a mixture of Cajun French and curses (both in English and Cajun French), and he appeared to hold nothing back, just as I had been told to expect. Second, he was not only angry and anguished about the current state of the shrimping industry but quite pessimistic about its future. Our three-hour-long conversation was dominated by the industry's troubles and its impacts on Glen and his family. He explained to me in colorful detail the hardships and emotional strain he'd experienced after the industry began to collapse under the weight of imports, and it was clear that he and his family had been enduring very real struggles.

Glen seemed to be one of those people who liked to shock and amaze with his stories and opinions, and while I was frequently astonished by much of what he said, I was most shocked by what he answered when I asked him if—given all that he had been through—he had any plans to leave the industry. He looked at me as if he were surprised I'd even ask such a question. "I'm not going anywhere," he stated. "I'm going to stay right where I am."

His dogged refusal to leave fishing was puzzling, especially given the abundance of job opportunities that were available right down the road in the oil industry. Glen was no stranger to working in oil. As a young man in his early twenties, he had worked for several years on tugboats, even obtaining in his thirties a captain's license that was still valid, and from time to time he would take a job on the tugs when extra money was needed. He knew from firsthand experience that captaining tugboats was not only very lucrative but compared to shrimp fishing much easier on the body.

I asked him to tell me about what it is like to work as a tugboat captain, and he replied with a hint of shame in his voice, "My hands turned back like a woman's—'cause I didn't trawl in a year, almost a year. Normally trawling, it's like you have some barnacles on your hands . . .'cause you always pulling on ropes, you always pulling, you always doing something. It's hard on your body." Having smooth, unblemished hands did not match up with the image Glen had of himself, an image constructed out of the intensive labor involved with running a shrimp boat. It was striking to hear folks such as Glen complain about *not* having to perform such physically demanding work in the times they were unable to trawl.

Glen was just one of the many shrimp fishers who steadfastly refused to leave the industry behind, even though he knew that other jobs were available. I was astonished to hear so many stories of hardships, to witness men I hardly knew break down in tears as they explained the difficulties they experienced as a result of their choice to stay, only to resolutely state that they had no plans to change course. How do people justify the economic and personal struggles that accompany their decisions to stay aboard a sinking ship when a lifeboat exists? What are they trying to preserve, and at what cost? The answers that shrimp fishers provide to these questions indicate the strength with which cultural identity factors into decisions that are made about economic well-being. Shrimp fishers are loyal to their way of life in large part because fishing is a highly valued part of their cultural identities as Cajuns. Work lives and family lives are intertwined, and the meanings given to each are forged out of a rich and unique landscape filled with boats, marshes, and a bounty of resources. Unraveling these important cultural elements—work, family, and landscape—would cause significant disruption to these identities. Many shrimpers were unwilling to part with a way of life that they deem as their life's calling, and their accounts of what they preserved by refusing to leave provide real-life examples of Friedland and Robertson's "other kinds of utility," as contained in the work that we do. These point directly to the relationship between identity and work.

Why Go Down without a Fight?

"So why do you stay?" I asked Glen and the other persisting shrimp fishers. There are multiple explanations for people remaining in a deteriorating situation when they do not have to. Before heading into the field I had assumed that most shrimpers would be making preparations to leave the industry because it made economic sense to do so. At the same time, I thought I might find a steadfast group who would be fighting for their work lives through some kind of political activity directed toward change, such as protests or other kinds of visibility campaigns. While I was surprised to find so many like Glen doggedly persisting, I was equally bewildered by their lack of social movement activity. What explains this lack? When I inquired, trawlers often said that they were simply too independent to ever come together, or too hardheaded and stubborn to ever reach a consensus on organizing activities. For example, J. T. and Donny, two lifelong trawlers, discussed why shrimp fishers haven't engaged in protest activities such as strikes.

> J. T.: What's our problem? We got a lot of people that got oil jobs and that got boats, they fish part time, they gonna go out. They don't give a care about us full-time commercial fisherman. And that would hurt us. One guy came up with a solution that would work. We gonna take all the boats and go to one shrimp shed to sell. Don't matter if it take you two days to unload, don't sell to anyone else. [Because it'd force other shrimp sheds to increase their price to fill demand] it's a solution that makes a lot of sense.
>
> Donny: It's just getting everyone together. We so independent. That's why we do this [fish for a living], we independent. I don't wanna work for everybody. It's hard to get us all together.
>
> J. T.: That's our biggest problem, we cannot get together.
>
> Donny: We don't like anybody telling us what to do.

Whether or not J. T. was correct in his assertion that part-time fishers would not respect a strike enacted by full-time shrimpers, their explanation about fishers being too independent to come together rang hollow for me because I knew that shrimp fishers successfully engaged in protest activity in the past when they felt their industry was threatened. Sociologists Anthony Margavio and Craig J. Forsyth's provocative book describes how shrimp fishers resisted the enactment of regulations that mandate the use of turtle excluder devices (TEDs).[1] Not only did they come together in regular meetings and planning activities, but they were able to engage in a series of highly coordinated protest activities that culminated in a thirty-six-hour blockade of waterways central to commercial activity. Although the shrimpers were successful in coming together, they ultimately lost the battle against the TEDs. The significance of the TEDs battle goes far beyond fishers having to comply with regulations directed toward saving valuable sea turtles; it and not a general stubbornness or individualism among fishers—goes a long way toward explaining their failure to engage in any meaningful activity toward reversing their current situation

It all began in 1987, when the federal government passed a regulation mandating that all shrimp trawlers install TEDs into their nets. The device is a grid of bars that is fitted into the nets to allow the escape of sea turtles taken incidentally through trawling. While these devices are effective at reducing the number of turtles caught, trawlers argue that they lose a significant part of their catch through the hole created by the TED. The extent to which shrimpers are upset about the TEDs cannot be understated, and in order to fully understand this, it is necessary to view the contentious historical background against which the TEDs regulations were enacted.

Beginning in the late 1970s, after the passage of the Endangered Species Act (ESA) in 1973, a number of environmental organizations launched a series of awareness-raising campaigns directed toward increasing protection for many species of sea turtles, especially the critically endangered Kemp's Ridley sea turtle. Because one of the contributing factors to turtle mortality is the unintentional capture of sea turtles in shrimp trawls, shrimp fishers became a symbolic target of the political campaign waged to protect the turtles. Not surprisingly, the shrimpers did not receive these accusations favorably. While it is incontestable that shrimp trawls sometimes do ensnare sea turtles and cause them serious injury or death, many trawlers felt it was unfair for them to bear the full brunt of the blame for sea turtle mortality. From the shrimpers' vantage point, many of the turtles they caught were unharmed or simply stressed and capable of being fully revived. They argued that the real culprits of sea turtle mortality were the oil and chemical companies, and it was these that should be forced to institute protective measures if the sea turtle population was going to be brought back.[2] Regardless of which group was to blame for endangering sea turtles, the debate was highly contentious and emotional from the get-go, and the ensuing struggle over how to protect the turtles was long and protracted.

In 1987 regulations mandating the use of TEDs were officially enacted, but the conflict was far from over. A bitter battle between conservationists, state and federal governments, and shrimpers continued to rage on. Shrimpers, particularly those from Gulf states, were outraged over the regulations and argued that the laws were enacted with no consideration paid to the technical and economic impacts that TEDs would have on them. Louisiana trawlers were especially aggrieved. They claimed that there was little evidence that they encountered the endangered turtles frequently enough to warrant being subjected to the same regulations as fishers from other coastal areas with more turtles. To this day they continue to argue that they should be exempt from the law.[3]

Over the next two years, a series of court battles were waged that pitted shrimpers against conservation groups, from some of which Louisiana trawlers emerged victorious. With support from their elected leaders, the fishers were successful in one court battle that resulted in the declaration that the enforcement of TEDs was illegal. Although this victory put wind in the shrimp fishers' political sails, it was only a temporary one; the decision was quickly overturned in federal court. In another court case, the shrimpers argued successfully that the enforcement of TEDs be postponed until sufficient evidence could be compiled showing the economic impacts suffered as a result of the device. They felt very confident that these studies would vindicate their claims that they lost a significant portion of their catch pulling with TEDs.

The shrimpers used the time allowed by postponement to grow their opposition movement. To coordinate their efforts, they formed an organization called Concerned Shrimpers of America (CSA), and as the date for scheduled enforcement grew nearer, their movement gained momentum. Their primary strategy was to disrupt the flow of commercial boat traffic in shipping lanes that bordered the Louisiana and Texas coasts through a series of blockades. In order to draw attention to their cause, they initially planned and executed a series of small blockades that were designed to minimally disrupt boat traffic. These smaller blockades led up to a massive protest held during the last weekend of July, when the regulations were scheduled to be formally enforced. During this weekend, CSA organized shrimpers from Texas to Florida to head to the closest port to block boat traffic, but they especially encouraged trawlers to go to Galveston, where the organization's main efforts were focused.

The blockade was a success. On that day, over four hundred vessels showed up in Galveston. Boats lined up side by side and blocked port traffic, greatly disrupting commercial shipping. The shrimpers refused to leave, despite threats from port authorities, and eventually the Coast Guard was called out to intervene. When the shrimp fishers continued their blockade, the Coast Guard used water cannons against them. But despite the force of water from the cannons, the shrimpers remained firm. In all, the blockade lasted thirty-six hours and was called off only after President George H. W. Bush agreed to review the regulations.

The shrimp fishers emerged from the blockade victorious, but only temporarily. Soon thereafter another round of meetings and legislative actions began: regulations were suspended, then reinstated; injunctions were filed and then dismissed. The back-and-forth finally came to an end a year later, when federal law made trawling without TEDs a criminal offense. This time fines and penalties for noncompliance were very stiff, and shrimpers were henceforth forced to observe the laws or pay the price. Eventually protest and noncompliance activity subsided, and three years after the blockade, the CSA formally disbanded.

Despite the shrimp fishers' frustration with the outcome, the TEDs blockades had been very large and well organized, and most of the shrimpers I spoke with had participated in several of them, most commonly the big one in Galveston. Clearly, they were proud of their efforts, and perhaps this is why the outcome was so disappointing. One of the most active participants in the blockade was a third-generation trawler named Teddy. He had a picture on his wall of a long line of shrimp boats blocking the port in Galveston. "That's me, right there," he stated proudly, going on to say, "For the blockade, I got everybody together, and we got everything shut down to the west. And they came with some barges and sprayed us with water, and all kinds of stuff. And we said we'd break the blockades if we didn't have to pull no TEDs. That was good."

Almost a decade later, in 1998, the National Marine Fisheries Service (NMFS) mandated the use of bycatch excluder devices, or BRDs, for all trawlers in the South Atlantic and Gulf of Mexico region. BRDs—pronounced "birds"—are similar to TEDs in that they consist of an opening in the shrimp trawl net that allows finfish and other acciden- tally captured aquatic animals to escape. When the NMFS enacted the BRD regulations, there was very little organized outrage on the part of Louisiana shrimp fishers. With the TEDs episode relatively fresh in their minds, many felt that engaging in political action was not worth their time.

Although a good deal of time had passed since the blockades when I conducted my field research, I found that most of the shrimpers I spoke with still harbored a great deal of anger about the TEDs, the establish- ment of the TEDs regulations often being cited as the first domino in what would become the eventual decline of trawling. Indeed, some trawlers left the industry after the TEDs drama played out, even before imports posed a threat. To be sure, the anger felt by the fishers was not born out of a dis- regard for the importance of protecting endangered turtles—by and large they agreed that turtles are worth trying to save—rather, they felt that the regulations had been passed without any consideration for the impact the TEDs would have on shrimpers.

The two major complaints trawlers had with the TEDs—that the devices allow a significant portion of their catch to escape and that they rarely (if ever) caught the Kemp's Ridley sea turtle the device is designed to protect—mean that some try to avoid complying with the regulations. But if they fail to do so, they are heavily penalized, as had happened to some of those I spoke with. Paul, a fourth-generation trawler, had been fined by the Coast Guard for not complying with the regulations in the past. As he put it, "I got stopped twice for not pulling the TEDs. But, you see, I don't catch turtles. At all. With those TEDs, you lose twenty percent of your catch. And you'll pull your hair out, because we don't catch turtles. I got caught twice already. Next time I go to jail. It makes my wife nervous, she's scared. And frankly I'm scared, too."

Teddy, the third-generation trawler mentioned earlier, echoed this statement and added that TEDs can be expensive to maintain. "We're al- ways fighting a losing battle. We lose a lot of money," he said. "Pulling the TEDs, you lose approximately twelve TEDs a year. You catch big tires, big oil drums, and they mess up the TEDs. Or you tear the trawl. Maybe, I would say about six trawls a year. When you mess up a TED, you got about six trawls broken, where sometimes you mess up just the TED. And the TED itself, they cost about three hundred dollars now. They were around two hundred before, and now they up to three hundred. And now we gotta pull *bigger* TEDs than we was before. That cost me a bunch of money again because [of that] I'm losing more shrimp."

Nick was a first-generation trawler who left the fishing industry in the late 1990s to work in the administrative department of a tugboat company. At the time he was thirty-eight years old. He'd gotten into trawling in his early twenties when he married his wife, whose father owned a trawl boat. Although he greatly enjoyed working as a trawler, the TEDs regulations—and the ordeal that led up to their enactment—led him to reconsider his career choice. He said, "The TEDs, that put a big hurting on us. And that was the beginning of it for me." Like the others, he was frustrated with the regulations because he claimed that he rarely caught turtles. "I didn't catch turtles, but I was only fishing for a relatively short time. I knew one trawler, I think he was trawling at that time about twenty-six years, and he said he caught two of those Kemp Ridleys his entire life. And he threw them back overboard. It's not like the trawl drown them. They're losing twenty percent of their catch every hour for something they catch once in a lifetime. That's what's not fair about those studies. I trawled for ten years and I never seen one."

The TEDs issue was a particularly salient one for a third-generation trawler named Albert. Albert was forty-two at the time and had trawled on his own boat for twenty-three of those years. He had very recently decided to get out of the industry. In fact, I met him through calling the number listed on the "for sale" sign he had posted in the window of his boat weeks earlier. That year was the first year he'd missed the opening of the season since he began trawling with his grandfather as a young boy. In the meantime he was working at the pool supply store that his father owned, and this was where we had our conversation about his experience as a shrimp fisher. During the conversation, his father, Larry, was also present, occasionally chiming in. Albert had been a trawler during the battle over the TEDs and participated in several of the local blockades. Like the others, he complained that TEDs were inefficient and often resulted in losses of both volume of catch and fuel:

> They make us pull these TEDs with these big holes in 'em. Me and you can pass through with no problem, okay? That's ridiculous! If you catch a crab trap or something, the flap stays open and everything goes straight out that's

in the bag [trawl net]. You drag it for nothing, you're burning fuel for nothing. Understand? So, you losin' that drag. You might pick up five or six bushels of shrimp on that side of the boat, and you might pick this side and there's a bucket, you know? How that makes you feel about pulling that TED, and you got a crab trap stuck in that damn thing? You drag it three or four hours, and you pick *that* up? I mean, you burn the diesel, it's gone and there's nothing you can do about it. And if you tie it closed or if you don't pull it, the Coast Guard comes and they seize the boat.

Like Nick, Albert also claimed that he rarely caught turtles in his nets. "I saw two turtles two times in twenty-three years," he said, "and it was a loggerhead both times. Now, those Ridley turtles? They're not around here. I've never caught one in twenty-three years."

Shrimp fishers' claims about not catching endangered turtles seemed odd to me, given what I knew marine researchers have found. According to the U.S. Fish and Wildlife Service, the warm waters off the Louisiana coast are among the turtles' major habitats.[4] "From what I understand," I replied, "isn't there a good deal of evidence showing that turtles do, indeed, live along the coast here in Louisiana?" Larry and Albert did not deny this, but I was not prepared for their explanation for why they believed the turtles could be found in Louisiana.

"The National Marine Fisheries," Larry began, "they passed the TEDs law. Right after that, Albert was trawling in [a nearby lake], which is west of here. All of a sudden, he seen a seaplane come and land in the water." His voice began to rise with excitement. "And guess what they was throwing out!? Turtles! Turtles!"

I was puzzled by this statement and shot Albert a look of surprise. Albert added, "They was dropping the turtles from the plane. I swear to God."

"Really?" I asked skeptically. "This really happened?"

"Oh yeah!" Albert replied.

Larry continued, "They all saw 'em with their binoculars. The deckhands and everyone, they all said they was throwing turtles in the lake!"

"I swear to God," Albert repeated.

Larry added, "And then National Marine Fisheries, Wildlife Fisheries, they come around and say, 'Hey pick up your rig.' But Albert *never* caught turtles before. Ever! That's because the turtles are over by the St. Padre

Island, way over there, because that's where they lay eggs. Okay? But they [NMWF] busted a bunch of people with the turtles! Now you tell me— how that happened?"

Their claim that the U.S. government had actively engaged in acts of sabotage directed at the shrimp fishers is certainly hard to believe, and initially I received this information with a high degree of astonishment. But I heard this exact story—or ones very similar—over and over again from both current and ex-trawlers, usually without provocation. Mike, an ex-trawler who had left the industry three years previously, was particularly adamant in his claims of turtle plantings. Mike had been one of the most politically active shrimpers on the bayou during the TEDs episode and had had an instrumental role in the organization of the Galveston blockade. I interviewed him in his living room, where a poster-sized photo of his boat being sprayed by a water cannon during the blockade hung in a prominent location. He told me he had rarely encountered turtles before the TEDs conflict grew tense, but that he and others had begun to catch them after the regulations passed.

"How does that make sense?" I asked. Once again, I was surprised by the response given.

He said, "You see some once in a while, lately. Before, when I first started trawling, when I was young and my daddy was young, you wouldn't see it. Now you started seeing them because they plant them. I was in the next town over trawling, and I saw a seaplane come throw 'em, the little turtles."

Bewildered, I asked, "You saw that yourself?"

"Yeah!" he shouted. "They drop them off. And, uh, in Texas, if the season opens like tonight, tomorrow night they come with a supply boat. The Wildlife and Fisheries and Texas A&M people. They come with cages full of little turtles. They would throw them overboard. We trawl in that! Then, uh, we catch them and they're dead. And sometimes it was proved that they would be dead before the season opens. Now, some of them *was* killed, like, maybe the wheel of the boat ran over them. But only some people were caught with a turtle in their net, ya know? Besides that, I never heard nothing about people catching turtles."

The frequency with which these stories were told was certainly surprising, as the accusations of sabotage might sound rather unlikely, if not paranoid, to some people. A few of the fishers recognized this. During one of my conversations with an ex-trawler named Lindel, I asked him if he had heard the rumors about turtle planting. "The first time I heard it was from

Albert and all," he said. "The first time I heard that I was like [skeptically] 'yeah, *maybe.*' But then, Mr. Gerald—you know, Mr. Cheramie?—he said he seen it with his own eyes. When *he* said it, then I kind of believed it."

Whether or not these accusations of turtle planting are true is not something that this analysis will pursue. However, the fact that so many trawlers believe and pass on this type of story is in itself significant for at least two important reasons. First, it illustrates the level of distrust and hostility that the shrimpers hold for governmental agencies and their involvement in regulating the industry. Perhaps more significantly, it helps us to understand why they have not engaged in a protest activity like the TEDs blockade to try to reverse the industry's present decline. The struggle over the TEDs issue—and the lasting perception that they ultimately lost the fight—had profoundly impacted the shrimpers who lived through the experience, instilling in many of them a lack of faith in their ability to influence decisions made by state and federal agencies. Not only did they believe their voices would not be heard, they became convinced that those with the authority to make decisions regarding their industry were *intentionally* acting against their best interests in order to push them out of the industry altogether.

The TEDs issue had certainly left its mark on the industry. Some fishers told me that they knew people who quit after the regulations were enforced, seeing it as an omen that more regulations were inevitable and believing that nobody with political power would fight for their interests. Still, despite their pessimism, most hung on. Then the import crisis hit in 2002, and the shrimpers were again faced with the decision to stay in and deal with the hardships or get out. Some chose to leave, and those who remained, generally lacking faith that anything in the way of a protest would be effective, had done very little to fight to save the industry. But the absence of activity did not mean that the shrimpers had failed to resist the deterioration of their industry. I show in the next section how their stubborn refusal to quit, despite all of the hardships and available employment alternatives, functions as an active form of resistance to the import crisis.

After the Collapse: The Difficulties of Staying Afloat

Over the course of my field research, I heard numerous stories of hardship and struggle from current and former shrimpers alike. As previously mentioned, the most noticeable consequence for the trawlers was the dramatic drop in dockside prices over a short period of time. The example of Glen illustrates just how dramatic this drop in prices has been for shrimpers. Glen owned one of the larger boats on the bayou, a steel-hulled vessel that measured around sixty feet in length. The larger boat allowed him to trawl farther out in the Gulf, although he stuck mainly to fishing the inland waters. While larger boats enable fishers to catch more shrimp, they are also much more expensive to operate and maintain.

Glen often trawled alongside his friend Arty, whom he had known since the early days of his youth. Both of them began trawling on their own boats before they graduated from high school. Glen spoke with great assurance about their abilities and skills, claiming that they were among the most highly skilled shrimpers on the bayou. "Last year," he told me, "in four days and four nights we hardly slept. We put 230 boxes, that's 23,000 pounds of shrimp, in my boat in four days. When we went to sell it, the shrimp buyer tells me, he said, 'Oh, Glen! You and Arty are my best fishers. Look what you brought in, in just four days!' He said that we're his best trawlers." But Glen's pride and confidence soon gave way to disappointment. "A number of years back that would have been $30,000 in four days' time. But the check he gave was only for $16,000." He raised his eyebrows and pounded the picnic table where we sat. "It should have been a $30,000 check! It would have been in years past."

Accounts such as this were consistent among persisting shrimpers, no matter the size of boat. Raymond and Ellen had trawled most of their married lives together. They were both third-generation shrimp fishers who learned the craft from their fathers and grandfathers when they were children. They trawled together for a few years after they got married and continued to do so even after they had children. Like many others, they trawled as a family. But when their children were still quite young, Ellen was diagnosed with cancer. The diagnosis proved to be a serious disruption to their lives, and they questioned whether they should continue as a fishing family given the uncertainty surrounding Ellen's health. Raymond said, "It was too much for her, so I got a land job to raise the kids. In case, uh, you know."

Raymond took a job working offshore on a rig, and although he didn't like it, it paid the bills. During this time, he still desired to be on the water. They budgeted some extra money and purchased a Lafitte skiff, a small shrimp vessel, so he could continue to fish. On his days off, Raymond and his son went out and caught shrimp, just enough to keep the freezer stocked and to give a little away to friends and neighbors. Fortunately Ellen overcame the cancer, and when she regained her strength, she wanted the family to return to their life as shrimp fishers, which was all they'd ever known. Raymond quit his land job, and they purchased the boat on which they still trawled, twenty-three years previous to our conversation. Their boat was smaller than the one they initially had. Raymond grew up working on larger boats, such as the one Glen owned, and while they wanted to purchase a larger boat, they decided to buy a more manageable boat because of the possibility for Ellen's cancer to return.

They mainly fished the inland lakes and did not venture out into the Gulf very often. But even though they owned a smaller boat, the import crisis made it much more difficult to maintain the standard of living they'd enjoyed a decade previous. "In years past," Raymond said, "I would trawl for forty pounds, fifty pounds of shrimp per drag. That's all I'd need to do. The price was there, they paid us, and the expenses were low. Now? No way. Now you've got to catch a lot of shrimp. I figure about, right now, you gotta catch about one hundred fifty to two hundred pounds per drag. You gotta at least average that. One drag you might make less, but the morning drag or afternoon drag might be extra good, so it accumulates. It has to average one hundred fifty pounds. You've got to do at least that much for it to pay."

Ellen added, "You've got to catch at least five hundred pounds a day."

The dramatic drop in dockside prices on its own is a serious challenge to persisting as a shrimper. But along with declining prices, overhead costs have skyrocketed. This combination has been a one-two punch that has knocked quite a few fishers out of the fight altogether. The increase in fishing costs has been driven by the rising cost of fuel, which has bumped up the price of just about everything else needed to make a fishing trip: ice, groceries, and hardware. Repairs have also become much more costly.

To remain competitive against these challenges, shrimp fishers must now work harder than ever. This point was emphasized by two shrimp fishers, J. T. and Donny, both lifelong trawlers in their early forties. J. T. and Donny had known each other since they were young kids, growing up down the street from one another. As kids, they learned how to trawl together from their fathers and grandfathers, and to that day, as in childhood, they were neighbors. Each man owned his own boat that sat docked side by side along the bayou's edge down the street from where they lived. I drove by their boats several times on my daily trek through town, and one very sunny and hot day I stopped after I saw them working on what turned out to be J. T.'s boat. They were preparing the boat for a trip they'd planned for the next day. After we chatted for a few minutes on the dock, Donny invited me on board. Over Coke and some homemade salted, dried shrimp, we talked about what it was like to be a shrimp fisher.

Like the other persisters I met, they described how dramatically the industry had changed, and how much harder it had become in the past few years to make ends meet. The low dockside prices were only part of the problem. If it was only the low prices that they were up against, they said they could probably make it. But the spike in overhead costs at the same time made it extraordinarily difficult to get by. J. T. explained to me part of what it takes to get the boat out on the water.

> I'm in a situation where I'm in a bind. And if the price keeps on falling, and the price of diesel fuel keeps going up, we ain't gonna be able to operate. Right now on *this* day, stuff is good, but if the shrimp gets real less, where you only catch two to three hundred pounds a day, we can't make it. No way. With insurance and all, or breakdowns? I mean, and the expense of diesel fuel, ice and groceries, and net repairs. If you lose a rig, that's it. Me, I pull aluminum trawl boards, those boards I pull, that's $5,000 a set. That's pretty expensive. People don't understand, it costs us to operate these boats.

In addition to overhead costs, shrimp fishers also worried about another very important element in the process of shrimp fishing: deckhands. Shrimping is an extremely difficult and labor intensive endeavor, and deckhands typically assist in a variety of duties, from loading equipment on board to unloading shrimp and cleaning up the boat after the trip is done. The more help on deck, the bigger the catch. Who fishers chose to bring on board depended on a variety of factors. Sometimes trawlers had sons or relatives who were willing to work as deckhands; in fact, most trawlers cut their teeth as deckhands before they went on to own their own boats. Other times, deckhands were roustabouts hired by going boat to boat asking if help was needed. Or trawlers in need of a deckhand spread the word informally. The larger the boat, the more help is required. Glen and J. T. both had larger boats, and each typically employed two deckhands.

Raymond and Ellen, who owned a smaller boat, served as each other's deckhands. Donny usually worked with just one.

Deckhands are typically paid a certain percentage of the total amount of the catch. Back when shrimping was in its heyday, working as a deckhand provided a pretty decent living for those who did it full time and was a surefire way to make a quick buck for those who did it only temporarily. When the season was at its busiest—usually during the first weekend or two of the season—shrimp fishers often looked for an extra hand or two. Back in 2001 when I worked for AmeriCorps, I had firsthand experience with the fast-money nature of working as a deckhand. That year two of my co-workers, who were brothers, worked as deckhands on their uncle's boat for the opening of the May season. Before they left for the weekend-long drag, one of them boasted about how much money he would probably make. He was well known for telling tall tales, so I more or less dismissed his claim as just another one of his exaggerations. When he showed up at the office on Monday morning, he pulled me gleefully aside to show me his weekend earnings, extracting from his pocket a thick wad of money that he said totaled thirteen hundred dollars for three days' work. Being that AmeriCorps workers received a very modest stipend, I felt envious of his newly acquired wealth and a little guilty for dismissing his claim. Although he was visibly excited by the money, he noted that he had expected to make a bit more and had earned upwards of two thousand dollars in a weekend in the past. "How can I get on one of those boats?" I jokingly asked.

The import crisis has made it much more difficult for fishers to hire and maintain deckhands. Not only must they pay deckhands a proportion of their catch, but for long-term, steady deckhands they must also provide health insurance, to guard against the possibility of high costs associated with injury. In recent years, as the industry has declined the cost of health insurance has soared. Before the collapse, it was commonplace for a deck-hand to work season after season on the same boat, allowing shrimpers and deckhands to forge relationships—and sometimes friendships—built on mutual respect and hard work. Working alongside hardworking and reliable deckhands is highly important to the fishing process.

J. T. recognized the value of working alongside good deckhands. He typically trawled with two steady deckhands and formed close relationships with both of them. In addition to his own family, J. T. also felt responsible for the economic well-being of his deckhands' families. The collapse of shrimping, however, hit him hard, and during our chat he worried that he would have to let one go. "We got crews to take care of and they're really good guys. With this boat, I don't just feed my family, I feed three families. I feel pressure to make money to feed three families. And it's hard. I don't know if I can do it no more, and it bothers me." With each unsuccessful trip out, he knows that there are others besides his own family who suffer the consequences. For J. T., letting go of a deckhand would not only result in more work for him, it would result in the unemployment of a friend.

There is another problem now besides being unable to pay for deckhands. As shrimp fishing has become less lucrative and more uncertain, many of those who worked as deckhands in the past have chosen to find employment elsewhere, usually in the oil industry. Shrimpers must therefore compete with both other fishers and other employers in order to attract and retain dependable deckhands. Teddy, a second-generation shrimp fisher, explained the difficulties involved with this scenario. "Right now, we have problems getting deckhands. 'Cause before to go work on the tugboat or in the oil industry, as like a deckhand or a roustabout, it don't pay that much. You understand? So before they could make more money on the shrimp boat. So it was easy to come by a deckhand. Nowadays you could make more money on a tug or in the oilfield as a roustabout than workin' on the shrimp boat, so it's harder to find people that wanna work."

This issue was particularly troubling to a fourth-generation trawler named Daniel. Daniel owned and operated a fifty-seven-foot boat that required the help of two deckhands. When I spoke with him, he had recently experienced a string of bad luck with finding and keeping deckhands. The problem, he told me, was just as Teddy described: deckhands who could be depended on to show up and work hard were more and more often choosing to go work offshore in the oil industry. Those who are left in the pool of available deckhands are often those who cannot find work elsewhere because of dependency issues or criminal records. "Yeah, the deckhands you find now, they can't go find a job nowhere else because they can't take no drug screen and all that. Most of them, you know, are addicted to drugs. Don't get me wrong, there's still some that are good. But I would say ninety percent of them, they're not good. But they can't find no other job, so they work as deckhands."

When I spoke with Daniel, he was preparing to leave the next day for a week out on the boat. He was apprehensive because he was going to take two new deckhands with him. He had just lost the deckhand he had fished with for three years to a heart problem that forced him to quit. Daniel was not looking forward to starting with two new deckhands, especially because one of them had a reputation for being a troublemaker. "He is a young kid and he had just been kicked out of the army," he told me, "but what else am I gonna do? I need help."

Trust in general was a major sticking point for the shrimp fishers. Many trawlers were reluctant to hire a deckhand with whom they were unfamiliar. If trawlers did not find a deckhand that they knew personally, they often found them through recommendations of other trawlers they trusted. Some trawlers outright refused to hire a deckhand with whom they were not familiar. Not only did they worry that a new deckhand might be lazy or unable to perform the strenuous duties, but they also worried about the quality of their character and whether they could be trusted not to steal, or worse. During a recent outing, Paul, a fourth-generation trawler in his mid-forties, opted to go out with only one deckhand instead of his usual two because he could not find someone that he knew and trusted was willing to work. He said, "I can't find a guy to work for me. Somebody I don't know I won't work with because they might cut your throat while you're sleeping and take your boat. I lose a lot on trips when I don't have a deckhand." Trust was so important to Paul that he accepted the consequences of being short a deckhand: more work for himself.

In addition to industry-related struggles—working harder for less, dealing with increased overhead costs, difficulty finding and keeping deckhands—shrimp fishers have also had to make real sacrifices in their lives outside of the industry in order to stay afloat. One of the most frequently cited casualties of the import crisis involved hunting trips. Hunting, especially for ducks and deer, is a popular pastime for people living in Bayou Crevette. Traditionally, trawlers made enough money in six months that they could spend the winter months hunting, trapping, and fishing before they had to get their boats ready for the next season. In Bayou Crevette, hunting typically does not entail taking a day or even weekend trip into the woods. Instead it involves owning or renting a hunting camp—usually a small cabin-like structure in the woods—and staying out for weeks at a time, usually with family or friends. Many fishers spoke about the importance of both hunting and trawling as a source of identity. As Donny put it, "We was born to hunt and trap in the winter and come back over here in the summer to shrimp."

Since the industry declined, many have had to sell their camps or skip the yearly rental. Daniel used to own a hunting camp in Mississippi, but he sold it a few years ago in order to cut back on his expenses. "When I first had my boat—twenty-six years I've been having my boat," he said. "We used to make some money and have a little bit of money on the side. We'd trawl for six months and we'd head to Mississippi for hunting season. We'd set up camp and enjoy life a little bit. Now? No. You gotta hold on to the couple of things that you got, to try to survive to the next season."

Rural sociologists have documented the significance of hunting to rural culture. The geographer Brian Marks notes that "for many southern men living in or close to rural landscapes, hunting . . . comes with the air and with the land and with the people who live there. Hunting is woven into the very fabric of personal and social history."[5] This statement fittingly describes many rural communities in Louisiana—a state that is known as "sportsman's paradise"—including Bayou Crevette. Many trawlers told me that they learned to hunt and fish with their fathers, and those who had sons often felt it their duty to pass along this knowledge to them. Glen discussed the importance of teaching his seven-year-old son to hunt. "He needs to know how to trawl so he can go catch some shrimp. He needs to know how to catch crawfish. He needs to know how to kill a duck. Kill a deer, catch a rabbit. He needs to know how to do that. And I need to teach him." He worried that the import crisis would make it so he would not be able to continue taking his yearly hunting trips, a concern spelled out in an exchange he had with his wife, Linda.

Linda told me, "In the wintertime, he'd go hunting for duck. And then after winter he'd go back to trawling."

"Yep," Glen said. "But I don't know if I'll be able to hunt no more."

For shrimp fishers, skipping the yearly hunting trip was no small sacrifice.

Another consistent pattern that emerged when shrimpers spoke about how their lives had changed involved another, somewhat stereotypical aspect of rural culture: their pickup trucks. Pickup trucks abound around the community of Bayou Crevette, a norm that is consistent with research documenting their importance to rural culture.[6] Pickup trucks are very practical vehicles. The dominant forms of employment in the community— oil and fishing—entail a great deal of hauling, for which pickup trucks are necessary. Furthermore, pickup trucks are also useful vehicles for popular leisure activities such as hunting, fishing, or canoeing.

Paul explained that it had been customary for trawlers to purchase a new pickup truck about once every three years. He lamented how the decline of shrimping had prevented people from buying new trucks. He argued that not only was this a hit to people's egos and pride, it was damaging to the local economy. "Every three years, you would go buy a new pickup. A $30,000 pickup truck times 40,000 people [the number of shrimp fishers Paul estimates is in the industry nationwide], well, that's a lot of money. And that's just pickup trucks! You need nets, and you need ice, and you need freezers, and you need trucks." Paul made the connection that the ramifications of industrial decline stretched far beyond the fishers and their families.

In addition to its practical value, pickup trucks served as an important marker of wealth and success. Daniel explained how driving an older truck might be interpreted as a symbol of financial struggle. He explained how in recent years he had been unable to purchase a new truck and that he was ashamed of this. "I have a seventeen-year-old pickup truck, that everyday I pick up a piece that fell off, you know? It's embarrassing." Driving an older pickup truck might not seem like a major sacrifice. Indeed, it was not the same as being unable to pay a light bill or one's mortgage. But for those I spoke with, going without a newer truck was significant as it signaled an inability to live up to cultural standards.

Thus far I have described the various work-related obstacles that shrimpers have been forced to struggle against since the industry has deteriorated: lower dockside prices, higher overhead costs, difficulty finding and keeping good deckhands, and sacrificing important cultural markers associated with the work. Those who chose to remain in the industry were working harder and harder for less and less. But what are the effects of this struggle for life outside of the industry? In the next section I describe how the deterioration of the industry has resulted in a host of personal and emotional problems for shrimp fishers and their families.

The Personal and Social Consequences of Persisting

Researchers who have studied occupational decline have documented how the process can be linked to increases in anxiety and depression for those affected.[7] Shrimp fishers on Bayou Crevette were no exception to this. Depression and melancholy were consistent themes that came up during our conversations. I was particularly struck by the number of times that the shrimpers—current and former alike—broke down into tears as they spoke of the prospect or actual incidence of leaving the industry behind. After all, shrimp fishing is a dangerous and physically demanding craft, and the men who performed the demands of the job possess qualities that conform to ideals of hypermasculinity: large physiques, being engaged in the pursuit of excitement and adventure, aggressive, fiercely independent natures, and expressing disdain for authority of any kind. For these men to be reduced to tears—in front of a woman they barely knew—was particularly powerful, very telling of their attachment to their occupational identities.

Such an incident happened as I spoke with two third-generation shrimp fishers, Randy and Keith. I approached Randy as he was attempting a small repair on board his boat, docked along the bayou. Keith stopped by later to ask Randy a favor and joined in the conversation. Randy, age fifty, had been trawling since he was nine years old. Like many others, he dropped out of high school to trawl full time, first with his father and then on his own boat. Keith, age forty, had been trawling full time since he graduated from high school. Both men had strong and hulking physiques, with calloused hands that matched Glen's observation that shrimpers' hands looked as if they were covered with barnacles. Their lifetimes in the sun had aged them beyond their actual years.

Similar to other fishers who had stuck it out, they discussed the difficulties involved with shrimp fishing and how much harder it had become since the decline. Like other trawlers, Keith touted the virtues of hard work, even coming across as boastful as he described the exacting nature of shrimping. He said, "We used to make some good money, and let me tell you, it ain't easy. It's hard work. I'm forty years old, and Randy could tell you, I'm like a seventy-year-old man right now. My shoulders, my neck, they always hurt. But we love to do it, you see. We work hard and now we go by ourselves a lot on these boats, without help, so that we can be able to afford to do what we do. And you know, we can still hang. A lot of people would have just left. But we stayed."

When I asked how things have changed since the decline, his confidence turned to sadness, and he became visibly upset. "When we was in good times with shrimping it was great. But my wife told me recently, she said, 'You know, you don't seem too excited.' And I'm not." He paused and put his hand over his face to conceal the tears. After a few moments, he went on. "We was on a high around here. When shrimp season was open, we was on a high. And now, they took that high from us."

Undoubtedly, the shrimp fishing crisis had been particularly hard for him. Unlike Randy, whose children were grown, Keith had several small children at home that he was supporting. To make up for some of the economic losses he had experienced, he had taken up performing odd jobs as a handyman. He had spent the past few days painting a house for a neighbor, an admission that explained to me the paint that spattered his clothes, face, and hair. Although the extra income served to ease his financial strain, being forced to go outside of shrimping to find other employment was something he was not proud of and contributed significantly to his feelings of melancholy and dissatisfaction. "My main income is shrimping. But I paint on the side because I got a lot of bills. I don't like it. But I got a family, I got two kids. I gotta keep it together. Randy's kids are grown, he don't have any bills. He can get by like that." Having young children at home to support not only increased Keith's financial burden but created time management issues that added to his stress and anxiety.

Since the decline, it had become necessary for shrimpers to work harder and longer to maintain the same standard of living enjoyed in years past. Working longer hours—many of them in odd jobs—decreased the amount of quality time they could spend with family, and striking a balance was tricky, if not impossible. This issue was problematic to Donny, who had three children at home, two daughters and a son. "When you're out there on the boat, you wanna be home with your family. And when you're with your family, you know you got bills to pay and you want to be out there. I been having trouble since the May season. I've been having trouble with my trawl, and the little bit of money I had, I spent it on my boat. I'm at the end of my rope, I ain't gonna lie to you."

Working harder for less, being unable to spend quality time with family, and having to give up important cultural experiences such as hunting had all certainly taken a toll on the bodies and minds of persisters. Taken together, the meanings attached to the occupational identity of shrimp fisher had begun to shift around for some who continued to tough it out in the industry. In the fight to stay afloat, egos had been bruised and battered. As a result, many shrimp fishers expressed sentiments that betrayed their wounds.

Daniel had been fishing since he was a young boy, learning all he knew about the craft from his father, who was present for the first half of the two-hour-long conversation we had on his front porch. After telling me about how hard it has been giving up hunting trips and doing without what he previously took for granted—like purchasing a new truck every few years—he admitted that his feelings of self-worth had been affected. "I used to be proud to tell someone I was a shrimper," he said. "But now, if you ask me what I do, I won't even tell them sometimes. I tell them I'm the scum of the earth, in trawling. That's how it changed." He stopped, and pointed to his father. "You met this old man who was sitting right here? He used to trawl. He got more money now than he can ever spend. But us? Now, we just struggle. That's the truth. I'm not bragging or nothing. That's how it is."

What Daniel was experiencing reflects what previous researchers have found regarding the impact of work problems on psychological well-being. As individuals struggle with feelings of inadequacy at the same time as financial hardships, their personal relationships with others may suffer. This is especially true of marital relationships and can explain why divorce rates rise during times of high unemployment or shortly thereafter. Shrimp fishers are no exception to this, and on several occasions they—or their wives—admitted to suffering through marital discord.

I met Charlene during my interview with Daniel. She was the ex-wife of Daniel's friend Arty—a fellow shrimper—and a very good friend of Daniel's wife, Caroline. She stopped over to pay Caroline a visit while Daniel and I chatted on his front porch. Daniel introduced me to her and told her that I was interested in what was happening to shrimp fishers. Before I could say anything, she immediately shared some very personal details about her life with Arty. It was clear to me that the decline of shrimp fishing was something very meaningful for her. With great sadness in her voice, she told me how the stress caused by the decline had become too much for her to handle. "You know, that's what broke up our marriage. It was just too much stress and he took it out on me, his stress about the boat, the shrimp prices. Thirty-five years of marriage. I gave him a choice, the boat or me. And he kept his boat. I didn't want to hear the boat. I gave him a choice. I didn't want him to do that no more. I had enough of being unhappy and struggling with the price problems. I had my own problems trying to raise the kids, and trying to carry the load." She became visibly upset and began to cry. "And I couldn't do it no more. And I *won't* do it no more."

Charlene, who said she was "forty-something," married Arty right after they graduated from high school. Both Arty and Charlene are from families with long histories in the shrimp fishing industry. As a young girl, Charlene regularly trawled with her three uncles on their boat. She always figured she would marry a shrimper, and after she married Arty, they had four sons. Her sons were all raised on board the boat—they trawled as a family—and shrimp fishing provided them with the means to earn a good living. They lived in a nice house, and she was especially proud of how she was able to be a full-time mother to her boys and not have to worry about working outside of the home. "I raised my kids on the boat," she told me. "I went trawling when my third son was nine days old. I went on the boat with him, a baby. I got pictures of it. Me and my brand new baby on the shrimp boat." She was clearly pleased with the life afforded by shrimping. It really was the only life she'd ever known. But only a few seconds after telling me how wonderful it was to be on the boat with her nine-day-old son, she added, "I sacrificed my life, and it didn't get us nowhere. Because of the prices now, you can't really make it."

She went on to explain how since the decline, her husband became more and more stressed and tense. He frequently worried about the prices, about the condition of the boat, and about how they were going to make ends meet with the high costs and low prices. Eventually, the constant stress became too much for her: "I think it was five years that he was a broken re-cord. 'Well,' I told him finally, 'go do something about it. Go find yourself a job.' Boy, he didn't like that." The thought of having to leave the industry to take work—even if only temporarily—was inconceivable to Arty, and Charlene's suggestions to do so were not favorably received.

To try to make ends meet, she picked up a part-time job waiting tables. She thought that the extra income would ease some of the financial burden and intensifying tensions. But Arty didn't see it that way. He saw Charlene taking a job as a sign of personal failure, an indication that his family couldn't make it on the income provided by the boat that he captained. He wanted to be the sole provider, just as he had always been. They fought frequently, and after years of frustration and argument, she issued him an ultimatum: the boat or their marriage. She wasn't prepared for him to choose the boat, but he did, and they soon divorced.

Charlene credited the demise of their marriage to Arty's dogged persistence in forging ahead with shrimp fishing. She also perceived it as a factor in what she described as deterioration in the relationship Arty had with their kids. He desperately wanted them to become trawlers, and they had all at some point served as his deckhands. But as the struggle to survive as a trawler became more and more severe—and as they witnessed how difficult it was to be a shrimper—they wanted to look elsewhere for ways to earn a living. "You know how they say you can unload to the ones you love?" Charlene asked. "It's true, but it makes you hurt so much. And my kids, he did it to my kids. He wanted to make them so tough and make them work, and make them trawlers." At this point she paused, looked down at the ground. "They couldn't take him. My little boy went trawling, and he don't want to be a trawler. I don't want him to be. I used to be on Arty's side and try to make the kids be tough. Well, I don't want that kind of life for them now."

Even though she left the marriage and was at the time living on her own, she still worried about Arty's health and well-being. Shrimp fishing takes a toll on a person's body, and as Arty was aging, she feared that the shrimping lifestyle—with all the struggles and strain—was going to be his demise. "That boat's gonna put him in his grave," she said. "It's gonna put him in there earlier than his time. It's so much stress."

Charlene's worries about her ex-husband's life were in part grounded in the stories and rumors that circulated around town about how other shrimp fishers were faring. The shrimping crisis, she explained, had been tough on many families around the bayou. The uncertainty surrounding the industry had pushed many out in search of other work, but she claimed that she knew others who had faced mounting financial and emotional struggles who chose to stay in. In an extreme case, she told me about the experience of one shrimper with whom she and Daniel were familiar. "Remember the case of Bernard?" she asked Daniel. "Oh yeah I do," replied Daniel. He then relayed the following story about a fisher who he claimed committed suicide after not being able to pay his bills.

[He] wasn't making ends meet. So he went and had to buy fuel from the man at the shed on credit. Fuel, ice, and hardware. The man said, "Sign this little paper, go and get what you need, and then you'll have to pay me." So he went on trawling, and was struggling. He couldn't pay the man, and the guy who let him charge fuel and supplies wanted his money. He was tired of not getting his money. So he borrowed money against his boat to pay the man, about $10,000, so he could be finished with that man, you know? But then he couldn't pay his boat note, he got his boat seized. He got it taken away from him for his $10,000. When the U.S. marshal came to seize the boat, the guy broke out a gun, he tied the U.S. marshal to the boat. Took the gun and shot him, lit the boat on fire. Took the gun and shot himself.

Surely this example lies at the extreme end of the continuum of shrimpers' responses to decline, and if it is a true story, it is an atypical one. Yet it is a powerful illustration of the desperation that people might feel when their livelihoods and way of life are threatened. And while most shrimp fishers are unlikely to engage in such behavior, the story itself illustrates that they do draw the connection between the new realities of shrimp fishing and suicide.

The stories I heard from shrimper after shrimper illustrate just how difficult it has been to be successful in the craft that most have pursued for their entire lives. The hardships have taken their toll on their physical and mental health, as well as on their relationships with family and friends. The suffering is clear. But we also must recognize that these individuals have *chosen* to struggle in these ways. There are numerous employment alternatives available to shrimp fishers; indeed, some have already exited. So why do they forgo these possibilities?

"I Don't Want to Do That, I Want to Do This"

It is clear that shrimp fishers had suffered in many ways since their industry fell into decline. But despite alternative employment opportunities, many simply refused to quit trawling, knowingly accepting the consequences. Their actions fly in the face of theories that predict that individuals by and large pursue economic incentives alone. Given the crisis of shrimping, rational choice theorists, for example, are likely to assume that because individuals seek to maximize personal profit, shrimp fishers would exit. What is more, because shrimpers have a plush economic cushion on which to land upon exit—because even though they are dealing with occupational decline, they have even better alternative employment options—some theorists may not deem them worthy of studying. What can we learn from such an uneventful transition from one form of employment to the next?

It has already been mentioned that those who chose to stick it out as fishers had many available alternative employment options; proportionally, Louisiana has more jobs for blue-collar workers than other parts of the modern United States, and most of these are concentrated in the south, including the southeastern area where Bayou Crevette is located.[8] While the fishing industry is deeply rooted in the culture and economy of the community, oil now employs more people than agriculture and fishing combined. Shrimp fishers therefore have friends, relatives, and neighbors who are employed by the oil or its attendant industries—some fishers have even worked those jobs themselves—and they know the good living that those jobs can provide.

During our conversation on his front porch, Daniel pointed out that his neighbor worked in oil. His neighbor's house was the largest and newest on the street, sitting on a very large lot complete with a fountain in the front yard. A shiny new Mercedes Benz was parked in the driveway. "See that house right there? That's oil money," he told me. Daniel has two brothers, both of whom left the shrimping industry years ago, even before the decline, for other employment. One of his brothers worked for a company that cleans up oil-related messes ("he deals with the oil slush"), while the other one got a job as a boat captain, and like many who do this, worked primarily running ships in and around the coast of Africa. It is far from home, but very lucrative.

"He gets five hundred dollars a day doing that," Daniel stated. He knew he could be making more money—and dealing with less uncertainty—if he left shrimp fishing, and he had friends and relatives who could easily get him a job. Despite this, he chose to continue doing what he loved and what he knew best. I asked him how long he would stay in shrimping. After a bit of a pause and a deep sigh, Daniel said, "For as long as possible. You know, this will tell you how things had changed: when we built this house, the first night I slept in it, it was paid off. Right now? I don't know if I could even make a house payment. That's how things changed. But I'll stay as long as I can. I will."

For Daniel, it wasn't that he lacked institutional access to other jobs. He had friends and connections in the industry, and he watched his brothers go through the transition and come out of it with more financial security. Other persisting fishers understood that their economic strain could be mitigated by taking other employment. Some of them even took the necessary steps to leave shrimping, at least temporarily. J. T., for example, had obtained a captain's license right when the industry noticeably changed for the worse. A captain's license is necessary to run tug or supply boats for companies, one of the most lucrative jobs to be had. J. T. remarked that "there's a lot of good jobs to be had in the oil field. If I tied this thing up right now, I'd go and make me three hundred dollars a day. I have my captain's license. But I don't want to do that. I have a captain's license, but I want to do *this*." J. T. knew that this license guaranteed him a more secure living, and he remarked that he had obtained the license "for backup if I ever needed it."

So it was not that shrimpers lacked the knowledge that they could make more money working in other jobs, or that they lacked access. In some cases they had direct experience working jobs associated with oil and knew firsthand the financial stability these jobs provided. Randy was among those who had previously worked in oil during times of financial strain. As he worked to repair his net, which had become snagged during a recent outing, he told me about a time when he'd taken a job offshore to make extra money. "I worked the oil fields. My bones got sore working offshore. I'm trying to do this at my own pace. I work when I want, do what I want. I love doing this." And then, acknowledging that working offshore is not only lucrative but also easier than trawling, "It's a lot of harder work than sitting offshore driving the boat, but I really like doing this.". "My bones got sore" is not a reference to hard, strenuous labor but rather to the idle nature of captaining a boat.

I wondered whether the shrimpers refused to leave because they of hoped that conditions in the industry would soon get back to what they used to be. Shrimp fishing requires a heavy investment of resources—the boat, the supplies, the know-how—and perhaps they were reluctant to jump to other jobs so soon after the collapse. After all, the industry had cycled through periods of boom and bust in the past. Sometimes crops are abundant and other years are scarce. Dockside prices have always fluctuated to some degree, resulting in variability of profit margins. Could it be that fishers were sticking it out because they hoped that conditions would improve?

When I asked them this question, they unanimously expressed great pessimism regarding the future of the industry; they did not think it would rebound, and most of them had braced themselves for economic conditions to *worsen* over time. J. T. and Donny recognized that boom-and-bust nature of fishing, but they differentiated down cycles of the past from their present predicament.

Donny said, "In the eighties, things got real bad. The price didn't drop that much, but shrimping was so bad. It was a bad year for shrimping. Banks was taking a lot of boats, people was losing boats like crazy."

"But even then," J. T. added, "the shrimp prices were mostly good, the fuel was low. Now though? It's unbelievable. The shrimp prices are so low, they're at the same price today that they were twenty years ago. And it's not gonna get better, it'll even get worse maybe."

This exchange highlights the two key differences between previous industrial downturns and the crisis of trawling that the shrimpers face today: fuel costs and imports. Before the decline, bad years were characterized by either low dockside prices that corresponded to an overproduction of shrimp or low yields due to insufficient numbers of shrimp. Sometimes a hurricane or other storm would come through and leave debris in the water (as Katrina did), but for the most part this was pretty easy to recover from. Problems such as these usually corrected themselves in a year or two, and shrimpers knew this, but the rising fuel costs and flood of imported shrimp have delivered an unprecedented one-two punch from which the industry may never fully recover. These are conditions over which shrimpers have little control, so they perceive their futures as uncertain and bleak—and they are worried.

I met Paul, the fourth-generation fisher mentioned earlier, through Larry and Albert. Albert and Paul grew up together and were still very good friends. I was fortunate to have traveled to Paul's house with Albert because it became fairly evident that Paul was suspicious of my intentions as a researcher. Like most of the others, he had lived through the TEDs battle and been deeply scarred by the outcome. He felt betrayed by politicians, who he felt sided with environmentalists and the federal regulating bodies. "It started twenty years ago," Paul told me when I asked about the shrimping crisis. "We got stuck with the turtle excluders. Our own congressman told us we couldn't fight the restaurant association, the environmentalists, the endangered species act. We were strong, and they killed us. We were strong."

Paul grew up in a fishing family, one of five brothers who all went on to run their own boats. They learned the craft from their father and grandfather, working side by side all summer long on their father's boat. As adults they often ran their boats side by side, sharing in the bounty of a "hot spot" where lots of shrimp were found. But the industrial crisis caused by imports broke up their family enterprise, as several of his brothers quit fishing and went to work in the oil industry.

"It's really bad," he said. "We was five brothers strong, and now three of us have got out. There's only two left."

"So why do you still do it?" I asked. "Why haven't you gotten out?"

"Only 'cause I love to do it," he replied. "If you don't like to do it, you can get out. The money is not there anymore." He went on to describe the financial problems involved with staying, and how it has affected his view for the future. "It's as simple as this: we get a dollar a pound and fuel is two-fifty a gallon. That's scary. I can't compete with that. Who knows what'll happen? I can make this story last a whole book, but it can be broke down to just that. And I'm scared."

High fuel costs and low dockside prices have put an unprecedented stranglehold on the shrimp fishing industry. As a result, shrimp fishers who wish to remain must deal with mounting economic, personal, and familial troubles. As conditions have continued to deteriorate, they have become more and more pessimistic regarding their futures. Why have they chosen to struggle when obvious solutions to economic uncertainty exist? What do they gain from dealing with the hardships?

If we are to recognize the full import of what is at stake in shrimp fishing's deterioration, we must begin by exploring the complex and deeply valued meanings that shrimp fishers attach to the work. While each shrimp fisher I spoke with had his or her own unique stories to tell, there are multiple similarities that weave through the narratives. In the community of Bayou Crevette, where the shared work of shrimp fishing has been so central, notions about the relationship between work, family, and place combine to provide a distinct and highly valued cultural identity. Shrimp fishers in this community essentialized their location in and affinity with their occupation. More than just a job, shrimp fishing fulfilled what they understand as their predetermined destiny as a Cajun, best described as a physical necessity akin to an addiction, as the basis for the social organization of the family, and as means to live off the land in the way that Cajuns have always done. These factors are powerful, and by elaborating on them we are shown a clearer picture of why fishers are so committed to their craft.

Going Down with the Ship: Nonmarket
Forces and Decision Making

While I emphasize the importance of nonmmaterial considerations to the fishers' decisions to stay afloat, I do not claim that economic factors do not matter to them. Economic aspects unquestionably factor into deciding whether to keep fishing or cut bait, so to speak. Among those I spoke with, there was great variation regarding economic factors that may make it easier to remain. For example, owning one's boat outright, having a working spouse that contributes to household income, or having children who are grown and no longer financially dependent surely make it easier to remain in the industry. Moreover, as the industry collapsed, trawlers who wished to get out faced difficulties with selling their boats, as few people were looking to invest in shrimping's future. Shrimp fishers looking to sell were reluctant to price their boats according to the low prices being offered these days. "I'm not just gonna give my boat away, no," I was told by those several of those considering exit in the future. Owing money on one's boat did not necessarily prevent a trawler from exiting. Some ex-trawlers had "tied up" their boats, meaning that they were no longer trawling and were looking to sell, but had not done so yet. In the meantime, they were working other jobs.

Although economic considerations surely factor into fishers' decisions to stay or go, they alone do not explain why persisting shrimp fishers choose to stick it out. If economic issues were the sole determining factors, then by and large shrimp fishers would have either already exited or be planning to do so in the near future. Among those persisting fishers that I spoke with, there was no real pattern regarding economic circumstance that emerged. Some had mortgages and boat notes (balances they owed on their boats), while others had no real debts. Some had young children at home, while others had no dependents. Some had wives who contribute to household income, some did not.

No, if we are to fully understand why shrimp fishers choose to stick it out and suffer the consequences, we must consider how economic *and* noneconomic factors combine to produce outcomes. Noneconomic considerations—emblematized through the phrase "it's in my blood" that I heard time and again—factor significantly into the shrimpers' decisions regarding their futures. Exploring on a deep level the loyalty of shrimpers to their craft and the meanings they attach to their life worlds shows us that their stubborn resistance to globalization and economic change is not an irrational act but is instead highly rational. It further highlights how local actors can be active participants in globalization processes and are therefore key players in shaping outcomes. Theories of globalization that strip local actors of their agency fail to understand the choices that they actually make, leaving us unable to understand why local actors so often obstinately refuse to acquiesce to the logic of the market.

"It's in My Blood": Family and Shrimp Fishing

Fishing has long been a way of life for Cajuns living in Bayou Crevette. From the earliest days of Acadian settlement around the swamps and marshlands of coastal Louisiana, harvesting from the rich natural resources of the unique environment has been an important part of life for Cajun people. The valuable resources supplied by the land have offered a means for both daily survival and economic livelihood; the bayous and marshes supplied by the Mississippi River contain a bounty of fish, shrimp, crabs, and oysters that could be caught for both consumption and the market. Forests and marshlands have provided an abundance of animal life to trap for both food and the fur trade. Wood from cypress trees has been—and remains—sought after for a variety of products (from boats to shingles to homes) because of its beauty and its resistance to rot and insects.

The rise of the Gulf shrimp industry in the early 1900s was important to coastal towns such as Bayou Crevette for several reasons. Economically, of course, it situated them within the larger context of the national economy. Many towns were built by the fishing and oystering industries. Commercial shrimp fishing became a viable way to earn a decent living. In addition to economic worth, the industry also played a key role in shaping the distinct, shared cultural identity that continues to thrive in towns such as Bayou Crevette. Researchers who have studied occupational cultures have found that those who work in extractive industries—such as fishing, logging, and mining—have strong identities that are characterized by a high degree of convergence between work and nonwork spheres of life.[9] The connection between shrimping for family consumption and shrimping for market consumption has provided a basis for cultural identity that still persists in present-day Louisiana. Preparing and serving meals in which many of the ingredients were gathered by the hands of either the cook or someone the cook knows is commonplace on the bayou and thus serves as an important cultural element.

Family has historically also served as an important component to the shrimp fishing process. In years past, all members of the family would typically lend assistance to fishing efforts in some way. Although trawling as a family has become less customary for U.S. commercial shrimp fishers as a whole[10]—as many women have opted to work outside of shrimp fishing or stay at home—recent research has found that it is still a fairly common practice among Louisiana shrimpers.[11] For the most part, fishers I spoke with either currently trawled with kin or had family members who had their own boats and to whom they frequently lent a hand.

The importance of family was typically referenced when I asked trawlers how they came to their profession and discovered that most of them had begun trawling with their families as young children. The extent to which this was common in the town is evidenced through school policies that dismissed male students (but not female students) from school a week or so early at the end of the school year so they could participate in the opening of the May season with their parents:

> J. T.: We been doing this since we been kids. Both our fathers had boats, and we went to work with them during the summer vacations. And for like the winter and Thanksgiving vacations, we went to work. And then, when we got out of school, this is what we did.
> Donny: They used to let us go early for the May season. This is almost thirty years, me and him. Since I was fourteen or fifteen years old, they let us out of junior high early to go help our parents out.
> J. T.: We used to work as a family, you know. My older brother worked, and when we got outta school, my mom would come, my sister same thing. That's why we built this boat. To be with the family.

For many like Donny and J. T., trawling was a family affair that included daughters as well as sons, and mothers as well as fathers. Family fishing outings not only served as a way to bolster family income (as there was no need to hire deckhands or at least as many of them as otherwise), they also provided the experiences through which the specialized knowledge and abilities associated with shrimping were passed from one generation to the next.

Glen also spoke about having learned how to work as a fisher from his father. He was the youngest sibling in his family. "It started with my daddy, ya see? I was the littlest one in the bunch. My daddy had a trawl boat. He grabbed me by the ear and said, 'you going trawling.' We'd spend the whole summer trawling, all through the brown shrimp season that started in May. When the white shrimp season would come along in August, you'd have to go to school. But you did it anyway. So as a kid when you finished school, you trawling, and when you started back school again, you trawling."

Surely, the deep cultural significance of shrimp fishing to self-identity resulted in part from this generational transmission of knowledge and skill. J. T. and Donny discussed the importance of the process.

> J. T.: Not too many people can do what we do. It's not easy work. The more you catch, the more you gonna make money. It's hard work. Sometimes you catch a lot and you can fill your hole, sometimes it's dirty. You know? Crabs, fish, it depends. It's not easy sometimes. People don't understand.
> Donny: You have breakdowns. Yeah, you don't just get shrimp anywheres. You got to know what you doing. If not, it's like Forrest Gump, you out there, and you can never catch any shrimp. Well, it's almost that bad sometimes, if you don't know where to get shrimp.
> J. T.: You gotta have the knowledge and all. And that comes from our parents. That's how we learned.

Donny referenced the movie *Forrest Gump* to demonstrate that shrimp fishing is not something just anyone can do. In the film, Forrest purchases a shrimp boat without any previous experience with or knowledge of shrimping. His primary motivation in purchasing the boat was to keep a promise to his friend, Bubba, who he met while he was in the army and with whom he later served in Vietnam. Bubba was a shrimp fisher from Alabama, and while in the army Forrest and Bubba pledged to buy a shrimp boat together as soon as they were finished with their tours of duty. Tragically, Bubba never made it home, as he was killed in the line of duty. When Forrest inherits money from a deceased relative, he buys a boat to keep his pledge. But he's very inexperienced, and when he first takes the boat out, he fails miserably at catching any shrimp—proving that to be a shrimper, one needs to have more than the funds to buy a boat. It's the skills and experience that are passed down from one generation to the next that provide shrimp fishers with the expertise required to be successful.

The most common way that the shrimpers explained their reluctance to leave the industry was by emphasizing its connection to family history. There was no phrase I heard more often throughout my conversations with both current and former shrimpers than "it's in my blood." They used this phrase to explain why, despite all of the hardships and struggles, they continued to try to make it as fishers, and with this simple expression they demonstrated that trawling was not merely a job or a way to earn a living. Rather it represented the foundation upon which family history had been forged. In that sense, shrimp fishing constituted what they considered to be their genealogical destiny. As Raymond put it, "It's in our blood. Our grandfathers did it. Ellen's daddy did it. And *his* daddy did it, you know. So I guess you could say it's in our blood. We love to do it."

Similarly, Daniel's wife, Caroline, emphasized the connection to family by describing why it is difficult for people such as her husband to quit. She said:

> From my perspective of shrimping, it's something that's in you. It's a part of who you are, it's what you love to do. And you know how to do it. It's like, sometimes you can't hardly find any shrimp, and it's like, how do they ever find this shrimp? It's a skill. What I see is it's like, in your blood, you know you work hard, and you buy a boat or you build a boat. You put all your energies into it. This is your life, it's a part of our culture and heritage. For Daniel, it's four generations. His daddy taught him how to do it, and his daddy's grandpa taught him how to do that. It's passed down. So It's hard for them to part with it. I had a trawler come over here yesterday, he said, "As long as I could still make a few dollars, I'm not getting out of it.". . . So, it's a culture and a heritage, and a way of living over here.

All of the persisting shrimp fishers I spoke with were second generation or more, meaning that at the very least their fathers worked as shrimpers. And most of the shrimp fishers I spoke with were in their mid-forties or older,[12] coming of age during the fifties and sixties, before the rise of the oil industry, when Bayou Crevette was primarily a fishing and farming community. However, even among younger trawlers—those who grew up after the oil industry expanded—I found consistency in the attribution of family history to the construction of occupational identity.

I approached a shrimp fisher named Tommy as he worked to repair a hole in his wooden boat, the result of a recent collision with a dock. At age thirty, he was one of the youngest fishers I encountered. His boat was docked alongside the bayou in a row of four large wooden boats, all belonged to members of his family: two of the boats belonged to his younger brothers, the other to his father, Vernon. Tommy was a fourth-generation trawler, and he took great pride in explaining his family's passion for using wooden boats. Most shrimp boats are now constructed using fiberglass and steel, and wooden boats have become something of a rarity. In that way, Tommy related wooden boats to shrimp fishers. "We try to hold on to them best we can," he said. "They're disappearing. Kinda like us." In his family, boats have been passed down along with the knowledge and passion for the work. When he graduated from high school, Vernon gifted him his old boat after building—in large part on his own—a new one for himself. And when Tommy's brother Eddie—twenty-six at the time of my interview—graduated from high school, Tommy gave him his old boat, and together with his father, built a new one for himself.

In all, there were five siblings: four brothers and a sister. Three of the brothers trawled, but the other left the industry to work for his father-in-law when he got married. Like the other persisters, Tommy and Eddie grew up on the deck of their father's boat: "When we was growing up we was the whole family on the boat, on my dad's boat. There was five of us. My mom still goes with my dad."

When I remarked that I had run across few younger trawlers like him, Tommy answered that younger folks, like his brother, often choose to work in the oil industry because it paid very well. He knew how much money he could make if he followed his brother, and that he would have an easier time paying his bills and not struggle to get by as he was at the time. But Tommy stayed because he could not envision doing anything else. "I have a couple more cousins, they're my age," he told me. "They still do it, but there aren't very many younger folks. There's a few. They just like me, they try, they struggle. But it's in our blood. And we're here because we don't want to do something else."

In addition to the blood metaphor, another form of imagery trawlers used to describe their connection to fishing was to liken trawling to an addiction. This metaphor is powerful, because not only does it describe how shrimping *is* part of them—as something that flows through their veins, like blood—it is also something that they perceive as a physical necessity. In the quote that opens this chapter, Glen used the metaphor to describe the control that shrimp fishing has over his decisions. He noted that, like

any addiction, earning a living as a shrimp fisher came with its fair share
of heartbreak and letdowns. "If there's a hundred things about trawling,
probably eighty to ninety percent stabs you through the heart like a vampire with a stick," he remarked. "But when you can win that one or two or
three times, it pumps you up! It's the greatest thing you will ever see. It's
an addiction. I love it."

The most poignant example of the addiction metaphor was given by
a second-generation persister named Alvin, explaining to me why he
found working in the oil industry—something he had tried—unacceptable.
Alvin was forty-five years old and had learned the trade from his father
and uncle and alongside his cousin and two brothers. He had five children of his own, ranging in age from ten to twenty-six. With that many
kids, extra money was always something he could use, and at one point
(before the collapse) he decided to try working a job in the oil fields because it was faster and more certain money. He worked offshore on a
rig for a season, but he just couldn't fight the desire to be out there on
his boat. "It's in my blood," he said. "In my blood, you know? Like a
crackhead. You always gotta go back for the hit of crack? I gotta go get
my hit of shrimp."

Similarly, Glen used the addiction metaphor when he spoke of struggling with the idea of leaving fishing behind for good. We were discussing
why so many fishers have a hard time leaving the industry, even if only for
a short while. He remarked that, like others, he'd given working on tugboats a shot. "I'm not too good at using some big words, but I learned how
to trawl with my father when I was a kid. My brother was some tugboat
captains. So I followed my brothers on the tugboats, but still I had an addiction for trawling."

Later on in our conversation, he used the metaphor again, this time in
response to my question about whether or not he wanted his son Marcus
to become a trawler. He talked about how he felt it was his duty to teach
his son how to trawl because through learning the work, his son would
also pick up important values such as hard work and responsibility. "I
think he needs to know [how] to catch some shrimp so he can feed his
family, so they can feed themselves." After pausing for a few moments,
he added, "But it's better he *don't* learn it, and get addicted like us. 'Cause
it's an addiction. Sometimes I think it's better for Marcus to not learn it
at all."

Metaphors such as these exemplify the degree to which shrimp fishers understand their work as an inherent element of who they are. And although some of them have an easier time persisting in a declining industry because of economic factors—a working spouse, fewer debts, no young children at home—their narratives regarding why they find it so difficult to leave for good are driven primarily by cultural factors.

Born on the Bayou: The Importance of Place

While family structure and history contributed significantly to the meanings attached to shrimp fishing, there was another culturally based element that was often cited: place. The swamps, marshlands, and bayous that surround the community produce an abundance of valuable resources for the community. Harvesting such resources as seafood and oil contributes greatly to state and local economies and is what makes Louisiana such an important player in the national economy. Often when Louisiana's natural resources are discussed, it is in economic terms. But the importance of landscape goes way beyond economic value. The rich and distinct environment serves as the tapestry against which shared cultural identity is forged.

When I asked both current and former shrimpers what it meant to be Cajun, most commonly people would respond with a remark about the landscape. "We live off of the land," was a phrase that was often offered to describe the Cajun culture. While this surely references how Cajun folks earn a living, it also suggests the rugged individualism and independence that is central to how Cajuns generally define their culture.[13] The rich and fertile land provides an abundance of resources that have given many people, such as the ones an ex-fisher named Jack, who left the industry a decade ago, describes below, the ability to subsist as well as the means to earn a living.

> My grandfather was a trapper, a fisherman, a shrimper. He lived off the land. He passed ten or twelve years ago. My uncle did the same thing. He trapped, he shrimped, he did some fishing. He had a summer garden, he had a winter garden, he had a calf that he grew every year. He had a hog, he had chickens, he had ducks. He went duck hunting, deer hunting. He lived off the land. The only time he couldn't live off the land was in March and through the middle of April. Nothing was in season then. During this time, he would carve wooden boats, he'd go to the shipyard and sell 'em. That's what he did.

Before the ascendance of the shrimp fishing and oil industries, hunting, trapping, and growing one's own food was a necessity for everyday survival. People built their homes and boats from the very cypress trees that they—or probably someone they knew—harvested directly from the swamps. The ecosystem of southern Louisiana is a harsh one, with very hot summers that bring humid, mosquito-dense air and winters that can get quite cold. Because the swampy land lies close to or below sea level, before the building of levees floods were commonplace, and so was the rebuilding process that followed. The tenacity with which Cajun people battled these severe elements continues to characterize how they view themselves and also serves as a source of pride. Of course, modernization has made it unnecessary to subsist fully on one's own through hunting and trapping, and building shelters and boats are no longer essential to survival. However, that doesn't mean these cultural pursuits are mere relics of the past. Now they constitute important leisure activities. Cajun people often fill their free time with hunting for deer and alligator, and although woodcarving and boatbuilding aren't nearly as popular as they once were, some folks pursue these as hobbies.

The importance of food to Cajun cultural identity has been well established by other researchers of Cajun culture.[14] A common phrase used to describe the region of southern Louisiana—including New Orleans—is that there people don't eat to live, they live to eat. An important element in bayou cuisine is that the ingredients are locally sourced, harvested from the surrounding estuaries, bayous, marshes, and the Gulf of Mexico. Shrimp, crabs, crawfish, redfish, alligator, and oysters are all key to the cuisine because they are found in abundance in the surrounding environment. Okra, mirliton (a pear-shaped vegetable), and cushaw (a crookneck squash) are also common ingredients used by southern Louisiana chefs because they grow in abundance in the subtropical climate.

These foods hold significance not only for how they taste but also because of how they are obtained. Catching and harvesting them require skills that are often passed on to young children. Glen described his experience as a child who was born on the bayou: "When I was a little bitty kid, my daddy did all kinds of things. And so when we was little, we was raised up doing that stuff: catching crawfish, perch, crabs, killing snakes. We did everything." He motioned toward his seven-year-old son. "When I was like my little boy right here, we was catching crawfish in the back near the canal that I showed you. We grew up on the back of the little shrimp boats. And we cooked what we caught."

The natural environment holds obvious importance to individuals and communities in southeastern Louisiana. The relationship between people and the environment is a reflexive one, that is, people shape the natural environment just as they are shaped by it. As shrimp fishing became institutionalized as a way of life for many in Bayou Crevette, the surrounding environment—and landscape—was altered to reflect the industrial importance. Scholars who study the relationship between people and environment draw a distinction between natural environments and landscapes. Natural environments contain the rocks, rivers, and mountains that make up the landscape, while landscapes hold the meanings attached to these objects. Landscapes can therefore be understood as symbolic environments that are grounded in culture and reflect people's self-definitions.[15] The natural environment and the landscape each reflected the importance of the Bayou Crevette community's shared dependence on the fishing industry. Even those who did not make a living as a commercial shrimp fisher recognized the centrality of the craft in shaping who they were and where they come from. Thousands of people turned out for the various shrimp boils and seafood festivals held in the town each year.

The fishing industry has contributed significantly to the landscape of Bayou Crevette. In addition to all of the shrimp boats that lined the bayou flowing through the middle of the community, the central function of many of the town's businesses was to provide support for it. The hardware stores, net shops, seafood docks, and icehouses all provided the community with employment opportunities as well as a distinct identity. Many trawlers worried about how the decline of shrimping would affect the overall landscape of the community. This concern especially troubled Vernon and his sons, the fishing family who operated on wooden boats.

> Vernon: You know, this bayou here, and some of the others nearby? That's all fishing industry right there. You got people that shrimp there. That's all we got, I mean, you take that out of the way, you get us out the way. If you take the shrimping industry out of here, you'd shut down half of the hardware stores on the bayou. And there's a bunch here. They got all the net shops. Those would be gone. You take out the fuel docks. What do you have left?

Eddie: And the icehouses.

Tommy: The boats that pass down the bayou, they don't fuel up here.

Eddie: No.

Tommy: They fuel up in Houma or New Orleans or somewhere else. They don't fuel up here. You can take that out of here. They would shut down the ice plant. It'd change this town.

Other trawlers commented on how the landscape had already begun to change in the relatively short time since the import crisis struck. The most remarkable change for many trawlers had been the decrease in the number of working boats traveling up and down the bayou that runs right through the heart of the community. The bayou is flanked on either side by the town's two main roads. In order to get across the bayou from one road to the other—something that is required quite a bit when traveling around town—one has to drive over a bridge. In years past, when the season was at its peak, there was a steady parade of boats coming in from or going out to the Gulf. Indeed, in 2001 when I was doing AmeriCorps and the industry hummed along as normal, I found the boat traffic particularly noticeable. The bridges in the town are either lift bridges or pontoon bridges, both of which are designed to let boats pass. Lift bridges are more modern and go up and down as necessary. Pontoon bridges are typically smaller, less-traveled bridges that float on the water and move back and forth when boats need to get by. As a land-locked midwesterner, I found the bridges to be unique features of the landscape, and I was initially charmed by them. However, there were quite a few times when they were sources of frustration because they slowed me down, much in the way of passing trains. During the height of the fishing seasons—May and August—as shrimp boats from all over Louisiana made their way back and forth to the Gulf, delays were very common.

But after the industry decline, while boats in general still passed with great frequency, there were quite a few less shrimp boats. Furthermore, there was an obvious drop in the number of boats that were docked along the bayou, where, in the off-season, shrimp fishers typically dock their boats. Many of those that remained had "for sale" signs in the windows, and some had fallen into disrepair. These types of changes in the landscape of the town had not gone unnoticed by folks in the community. As Daniel stated, "You go up and down the bayou, and ten to fifteen years ago you saw a lot more boats than you see now. It's sad."

The importance of family, environment, and work combined to create a deeply meaningful cultural significance that was often used by fishers as a rationale to forge ahead in the dying industry. Paul, introduced earlier in the chapter, was among those who felt that way. As we wrapped up our conversation, he summed up his feelings about why he stayed in. "I wouldn't want to live anywhere else," he said. "It's a heritage we have. I did it, and my dad did it, and *his* dad did it. It's in my blood and I love it. But you've got to work so hard, they're making us work extra hard. I might catch two hundred thousand pounds now, and that's a lot. You got less boats out there, and less competition, and that means more shrimp. But they keep pushing the price of shrimp down, down. From a dollar thirty, down to a dollar, or less. It's hard for us. I'm going to keep going, though."

The Meaning of Work

"For a Cajun the business of life is not business; it is living."[16] This simple phrase written by the sociologists Anthony Margavio and Craig Forsyth beautifully sums up the absence of boundaries between work life and home life. Bayou Crevette has built its identity out of the types of work that are performed there. When Acadian settlers were initially established in the swamps of Louisiana, most made a living through extracting valuable resources from the rich natural environment. This often resulted in a person being self-employed in some way: selling shrimp, fish, or crabs caught by hand; carving boats or making homes using cypress trees that were cut down by oneself with one's family; selling food or hide or other supplies (such as ice) to those who needed them to make their living. In the earliest of days, there was a high degree of self-employment, as most people sold the goods they grew, caught, or trapped. By the middle of the twentieth century, however, the offshore oil industry began to rapidly expand. The pursuit of oil threatened to replace cultural values that were not traditionally guided by the marketplace—those based on the importance of close-knit family bonds—with those associated with the modern spirit of capitalism that emphasized mass consumption and material gain. The growth of oil also led to an influx of nonnative workers who were attracted by a wealth of employment opportunities. Because the region was so isolated by swamps and lowland marshes, up until then it had remained culturally homogenous, and those native to the region were often worried about what the arrival of outsiders would mean for their communities. Within the community, the promise of high wages lured many away from such traditional occupations as commercial shrimp fishing.[17] While we might expect the development of oil to bring about significant changes in the meanings Cajuns attached to work and their communities, by and large it adapted to these economic changes in ways that reinforced cultural values.

Margavio and Forsyth found that flexibility in the structure of both the oil and shrimp industries led to a relatively peaceful coexistence as shrimpers adapted to changes brought by oil:

> Evidence suggests that Cajun culture has not been dismantled by the coming of offshore oil. Although in many ways Cajuns have resisted modernization, the relationships between offshore oil and traditional culture of South Louisiana has been, at least to some extent, congenial. No other industry would have allowed culture to survive, and no other culture would have given the industry such an accommodating workforce. Even in economically depressed times, the father's altered working pattern left the family intact. The family also remained geographically in place, not disrupting the community.[18]

Even though many people on the bayou now earn a living through working for others, the value of self-reliance and independence was still touted as an important feature of what it means to be a Cajun. Trawling is, by all accounts, a strenuous—even grueling—occupation. Many such as Glen, who portrayed his hands as resembling barnacles, vividly described the laborious nature of the craft. Daniel told me, after returning from a trip out the day before, "Man, last night I hurt bad, I was walking around like I'd been riding a horse for three months," to which his wife added, "Last night he made the whole room smell like that stuff he was rubbing all over for hurt muscles, for ankles and backs. You know that stuff?"

I responded in the affirmative and then asked him what it was about trawling that shrimpers found so appealing.

"Well," he said, "I'm my own boss, for one. So I don't have to listen to nobody. And I work at my own pace, which is worth it. I mean, when the season opens I don't come home for a bit, you know, I stay gone. I just come in and go out. And, I mean, that's how I like to work."

'"I'm my own boss" was a phrase I heard nearly as often as "it's in my blood" when trawlers talked about sticking with the craft. Working in a craft where one can be one's own boss has numerous benefits, including working at one's own pace, setting one's own hours, and making important decisions regarding the way the ship is run. Shrimp fishers do not have to ask a boss for the day off or request a certain week off for vacation. And these qualities are associated with cultural values on which Cajuns place a premium: freedom, flexibility, and self-sufficiency. For shrimpers, working hard has a direct payoff: the harder one works, the more one earns. One of the reasons fishers cited for not wanting to take a job in the oil industry was the set hourly wage. Many trawlers expressed reluctance to take a job where they can work as hard—or as little—as they want and at the end of the day have the same amount of money in their pockets. This issue was a sticking point for Tommy and Eddie.

> Tommy: That's the thing. From the tugboat job to this job. On this job, the more hours you stay up and the more hours you put and the harder I work, the more money I'm gonna make. The other way, you know, you get a set price no matter what you do.
> Eddie: Yeah, you could have an easy job or you could have a hard job. Stay up many hours at a time, like you might now as a tugboat captain, but you get paid the same no matter what you do. You might sit around, or kill yourself, and still get the same check at the end of the week. With trawling, the harder you work the more you get paid.

Eddie described what shrimp fishing was like before the collapse. Since the collapse, the payoff was far less certain. Working as hard as one can no longer guarantees that fishers will have money in their pockets. J. T. and his friend Donny were among those who mentioned this.

When I asked them to talk about what aspects of fishing they really enjoy, J. T. brought up how much he valued the fact that hard work has a high payoff. He said, "What's so exciting about this business is that the harder you work, the more money you can make so you can better yourself. It's not like you getting paid ten dollars an hour no matter what you do or how hard you work. If you don't work hard you won't make no money!"

Donny chimed in, "The more shrimp you catch, the more excited you get."

"You get excited because you have a good drag," J. T. added. "You see it on the deck, you knew it was more money. And you wanted to drag even more."

"I always said that it's an honest living," Donny stated.

Then J. T. paused, took a deep breath, and let out a sigh. "But it's not like that no more."

The value of hard work was perhaps most evident throughout the numerous accounts that indicated a disdain for laziness. One of the best examples of came from the ex-fisher Jack:

> Those of us that did well in the shrimping industry, we got up and went to work every morning. Got up, went to work. I do the same thing today. I tell you a for instance. When we, I guess, maybe thirteen or fourteen years ago, we went out on the big boats, we was having a tough year. We were on one of five boats that were running side by side, all of us friends. We were looking for shrimp. When you're looking for shrimp, you run fifteen minutes, then you slow down, you put your test net in the water, and you pull your test net up. Unless you super tired, the engine noise or whatever, it breaks up your sleep. It's hard to rest. And we had been doing this for probably thirty hours. One of the boats, there were two other guys, it was about two in the morning. We was about to call it quits for the day. We're tired, you know, the noise and all? The four of us [each on his own boat] had payments to make, we had kids to raise. We kept going. Well, about midmorning, we hit some shrimp. The four of us found some shrimp. We were four friends running side by side. The other guys were thirty or thirty-five miles behind us. So we changed channels on the radio. We all shut up. We were very careful what we said. We didn't want them to know about the shrimp. They called, and they called, and they weren't sure where we were at. They found us, twenty-four hours later, I had ten thousand pounds of shrimp in the hole. They were hot. They were mad, and you know, when they finally came on, we had to talk to them. They was cussing us. But I said, "Whoa, whoa, whoa, whoa! You slept for six hours. We didn't sleep. We haven't slept yet. You all was getting sleep. Why would we get on the radio, and tell you what we're catching? So everybody can come in on us?" The four of us kept going. That's how you make it.

Jack's anecdote is particularly compelling because it demonstrates that even the bonds of friendship could not withstand the weight of a hard work ethic. Jack and the other three boat owners agreed not to share their bounty of shrimp with those they felt did not earn it. "You have to work hard for what you have," he told me. "Are we gonna let ourselves become a welfare nation?"

Perhaps work ethic was so highly valued among fishers because—like the knowledge and skills necessary to be successful—it is also a value that gets passed down from one generation to the next. In fishers' eyes, it is something to revere. At times, they talked about learning a work ethic as if they were among a sacred few bestowed this wisdom by their elders, and they felt as if they had a duty to pass it along to their own kids. As such, they understood the family as an important mechanism through which a work ethic is learned. But many trawlers feared that the collapse of the shrimp fishing industry would likely weaken this work ethic in younger and future generations. A persisting fisher named Henry was among those who expressed this concern when he said:

> Kids nowadays, all they want to do is play on the TV, or play sports at school. That's no good for the kids, unless they're really good at sports. It makes money for the school, and if he makes the coach win, fine, but after the sport is finished, it does them no good. You gotta teach your kid how to work, especially boys. If you don't teach your boy how to work, he won't know the world. I take [my ten-year-old son] out trawling the day school is out. As a matter of fact, I took him out two days before school ended. He made five trips in a row with me. He didn't want to go play with his friends, he wanted to come trawling with me. He loves to trawl. And he works, too. He don't just come and do nothing.

Not only did Henry find his son learning to value hard work, he also attached importance to the experience of passing on a solid work ethic to his son. He thus drew a distinction between his son and other nontrawling children his son's age. In his estimation, those other kids were losing out, wasting their time watching TV or playing sports.

Summing It Up

As the pink tsunami crashed ashore and caused considerable—and permanent—damage to the domestic shrimp industry, some fishers decided to stay afloat in the rough waters, suffering the consequences of their decision. What makes this case so compelling is that their choice to stick it out despite the ensuing struggles was an active one, as they willingly chose to forgo the better employment options that are available right down the road. They did it without engaging in any kind of meaningful political action to fight to save their industry, and they did, in fact, hold out very little hope that their situation would—or could—improve in the future. Low dockside prices and high overhead costs—the one-two punch that nearly knocked out the industry altogether—were perceived as permanent parts of fishers' daily realities. Why did they persist when they didn't have to? Their decisions to doggedly stick it out were grounded in a calculation that prioritized noneconomic considerations. The people who shared their stories understood shrimp fishing as genealogical destiny (part of their Cajun identity), as physical necessity (addiction), as the basis for the social organization of the family, and as a way of life that enabled them to live off the land (their deep identification with the "landscape"). The means by which they naturalized their place within their occupation was, at least in their view, a significant reason they were committed to the work and loath to leave it behind.

By drawing attention to these shrimp fishers' dogged persistence in the industry, I also argue that they are not passive victims of globalization, as workers are often portrayed in cases of industrial decline. Shrimp fishers know they can leave, and that they could be making better money in other jobs pretty easily, and yet they *actively* persist and deal with the hardships. I argue that, rather than victims, they are better understood as globalization's *martyrs*. They had chosen to suffer for what they love, *even when they don't have to*. Of course, not all individuals facing occupational decline are fortunate to have alternative options. Steelworkers, for example, did not have the option to stay in steel or work at another job when they were told that their plants would close. But the uniqueness of this case reveals what is hidden even in places where people do not have economically attractive alternatives.

3

Loss

Jumping Ship for Higher Ground

Losing my boat is like losing a baby. It hurts, you know? Like losing a baby.
GERALD (EXITER)

Gerald was an ex-shrimper who got out of the industry in 2003, just as it began to collapse. I met him and his wife, Diane, at a shrimp boil I'd been invited to by another ex-trawler named Lindel. Earlier that day I had spoken with Lindel—who now worked for an equipment company that supplies offshore oil rigs—and he'd encouraged me to attend that evening's festivities. He promised that I would find "lots of former trawlers like me who'll talk your ears off. And beaucoup shrimp to eat!" I followed Lindel's advice and headed down to the coast. Before I even stepped out of my car, my senses were assailed by the smell of fresh-boiled shrimp and salty sea air, hanging low in the sky of the extremely humid summer evening. Crowds of people two-stepped to the beat of Cajun French songs being played by a local swamp pop band. Dinner plates were piled high with Gulf shrimp, French bread, and vegetables.

The shrimp boil, sponsored in part by a local energy company, was being held under a tent near one of the company's main offices, located in the heart of the oil industrial complex along the coast. The location of the shrimp boil beautifully emblematized the harmony between the seafood and oil industries, showing how neatly they blended to become part of the community's shared identity. The smells, sights, tastes, and sounds of Cajun culture filled the air, but all the while we were surrounded by the imposing infrastructure of the oil field. Towering cranes and other large machinery, semitrucks, and tin-roofed warehouses provided the backdrop for this Cajun celebration. Tugboats and shrimp boats were docked along the water's edge, side by side. This is modern-day Cajun Louisiana.

Shortly after I arrived at the shrimp boil, I spotted Lindel in the crowd. This wasn't difficult: he was a big man with a loud voice that lifted over the sounds of the fiddle, accordion, and laughter of the crowd. He was chatting with his long-time friend Gerald, a much smaller and more soft-spoken man who wore a trucker's cap and blue work pants. I introduced myself and told him that I was from up north.

"You're from Ohio?!" he exclaimed. "What are you doing all the way down here? But more importantly, have you had any shrimp yet?"

I explained that I was a researcher who was looking to speak with ex-trawlers about what their lives were like after they got out of the industry.

"Oh lord," he said, "it was for thirty-three years that we did that."

He explained that he learned how to shrimp as a teenager from his step-father, a man he credited with all his knowledge of shrimp. He purchased his own boat around the time he got married to his wife, Diane, whose father was a lifelong trawler of fifty years. Although she'd grown up in a fishing family, she'd rarely trawled with her father and only occasionally went out with Gerald. "It's too hard of work," she explained to me when I met her. "But sometimes I'd go out on the weekend with him, because I wanted to be with him." They had two children, both daughters, but neither of them spent much time on the boat.

Gerald and Diane told me the same story regarding the declining state of the industry that others had, about prohibitively high gas prices and the problems with imported shrimp. Gerald expressed with great enthusiasm how much he loved trawling. He emphasized that he'd never wanted to leave it behind, but his enthusiasm dissipated when I asked him what it was like to leave the industry: "Oh no, leaving was heartbreaking. But, uh, what you gonna do."

He described how the prices had dropped too appreciably in a very short amount of time. Although price drops weren't uncommon from year to year, he explained how this time it was different, how rumors had swirled among shrimpers that the unprecedented surge of imports would keep the prices low permanently. When prices did fail to rebound, their fears became a reality and panic set in. Around the same time this was all happening, an acquaintance offered Gerald a job as a seafood wholesaler. It seemed to him too good and too timely an opportunity to pass up, so he took it and put his boat up for sale. When I asked him how he had fared since leaving shrimp fishing behind, he admitted that he had been doing fairly well financially these days. But he quickly added, "I'd much rather be shrimping because that's what I love to do."

As we spoke, it became clear that for Gerald and Diane shrimp fishing was more than a job. Their attachment to the industry crystallized when I asked them to tell me about their boat. "Oh yeah, we had a big boat, a beautiful boat," he told me proudly. They had owned and operated the same boat for thirty-three years, and because they were always sure to perform the yearly maintenance necessary to keep it in good shape, when they sold it, it was in nearly perfect condition and came accompanied by a meticulously kept history of maintenance and repair. Their story matched what was told to me time and again by other ex-shrimpers, how selling the boat was one of the most difficult parts of leaving the industry.

The process was particularly difficult for Diane. As she told spoke about their boat, her voice began to crack. "I was sad. I didn't want him to get rid of the boat," she stated. At that point in the conversation, she reached into her large purse and pulled out her wallet. "It was so hard, you know. I have a picture of the boat in my wallet. Do you want to see it?"

"I would be honored!" I replied.

Much as a proud grandmother might, she showed me the dog-eared, wallet-size photo of their boat. It was named after Gerald's stepfather, who had taught him all about shrimping. Although it had been four years since they sold the boat, she beamed with pride as she described its unique features. It was exactly as if she was bragging about a grandchild. After Diane returned the photo to its safe place in her wallet, Gerald stated, "Losing my boat is like losing a baby. It hurts, you know? Like losing a baby."

To Gerald and Diane, the boat was more than a fishing vessel or an object that enabled them to make a living. To them—and to many of the shrimpers I spoke with—their boat was part of the family. "I really do miss it," Diane stated solemnly.

When the shrimp fishing industry fell into collapse, Gerald left it for a more certain and economically sound employment alternative. And so far that decision has paid off for him in a very literal sense. His new job as a seafood wholesaler paid fairly well and offered employment benefits and a sense of security as well. Given this, it may tempting to regard Gerald— and those like him—as success stories in the fight against globalization, since most documented cases of industrial decline focus on the economic hardships and survival strategies of those who suffer the many resulting problems associated with unemployment. Gerald and many other ex-fishers have avoided the protracted experiences of uncertainty or financial hardship because there were job opportunities waiting for them upon their decision to leave the industry. As a result, folks like Gerald might not otherwise be given a second glance by deindustrialization scholars because they avoided the misfortune that most suffer when a local industry collapses. Unlike so many others impacted by industrial decline, ex-fishers do not have to turn to Wal-Mart or other low-wage jobs to attempt to piece together a living, nor do they have to use government assistance or welfare programs. The jobs available to shrimp fishers require skills and specialized knowledge that trawlers already possess (captaining a boat, welding, repairing machinery). These are "good" jobs, in the sense that they are well paying, offer decent benefits, and are relatively secure (at least at the current time). The process of shrimp fishing is physically demanding, and in some cases ex-shrimpers who take work on oil rigs or as tugboat captains make *more* for working *less*, or at the very least for working less hard.

Of course, it would be a mistake to ignore the good fortune of having access to alternative income opportunities. But would it be accurate to understand these ex-shrimpers as victors over the forces of industrial decline? We might do this if our understanding of what it meant to be victorious was couched solely in economic terms. As I emphasize in this chapter, focusing solely on economic outcomes of industrial decline obscures the importance of other, nonmaterial effects even for those who obtain better-paying or more stable work. By digging a little deeper into the process of transitioning into new forms of employment, we can see what the ex-shrimpers' stories reveal: that even though most are better off financially, many experience exit as a personal tragedy and describe what is lost when deeply meaningful occupational identities are abandoned.

Jumping Ship for Higher Ground: Ex-Fishers and Market Logics

Dave and Lynette had been married for thirty years when I spoke with them at a local diner. They had trawled together for most of their married life. Dave, a third-generation shrimp fisher, began trawling with his father when he was a teenager. Lynette's father, Jesse, worked as a tugboat captain for most of his life. As someone who did not fish for a living, Jesse worried about the general uncertainties associated with being a shrimp fisher, and when Dave and Lynette got married, he pressured Dave to acquire a captain's license to use as a backup to shrimp fishing, in case there was ever a need for extra money. Dave was reluctant to do so because he couldn't imagine a time when fishing wouldn't be viable, but eventually, and with a lack of enthusiasm, he obliged.

As was true of most shrimp fishers, Dave didn't like to work during the off-season. For most of the year—from May until November—he and Lynette trawled the in-shore waters on their fifty-foot steel-hulled boat. When I asked him what he did during the remaining months of the year, he replied, "If it was a real good year, I like to hunt. I'd go hunting, and then work on my boat. If it wasn't much of a good year, well, then I'd go to work on the tugboat, go hunt, and then I'd work on the boat. I'm *always* working on the boat. In February I start getting the boat ready for May." Because Dave had followed Jesse's advice, he had a captain's license and thus the option of working during the off-season to make extra money. But generally he chose not to, since as was true of other trawlers, hunting was one of his off-season priorities. And before the shrimp industry collapsed, there was no financial need to work on the tug, as they typically earned enough money during the shrimping season to last until the next one.

As the industry began to decline, every year became a little more difficult, and Dave found himself working on the tugboat more and more often. Eventually he realized that he was making more money on the tugboat than he was on his shrimp boat. It wasn't that the money he made on the tug got better, it was because the shrimping got worse.

> I remember when the fuel was like twenty cents, thirty cents, thirty-two cents a gallon, compared to the two dollars-plus a gallon that it is now. The ice was two or three dollars a block. And now, it's eleven-fifty. The small shrimp, the eighty/hundreds [shrimp per pound], was always right around

a dollar a pound, and now it's forty cents a pound. When it was good, we'd catch seven or eight hundred pounds a day. But we'd have five hundred dollars of expenses instead of fifteen hundred of expenses. We'd get one dollar or more a pound instead of forty or fifty cents a pound. Did you know that shrimp pays less now than it did twenty years ago? That's just in raw numbers, not even including any kind of adjustments.

Lynette added, "When you sit there and realize that you're working for fifty cents a pound, you're ready to shovel it all overboard."

Dave and Lynette had been frustrated for several years with the depressed state of the industry. Because Dave had a captain's license and experience working on tugboats, they knew that they could avoid financial struggle if they tied up their boat for good. When Jesse had pressed Dave to get a captain's license all those years ago, he'd felt frustrated, never believing that he'd one day need to get out of fishing for good, but in retrospect Jesse's insight was prescient. Dave took full-time work as a tugboat captain and soon they put their boat up for sale. When we spoke, it had been three years since they sold their boat and Dave was still working on the tugs. Lynette was no longer employed, but Dave's salary provided more than enough for the two of them, as their children were grown and they lived alone.

Those I spoke with who left the industry for good most often cited the combination of low dockside prices and high overhead costs as the primary reason for why they got out. The dramatic spike in fuel costs was especially emphasized, as it had not only affected the shrimpers' ability to fill the tanks on their boats, but had also pushed up the price of most consumer goods as well. Ex-fishers complained that the decline had damaged their purchasing power as consumers to the point where they were no longer able to maintain the same standard of living as before.

This point was illustrated by Wendell, a first-generation trawler who left fishing to work for a company that equips offshore oil rigs, deciding to exit when he realized that he was working harder but consistently making less. "With shrimping," he said, "if you're not making the price, you're not making the money. But everything else is going up. When I was doing it, you could go and buy a brand-new truck for ten thousand dollars. You can't do that now. It's thirty-five thousand for a full-size truck. The economy is going up, but not the shrimping. It's not keeping even, not even close. And now you got to get a good catch every single time you go out. I couldn't do it."

Wendell's description is telling for several reasons. First, it illustrates the cost-benefit thinking that has guided shrimp fishers out of the industry. Yet it also reinforces the significance that owning newer pickup trucks holds for the fishers. Trucks cost money, but they also hold symbolic value—here as markers of success—that is not so easily quantified. Wendell's inability to afford a new pickup truck—and thus maintain the proper image of Cajun shrimp fisher—served as a warning to him that the industrial crisis was indeed quite considerable and carried great costs. Wendell got out after the 2002 season when his next-door neighbor offered him a job in the oil-related company for which he then worked. It was an offer Wendell could not refuse.

Family Legacy and Market Logics

Ex-fishers eventually chose to take a different path from the one chosen by persisting fishers, but they traveled on the same bumpy road for quite some time. Like persisting fishers, they shared with me stories of struggle, heartache, and loss. They also discussed their frustration with what they saw as the growing regulations with which they had to comply, such as TEDs, and how these serve to threaten the industry's future. Current and former fishers alike knew that in order to survive in the industry they would have to deal with the reality of working harder and harder for less and less. They also described in painful detail how the import crisis had taken its toll on them both physically and emotionally. So why did some choose to stick with shrimp fishing while others sought work elsewhere?

One possible answer to this question is that perhaps persisting shrimpers as a group enjoyed some kind of economic advantage: a working spouse, no or few dependents, and/or a lighter debt load. Rural sociologists who have studied how small-scale and family farmers adapted to the farming crisis of the 1980s have often pointed toward this type of economic explanation. Relying on a spouse's income, working a greater number of hours, and cutting back on household expenditures are all ways that farmers have adjusted their practices in order to continue farming.[1] Farmers who did not have a spouse who could contribute to the household income—or those who carried a higher debt load—were in a less advantageous position to continue farming than those who may have had those benefits. Could it be that persisting shrimp fishers were in a position of economic advantage?

I took this question seriously, and after revisiting the interview transcripts to look for answers, it became clear that there was no clear-cut pattern that existed among those I spoke with to be able to say for certain that economic context alone—or even primarily—determines whether one will stay in or exit. Some persisters had wives who were employed outside of the industry, had boats that were completely paid off, or had no dependents at home. Others did not have spouses who worked outside of the home and also carried rather expensive boat notes. Some current fishers had young children at home, but some of the ex-fishers chose to tie up their boats well after their children were fully grown. Without a doubt, economic factors weighed significantly into decisions to stick it out or leave, but this does not mean that their decisions were made with only economic considerations in mind.

Because family is such an important element to Cajun ethnic identity as well as to shrimp fishing itself, I went back to the transcripts to see if there were any differences regarding how deeply rooted particular shrimp fishers were in the industry. What I found was fascinating. There was a clear pattern linking family history with the decision to remain in the industry. Ex-fishers' familial roots in the industry did not go nearly as deep as current fishers' roots did. Of the seventeen ex-fishers I spoke with, only six were second generation or more. In other words, only six of them had fathers or grandfathers who also worked as shrimpers. Most of the remaining ex-fishers were men who had married women whose fathers had trawled, and they took up the work only after they got married. In contrast, *all* of the persisting shrimp fishers were at least second generation or more, and most of them had roots that went three or four generations deep. There wasn't a single persister who had gotten into shrimping as a result of marriage.

What does all of this tell us? Although my sample is somewhat small and perhaps not wholly representative of Louisiana shrimp fishers, it appears that having a deeper personal and cultural investment in the industry may act as a barrier to exit. Lifelong, multigenerational trawlers have accumulated a lifetime of experiences that are grounded in the work that has historically been performed by family members, and family relations have been powerful in shaping their sense of purpose and the meanings attached to their everyday lives. Because shrimp fishing is a locally specific occupation, their understanding of community is also understood largely on the basis of work. As such, their stake in the continuation of shrimp fishing is likely greater than that of those individuals whose family histories are grounded in other occupations, such as the oil industry.

The Highs and Lows of Exit

What does it mean to walk away from one's livelihood for good? The answer surely depends upon whether or not a person chooses to go. In most cases of industrial decline, workers are forced to find other work when factories close up shop. The sudden economic dislocation is associated with a host of problems as people scramble to try to make ends meet amid great uncertainty. Bills go unpaid, families go without, and depression and anxiety mounts as people figure out what to do next. But what about those instances where people are given a choice to stay or exit? Admittedly, this is a rare event. The sociologist Ruth Milkman studied one such event when workers at a New Jersey General Motors plant were given the option of taking a cash buyout and leaving the factory or keeping their job and dealing with significant changes that the company planned to implement as a means of remaining competitive. She found that several years after workers made their choices, those who took the buyout were by and large much happier with their lives than those who stayed in and stuck it out. The buyout takers expressed little nostalgia for the way of life provided by work in a factory. In retrospect, they understood their lives in the factory—and the boring, routinized work they performed there—as being degraded by their conditions of employment. The humiliation they felt was not so much the result of the routinized nature of work as it was the oppressive, authoritarian supervisors under whom they were constantly surveilled. Those who stayed on the job echoed the ex-employees' feelings of humiliation, but they grounded their justification to stay in purely economic terms. The job provided them the ability to live a middle-class lifestyle despite their relative lack of higher education or other marketable skills that are typically required to obtain "good" jobs. For those who stayed put, there was just too much uncertainty regarding what would happen to them post-buyout for them to take the leap.[2]

Milkman's study suggests that it is misguided for deindustrialization scholars to emphasize nostalgia for the industrial past. Indeed, that type of work is often gritty and dangerous, and it can be very hard on the body as well as on one's feelings of self-worth. Just as the buyout takers at GM did, ex-fishers have also made the choice to leave their way of life behind. But shrimp fishers differ from GM workers in several important ways. First, the industrial structure of shrimp fishing is quite different from auto manufacturing in that shrimpers are owner-operators of their boats. As such, they do not work under a supervisor, they are their own boss. In that sense, most often leaving fishing means that they transition *to* waged labor, and not out of it. Another key difference is that shrimp fishers live in a region surrounded by rich oil reserves that provide a number of employment opportunities. They are therefore fortunate not to have to cope with the economic uncertainty that many of the buyout takers faced. Given all of this, there are several important questions that emerge when considering the case of ex-fishers. How have they fared upon exit? How do they understand the decision-making process that led them to permanently retire the white rubber boots that are characteristic of Louisiana shrimp fishers? And what can they teach us about the significance and endurance of occupational identities?

The Benefits of Life on Land

As I set out to find ex-fishers who could provide me answers to these questions, I recognized quite readily that tracking them down was going to be a great deal more difficult than finding current shrimp fishers. The reason for this is that they were way less visible in the community. I was able to connect with many current fishers by stopping by their boats when I saw people working on them. Ex-trawlers could be anywhere, and often it was only through happenstance that I was introduced to one. Such was the case with Lindel, the ex-fisher mentioned earlier who was working at a company that supplies equipment to offshore rigs. I first met Lindel when he was shopping at the retail store where an ex-fisher named Albert worked. I was chatting with Albert about his thoughts on life after fishing when Lindel walked into the store. Lindel overheard Albert talking about how things had become so difficult that he was forced to sell his beloved boat, at which point he came over to where we were, apologized for interrupting, and said, "Oh, I love shrimping and all, but you gotta make money to survive. That's why I left." His interruption was greatly welcome as Lindel later became a key informant in my study. He was instrumental in getting me in touch with other ex-fishers he knew who worked in oil.

Albert was clearly distraught, nearly tearful, as he told me that he didn't know what he was going to do now that he was trying to sell his boat. Lindel was quick to interject that for him there were benefits to getting out, first and foremost that he was making more money now that he'd left than he ever had as a shrimper. The dissimilarity between their points of view revealed the real difference between Lindel and Albert. Lindel was a first-generation trawler who got into it full time only after he married his wife, whose father was a lifelong trawler. Albert learned the trade from his grandfather, who was taught by *his* father, so his roots in the industry went deep.

Lindel had a much easier time discussing the benefits of leaving fishing than Albert had had. His father was not a trawler, but he grew up working as a deckhand for neighbors and relatives who were full-time fishers. It was a way to make quick money, and the experience provided him with the skills needed to run a boat independently. When he graduated from high school, he followed his father's advice and took a job as a deckhand for a tugboat company. Because he thoroughly enjoyed trawling, he continued to work on trawl boats whenever he could, and it was through shrimping that he met his future wife, the daughter of one of the trawlers who had hired him as a deckhand. His father-in-law helped Lindel transition to becoming a full-time trawler on the boat that Lindel later went on to run as his own.

Even though he trawled full time during the shrimping seasons, Lindel also continued to work the off-season in the oil industry, wanting to make extra money for his growing family. When I asked why him why he decided to finally leave shrimp fishing behind, his answer focused on the economics of it. "Probably when I started making more money in the oil fields. That's probably it, when I started making more money," he said. "And there were times in shrimping I was doing real well, like I said. In ten days I made like five thousand dollars. And I can't do that in the job I work at now. But I'm doing real good now. Making that kind of money in fishing was when it was good at that time. That's not now. This job I have now is a *steady* check. There's no guessing, like in trawling."

By maintaining his previous connection to the oil industry even after he became a full-time trawler, Lindel was provided with a lifeboat to jump into as the shrimping industry began to go under. When he decided to leave trawling, he used these connections to obtain a job in the company for which he now worked. Because he had previous experience with the company and the oil industry, he moved up the ranks fairly quickly, and at the time of the interview he was the head manager of operations. He was now the boss to many people. In addition to the steady paycheck he mentioned above, he listed other perks his job offered that were absent in shrimp fishing. "The benefits of leaving? Well, I think that workin' with a company like what we're working for, we got the option for hospitalization and a retirement plan. We got safety bonuses. We got, uh, some program where every quarter, or every three months we get performance bonuses. So, for our company, depending on what people make, we get a bonus every three months. That's one thing, as a trawler, the only bonus you getting is some fish and some crabs! But, that's pretty much it."

Because shrimp fishing on Bayou Crevette is primarily an owner-operator venture, shrimpers receive no health benefits or pension plans. They must pay their insurance costs completely out of pocket, a reality that current fishers readily recognize. These out-of-pocket costs were described by Daniel and Caroline, a persisting fisher and his wife. Caroline was particularly aggrieved about these expenses since she was in charge of the household's finances.

Daniel stated, "I don't want to know how much a year I pay in insurance. You got health, car, and boat."

Caroline added, "I feel like I'm writing a check every other week for insurance."

"Yeah," Daniel replied. "One thing good about working for a big company is just for the insurance, sometimes. We're up to seven hundred dollars and something a month, for all of us. Seven hundred and something for health insurance. Some guy might have a little job making two to three hundred dollars a week, but they have insurance. They make a couple hundred dollars a week, but the company pays for the insurance."

Steady paychecks and employer-provided benefits were just a few of the advantages ex-fishers listed. Another advantage reflected the importance of family in Cajun cultural identity. Because it has become less common for entire families to trawl together, being out on the boat may require trawlers to spend time a significant time away from their families. This is especially true for those with larger boats that trawl farther out into the Gulf. Both Lindel and his co-worker Kurt, who was also an ex-fisher, trawled on larger boats and would often be out for up to twenty days at a time.

Kurt said, "You gotta put more hours into it. More hours in the day, the day and night, you do what you gotta do. And also, you know, Lindel trawled on big boats and I trawled on big boats, and I know we used to leave the dock and go out like fifteen or twenty days, that's like fifteen or twenty boxes of shrimp a day. You would stop, throw the anchor and check the engine, and change the oil, and you're back at it again. It's rough."

I asked him, "Do you think with what you do now you get to spend more time with your family?"

"Oh, definitely," he said. " For sure."

The importance of family time was particularly salient for an ex-fisher named Jack, a third-generation trawler who got out of the industry in the 1990s after the TEDs regulations were passed but before the collapse. While he started out trawling on smaller, wooden boats mainly in the inshore waters, he eventually purchased a larger, steel-hulled trawl boat that allowed him to trawl year-round in the Gulf. He made a very comfortable living as a trawler, but it required him to be away from his family for long periods of time. He found this to be an unattainable way to maintain the kind of family life that he wanted.

> When we were shrimping, a long trip was thirty days. We stayed thirty days. And a lot of times, I'd make a trip, say in the Texas area. I'd go my thirty days, unload my shrimp, I'd get ice or whatever I needed, and I'd make another trip and come home. Sometimes it takes me sixty days before I'd come home. That's just the way we worked in those days. That's the way my dad worked. My dad didn't have the boats we had, he had a wooden boat. It wasn't as good. They could hold shrimp probably ten to twelve days. . . . When we went from the wooden boats to the steel boats, we could carry a lot more fuel, better insulated boats, the ice would last longer. We went from staying ten days offshore to staying thirty days offshore. Instead of coming to the dock three times a month, we coming to the dock once a month. We made real good money in the sixties and seventies because of the amount of time we spent on the boats. My wife and I went nineteen weeks, I was home two nights in nineteen weeks. That's what I had to do. That's where I made my living, that was the only thing I knew.

After the TEDs regulations were enacted, Jack began to worry about the industry's future, telling me that he sensed trawling was going to become more difficult. Eventually he was approached by an oil field representative about using his trawl boat to remove debris when offshore oil rigs were dismantled. As Jack explained, "Once they remove a platform, we're supposed to sonar it and dive on it. You get a trawler to trawl the area, in a mile radius, to make sure all the debris has been picked up." Oil companies paid him handsomely for his services, and eventually he became involved in site clearance full time. After almost a decade, he developed his own company, which builds new boats—and transforms old trawl boats— to perform site clearance duties. His wife works at the company, as do three of his five children. He enjoys being able to spend time with them throughout the day.

The Costs of Exit

In the previous chapter, I discussed the value shrimp fishers place on "being my own boss." The freedom and flexibility that accompany this valued feature of their job serve as a barrier to exit, as they are loath to leave that important part of their occupational identity behind. As owners of their own vessels, shrimpers are in charge of making all the decisions relating to the production process. Leaving the industry behind would likely entail moving from self-employment to waged labor and thus reduce the degree of control they have over their working lives. Rural sociologists who examine the decline of family farms have shown how farmers' reluctance to move to waged forms of employment is significant to understanding why they continue to work harder for less.[3] In this way, shrimp fishers and farmers are similar. But some fishers have chosen to leave the industry. How have they made sense of their new realities as waged workers?

Many ex-shrimpers I spoke with freely admitted that they would much prefer to be their own boss. When I asked them about the loss of autonomy involved with transitioning to waged labor, many replied with statements that emphasized the benefits of waged employment rather than addressing the loss of self-directed employment. Some ex-fishers redefined their occupational identity by focusing on aspects of their new jobs that allowed them to maintain that sense of autonomy in their newer positions. This was especially true for those who, like Dave, left fishing to work as tugboat captains. Dave emphasized his position of authority when he discussed his life after fishing. "You're a captain," he said, "and so you're the boss of the boat. Now, you might take orders from the office where you work for. Like, they might tell you to take this barge and go over there and load it. But, you know, *you* have got to run the boat. *You're* in charge of the boat."

"So do you perceive yourself as still maintaining a semblance of being your own boss?" I asked.

Dave replied, "Well, yes. The only thing is, I can't get off the boat when I want. I work a schedule, seven and seven. Seven days on and seven days off." While Dave admitted that he lacked ultimate control over the conditions of his employment—such as when he chose to work—he still perceived himself to be boss. He was the captain of the ship in a literal sense. The work of a tugboat captain was difficult in some aspects, but it was not nearly as physically demanding work as shrimp fishing. Working as a tugboat captain is a great deal easier on the body and comes with a lot less stress and uncertainty.

Like Dave, Lindel also enjoyed an authoritative position in his current work. He was a supervisor and the most highly ranked person in his office. While he had a boss to answer to, he was also the boss of many others, and as such he had a high degree of power and more flexibility than nonmanagers. He set the schedules, was in charge of hiring and firing, and had considerable say over day-to-day operations. Most of his days were spent working behind a desk, which, when compared to shrimping, was on the other end of the physical labor spectrum. Even so, he admitted to being paid very well. "When we were younger, if you ask us if we'd be making the money that we are now, I'd laugh. No way, I wouldn't have believed it."

Folks like Lindel and Dave enjoyed what they understood as the perks of life after shrimping: a steady income, employment benefits, less physically demanding work, and reduced stress regarding how much money they would have at the end of the month. Dave had even maintained the sense of autonomy that so many farmers and fishers fear losing. Based upon this, we might be tempted to hold them up as survivors of globalization's mighty waves, and maybe even as victors. I wondered about this as I spoke with Dave.

After he described to me what his life has been like after exiting, I asked him, "Dave, it sounds like your life is pretty good right now. But if you could still be trawling, would you?"

He replied quickly. "Well, sure. No doubt about it. 'Cause it's in my blood."

I asked Lindel the same question.

"As far as doing it and *liking* it," he replied, "I'd much rather trawl then do what I'm doing now. Even though over here, you come to work, you're guaranteed a check. You go out on your shrimp boat, you're not guaranteed. You gotta go out and catch shrimp."

"But do you like what you're doing now?" I asked.

"No, not really, I hate it. I'm the boss. Where I work, I'm the boss and I hate it. I'd love it if I could make it with shrimping. I'd give up sitting behind the desk to go out there."

Of course, it is much easier to make statements such as this while simultaneously reaping the benefits of waged employment. But like those who continued to struggle to survive as fishers, Dave understood the work as something that he was born to do. Failing to live up to personal expectations can serve as a point of dissatisfaction.

Perhaps no shrimp fisher described the pain of failing to fulfill one's expectations in as vivid detail as Albert. From the outset, he made no attempt to hide the grief he felt upon just having made the difficult decision to sell his boat and leave the industry. When I called the phone number I'd copied from the "for sale" sign in the window of his boat, he encouraged me to come and meet him right then. "You can come on down now. Now that I'm not fishing, I'm always around," he told me.

I got in my car and drove to his father's store where he was working in the meantime. It was an extremely hot and balmy day, typical of July in southern Louisiana.

It didn't take long for Albert to open up to me, and he was frequently emotional during our three-hour-long conversation. The wounds created by his decision to quit were still very fresh. He had made the difficult decision to leave the industry only a few months prior to my phone call. He admitted that he'd been thinking about quitting for years, not because he wanted to, but because he feared he would have to. He dreaded the day that finally came, when he placed the "for sale" sign in his boat's window for the first time. Albert explained that he had gone out trawling for the opening of the most recent May season, just a few months earlier, hoping he would do well enough to quell the ever-growing doubts that he had about his future in the industry.

The previous year had been a particularly rough one. He hadn't made enough money to break even on what it cost to go out fishing. He hadn't been able to pay his debts on his own, and this deeply troubled him as it didn't line up with the ideal of self-sufficiency that was central to his values, something that gets to the heart of Cajun cultural identity. Albert explained how in the past, repaying the people around him who lent him money—especially his father, who often lent him money at the beginning of the season—was always his first priority. He mentioned how the owner of a local hardware store, a man named Eddie, always gave shrimpers a line of credit before the opening of the May season because he knew that he'd get paid back pretty quickly.

> At the end of the year, I pay my daddy and all, what I had in my account. Then, I'd save enough just to get my boat ready, and then I'd pay my taxes and whatever. And if I didn't have enough money, then I'd go and I'd charge it. Eddie said, "Don't worry about paying me till the season is over." And I'd run up a bill of six, seven, eight hundred dollars. And he wasn't worried about it. I'd go out for the opening, and bam! I'd come in and pay my bill. But now? It's not like that. I mean, when I go over there, I mighta spent two to three hundred dollars. I watch what I'm doing, and then I go pay $60, $70 here and there, and $60 here, until the bill was paid. It took me a month, it took me four weeks to get the boat painted, where it normally takes me about ten days because I didn't have the money to do it.

Albert was not alone in this. Since the crisis, many shrimp fishers have struggled to pay their bills, causing significant delays in their preparation for the season and burdening them emotionally with worry and stress. The inability to pay back debts is not what shrimp fishers are used to; it doesn't fit the definition of the "honest living" revered by so many of them.

When the previous year's season ended, Albert was so in debt and frustrated that he questioned whether or not he should even try to go out for the following May season. Over the winter he decided to put his boat up for sale to see if there would be any interest. But when signs of spring began to appear, he couldn't resist the urge to give it one more go. He wanted to see if he could make enough to convince himself that he should stick it out, to make enough so he could take the "for sale" sign off his boat, as it served as a constant reminder of what was at stake—the imminent loss of his boat. So, just as he had always done, he embarked on the spring ritual of getting his boat ready for the season: he made sure the engine was properly functioning, applied a new coat of paint, and repaired nets and hardware. He scurried to assemble a team of deckhands, all the while acutely aware that this might be the last time he made a trip with the boat he had owned for twenty-two years.

About a week before the May season opened, Albert noted the dockside price of shrimp. He imagined that he would mostly catch the 80/100s (the smaller shrimp that run eighty to a hundred per pound), and for these the docks were offering about a dollar per pound. This price was a good deal lower than what had been offered in the past, but deeming the price to still be worth the effort, he forged ahead with his plans. The day before the opening, however, he noted a severe drop in the price. He told me, "They dropped it down to thirty and forty cents a pound! You've got to fill that boat up just to pay the expense, and to make just a couple of dollars. It's almost like, you know, I'm not even going to go to the opening because I got to fill the boat twice just to pay for the expense! You know? You can see where it's at, huh? In the toilet!"

Albert perceived the sudden drop in price as shrimp processors and dock owners gaming the system. He noted that it wasn't uncommon for dock owners to drop the price right before the opening (generally what I heard from most of the other fishers, who typically held very unfavorable opinions of shrimp buyers and processors). However, since he was already set to go out, he decided to give it his all and accept the low price. He and his two deckhands left on opening day and stayed out for almost a week. When they returned, they had a good crop of shrimp, but they were forced to accept the low dockside prices, leaving Albert unable to cover the full range of his expenses (fuel, ice, groceries). When they came back from that single trip, he decided that he could no longer make it, and with great disappointment and a very heavy heart, he left the "for sale" sign in the window of his boat.

Before the industrial collapse, Albert had never imagined what it would be like to leave shrimp fishing behind. He explained that the hardest part of leaving was the process of selling his boat. As he explained to me his connection to his boat, he became visibly upset, and frequently broke down into tears. "My dad and my grandpa built that boat with me. And I *never* wanted to sell my boat. So I built it with the best stuff I could, you know?" At this point, he paused and began to cry. After a few moments, he continued. "Grandpa died. But I built this to keep. It was never my intention on selling this. Like I told you, when we first started shrimping, and I built that boat in eighty-five, and we used to go out and we was getting paid like a dollar fifty for forty/fifties [shrimp per pound], and it even went up to two forty and two fifty for forty/fifties. Right now I think it's eighty cents. And it goes down, it doesn't go up. Nothing goes up."

Much like Gerald and Diane—whose story opened this chapter— Albert's attachment to his boat was made strong by its connection to his family and to his personal identity and feelings of self-worth. Besides being the vehicle through which he earned his living and enabled him to fulfill his calling to fish shrimp, it symbolized his connections to his past and to family members who have passed on, especially his grandfather, for whom the boat was named. Albert was extremely close to his grandfather, the person who taught Albert to shrimp. Albert's father was never a trawler and as a young man chose to go into business selling tools and pool supplies. When Albert was little, he would go out trawling with his grandfather. He found he loved to trawl, and when he graduated from high school, his father and grandfather pulled together the funds to build Albert his own boat, a wooden boat, and they spared no expense when they built it, together. "That boat's built with brass, stainless. It's built with five-quarter Spanish cedar, three-by-ten cypress ribs, a solid deck that goes all the way to the back. There's no hole under the cabin, or nothin'. You got to bust through the ice hole to pull the engine out. That's a solid deck boat. I built that to keep. I never wanted to sell that. But I can't work it. I can't do it no more. And the way prices and things and stuff are, I just, see where it's at? That's it."

Eventually, his grandfather became too old to trawl on his own, so he would ride along with Albert, offering what assistance he could. Later in the our conversation, Albert pulled out old photographs that depicted some of their most successful trips on board the boat. In the photographs, Albert stood among shrimp that were piled so high they came up to his knees and covered the entire deck. He was once again moved to tears when he pointed out his grandfather, a man he greatly resembled. He also had pictures that documented the care he put into the boat in the off-season, when it was dry-docked to give it fresh paint. He was clearly very proud of the photographs and the life they depicted.

After he left the industry, Albert worked in his father's retail store. He told me that it was just for the time being, as he hoped to eventually find work as a diesel mechanic. Years ago he had become certified as one, not to use as a backup to shrimp fishing, but so he would be able to work more effectively on his own engine. The certification would now come in handy in his search for new employment, and he was confident that he'd eventually find a decent job. In the event that he did find another form of steady employment, it would be inaccurate to depict him as a success story, as a victor over the foe of occupational decline. As others had done, Albert understood shrimp fishing as something that was physically part of him, something that flowed through his veins. "Once it's in your blood, it's hard to get it out," he told me. "You know, it's, if I could be doing it, I'd be doing it right now."

To walk away from shrimp fishing as a lifestyle was not an easy process, nor was it a choice that was made without serious consideration. Lynette and Dave had also experienced difficulty with making their final decision to quit. When we spoke they were both in their early fifties. Through thirty years of marriage they had had three children, two sons and a daughter. One son was a mechanic, and the other one had a job in the oil industry. Dave obtained his captain's license years ago when he and Lynette first got married. He sometimes worked as a tugboat captain in the off-season, mostly to make a few extra dollars to get them through until the next year. His familiarity and experience working outside of the shrimping industry minimized some of the uncertainty that shrimp fishers who never worked outside it may go through. But this does not mean that the decision was easy.

For Lynette and Dave, like Albert and many of the ex-trawlers, the most difficult part of leaving the industry was selling their boat. Lynette and Dave had a particularly strong attachment to their boat, as they'd built it using the money they received when their only daughter was killed in an accident. Before revealing their daughter's connection to the boat, Lynette talked about how hard it had been for her to part with it.

"What was it about your boat that you found to be so special?" I asked.

Lynette looked down and then at Dave. He grabbed her hand and said, "Go ahead, tell her."

"You see," she began, " the boat was named after my daughter. And she was killed in a car accident. So when that happened, that's when he bought the boat."

"The insurance money," Dave added in a hushed voice, "I bought the boat with that." Lynette added, "And it was named after her, it was the *Miss Gloria*. That was her name."

Dave nodded toward Lynette and said, "She didn't want me to sell it. But it was costing me money to keep it every year in front of the house when it wasn't making no money. I said, 'I gotta let it go.' I didn't get what I wanted for it."

"No, he gave it away," Lynette said.

Lynette shared with me what she found to be one of the most diffi-cult realities of being an ex-shrimper: hearing what happened to their boat after they sold it. They sold it to someone who was not from their com-munity, but from one about an hour away. They considered this a blessing because they did not want to be reminded of the boat. It would have been difficult for them to have to drive by it on a regular basis. Their son Tom sometimes visited the community where their boat ended up, so from time to time he saw the boat when he passed through town. According to Tom, the boat had not been well maintained by its new owner.

This upset Lynette. "I tell you what," she said, "the story that Tom told me about the boat . . ."

Dave cut her off. "Ah, don't worry about that. That's him, now."

Lynette said, "It breaks my heart because the guy who bought it just about destroyed the whole boat already."

Dave added, "He tore the boat up."

"Oh yeah, Tom said that he saw that boat. He said, 'Mom, you'd have died if you seen that boat.' I told him, 'I don't want to hear anymore.' We took such good care of that boat. I mean, that was the home away from home, you know."

Dave agreed. "That right there had air conditioning, hot water heater, a stove. The only thing we didn't have was an icebox. We lived out of ice chests. But it was home away from home."

Their boat not only symbolized their independence and cultural heri-tage but directly symbolized their daughter. From the tragedy that took their daughter's life, they were able to build the boat that they always wanted, and on which they presumed they would trawl for the rest of their lives. Fishers' boats are not merely vehicles that enable them to live middle-class lifestyles. Each has a history, and it carries not only the weight of the latest catch but years of memories. Family often provides the inspiration for what shrimp fishers name their boats, after specific family members or a reference to family history of some sort (e.g., one trawler's father's boat was named after the trawler's favorite TV show as a child). While it is possible for them to put a price tag on their boats through the selling process, it is impossible to quantify the boats' true value.

Summing It Up

The industrial crisis brought about by imports and escalating fuel costs has been too much for some to bear. Fortunately, most ex-fishers were able to obtain employment in the oil industry or in companies that support it. For the most part, their decisions have paid off, as most report satisfaction with the stability and certainty that a weekly paycheck provides. Without fully considering the process and consequences of exit for shrimp fishers, we might be tempted to consider them as fortunate survivors—or even victors—of industrial decline. But while they described the economic benefits of their new jobs, they were also quick to discuss important nonmaterial costs of exit. They did not arrive at their decisions to quit lightly; rather, their choices were made only after considerable deliberation and often as a last resort. And although many were enjoying the financial benefits of their decisions, they had also experienced real loss.

There is much we can learn from both current and former fishers, especially about the power that nonmaterial factors can have in motivating our decisions and how we make sense of them. For persisting fishers, real material costs were involved with the maintenance of occupational identity. But for ex-fishers, there were other kinds of costs associated with leaving this identity behind. Their stories of what they had lost by tying up their boats for good emphasized the noneconomic costs of industrial decline and economic dislocation. Although staying or quitting are two obvious choices fishers faced as their industry collapsed, they had at least one other option. In the next chapter, I describe how a small but enterprising group of shrimp fishers have changed their practices to adapt to the decline in a way that allows them to preserve their occupational identity while also maintaining economic viability.

4

INNOVATION

Changing Course on Choppy Waters

Most people just dread the future, I see a shining light. If we can ever break
this cycle, this is what has to be done.

JACOB (INNOVATIVE ADAPTER)

When I first met Jacob in the summer of 2006, I presumed that he
would be like most of the other trawlers I had met up to that point. A
multigenerational trawler, he had dropped out of high school to work as a
deckhand on relatives' shrimp boats, and by age twenty he owned and operated his own boat, named the *Miss Mary Ann* after his mother. He liked
to hunt in his spare time, and he talked at length about how much harder
he had to work now that shrimp prices had fallen and expenses soared.
He also proudly identified as Cajun, and like so many others he equated
his ethnic identity with the work he performed. "We live off the land,"
he told me. "Being Cajun is kinda like what we were brought up doing.
Not everybody's fortunate to be able to keep doing what they was brought
up doing." But as the conversation unfolded, it became obvious that there
was something different about him, something that set him apart from
the other shrimpers that I got to know. Demographically he was in his
late thirties, so he was younger than most of the others I had met. But it

wasn't just his age that made him stand out as different. It was something less palpable than age or any physical characteristic.

What, exactly, was it about Jacob that set him apart from the other fishers? For starters, Jacob approached the production and sales aspects of shrimp fishing much differently than other shrimp fishers. When I arrived at his home for the interview, he had just returned from a farmer's market (almost two hours away) where he sells his shrimp every Saturday. "I sold out of shrimp again," he told me proudly. "We do real well up there. We sell out just about every week." Most trawlers sell their catch to the seafood docks, not directly to consumers. In doing so, they must accept whatever price the buyers are willing to pay. But as I came to discover over the course of our conversation, Jacob marketed most of his shrimp himself. In addition to the farmer's market, he also sold his product to several local grocery stores. And perhaps most uniquely of all, he had a fully functioning website through which he sold his shrimp to anybody across the United States that would like to buy it. He shipped his shrimp nationwide.

Jacob also boasted about the higher quality of his shrimp as compared to most other trawlers. Several years ago he had invested in on-board freezer technology that allows the shrimp to be frozen immediately after it is caught, often in their live state. Most other shrimp boats store their catch in a hatch filled with ice until they are able to unload it at the dock. The shrimp might sit in the ice hole for days at a time, but because they are not frozen, they deteriorate in quality over those days. Because his shrimp were quick frozen and thus higher quality, Jacob was able to sell his product for a higher price. What is more, because he bypassed the shrimp processor and sold directly to the consumer, he profited even more.

Clearly, Jacob had chosen to take a different path than the exiters or persisters. But it was not merely the way that Jacob caught and marketed his shrimp that set him apart from others. Perhaps the most telling difference was his contented optimism regarding his future within the industry. As did others, Jacob had his fair share of complaints and frustrations with what had happened to his industry, and he, too, endured struggles as a result of the crisis. But instead of trying to persist, treading in the same choppy waters, he made the decision to change course in order to adapt to the new realities of shrimping. And at that point the decision had paid off.

During my research on the bayou, I encountered two other individuals who, like Jacob, had changed their practices to adapt to the decline. And to some degree they all achieved success as a result.[1] These individuals, the "innovative adapters," had successfully adapted to the logic of the market in ways that allowed them to remain viable producers while simultaneously preserving the meaningful occupational and cultural activities associated with their way of life. In this chapter I focus on the process and consequences of changing to adapt. By using the internet to find new and lucrative markets for their high-quality catch, as well as taking advantage of production and shipping technologies, these local actors are not only fighting against global forces, they are using globalization in judo-like fashion to advance their own agendas. And while this option may not always be available to individuals facing unemployment, I argue that innovative adaptation in place may be an important form of agency in many organizational settings.

The Elements of Innovative Adaptation

How, exactly, does the process of catching and selling shrimp differ between innovators and noninnovators? The traditional way that in-shore Gulf shrimpers catch and market their shrimp is fairly straightforward. After shrimp is caught and sorted from bycatch and debris, it is stored in the boat's ice hole. The ice hole is a large, insulated hatch located under the back deck of the boat that is filled with ice before the trip. The shrimp remain on ice in the hole until it can be unloaded and sold to seafood docks or shrimp processors. Usually, this is where the process ends for shrimpers. Once they have their money from the processors or buyers, they start the process over again. The processers are the ones who typically clean, freeze, and package the product in order to sell it to the buyer (such as seafood wholesaler or grocery store owner), who then prices it to sell to the consumer. In this way, processors have a great deal of control over setting the price that shrimp fishers receive at the docks. Because shrimpers are at the mercy of the processors' price decisions, there are tensions and often conflict between the two groups. All of the shrimp fishers I spoke with blamed processors—and not the imports—for the low prices and ensuing difficulties with making ends meet. Most fishers plodded on, accepting the low prices out of necessity. But a few intrepid fishers were dissatisfied with the imbalanced arrangement and motivated to find a way around it.

On-Board Freezers

The key to possessing the ability to successfully market shrimp to consumers is in the investment in on-board freezer technology. These large freezers take the place of the ice hole and instantly freeze the shrimp until they can be unloaded. There are multiple benefits to having on-board freezers. The first involves the storage and quality of shrimp. On-board freezers can be used to produce a higher-quality and value-added product, known as individual quick frozen (IQF) shrimp. Most of the imported shrimp that consumers buy in the supermarket today are frozen according to IQF specifications, but much of the imported shrimp contain traces or even high levels of antibiotics and other chemicals, some of which are illegal in the United States and Europe.

IQF shrimp are a value-added product for several reasons. First, during the freezing process, the shrimp are spread out evenly to prevent clumping, so each shrimp is individually frozen. Unlike shrimp that are frozen in large blocks (as is traditionally done for shrimp caught on boats without freezer technology), individually frozen shrimp can be sorted according to uniformity of size and/or quality. Uniformity is especially important to chefs, restaurateurs, or buyers at retail markets who rely on product consistency or are interested only in purchasing a particular size of shrimp (say, the larger ones). Furthermore, because IQF shrimp can be thawed individually, they are more convenient than shrimp purchased in a block. Block-frozen shrimp must be thawed in its entirety and thus are more perishable if not used right away. IQF shrimp can be thawed individually, so a consumer can thaw eight shrimp or eight pounds of shrimp depending upon need, thus reducing the likelihood of waste.

One of the most important features of IQF shrimp are their superior quality.[2] During the freezing process, the shrimp are flash frozen very quickly using carbon dioxide, which preserves the shrimp's moisture and texture. Because they are frozen so quickly after or even during their live state, the quality of the meat is typically higher than that of shrimp that sits in the ice hole for days at a time—up to as many as twelve—before they can be unloaded at the dock and fully frozen. Higher-quality IQF shrimp are thus sold at a higher price than block-frozen shrimp. Enhancing the quality of shrimp has been the primary focus of innovative adapters precisely because they can yield a higher price.

In addition to the value-added features of IQF shrimp, freezer boats provided another—perhaps even more significant—advantage: they enabled shrimp fishers to reduce their dependence on shrimp buyers. Shrimpers without on-board freezers are hamstrung: because they need to unload their shrimp, they are forced to accept the low prices offered by the docks so they can clear out their boats and head back out to catch more. On-board freezers, on the other hand, provide shrimp fishers the ability to package and sell their shrimp directly to the consumer, yielding a greater profit. Bypassing the processor or buyer—or cutting out the "middle man"—can really add up, because commercial shrimp fishers typically deal in very large quantities of shrimp. A fisher selling shrimp directly to the consumer for one dollar *more* per pound when selling ten thousand pounds profits an additional ten thousand dollars over a fisher forced to take the lower price. One significant drawback to installing freezers (to be discussed in greater detail later in the chapter) was that they are quite expensive to install. But the returns had been promising.

Bending the Forces of Globalization: Using Technology to Market Shrimp

In addition to installing on-board freezers, innovators also changed the way they marketed and sold their products. Instead of selling all of their catch to docks and/or seafood processors, they took on the responsibility for marketing and selling their own shrimp. There were several ways the adapters did this. First, they engaged in face-to-face marketing of their product. All of them have used farmer's markets as a place to sell their shrimp. Jacob regularly went to several farmer's markets around his community, traveling as far away as two hours to participate in the largest (and in his opinion the best) markets. Of the other innovators I interviewed, Charles sold his shrimp at a popular outdoor roadside market that takes place during weekdays and Lori only occasionally went to farmer's markets to sell her shrimp but said she would do it more regularly if she had the time.

Innovators also marketed their shrimp to local grocery stores. Jacob reported that he regularly sold his shrimp to two of the state's three Whole Foods Markets, a chain of grocery stores specializing in natural and organic foods and locally sourced products. All three innovators—Jacob, Charles, and Lori—supplied one or more of the local grocery store chains with their shrimp. In order to forge these kinds of connections, innovators had to go out and establish networks with the store owners and seafood purchasers who supply the local market. Marketing is not typically part of the fishing process for trawlers and is therefore unique to adaptive innovation.

Two of the three adapters—Jacob and Lori—developed their own marketing companies through which they promoted and sold their shrimp. Both had fully functioning websites that facilitated marketing and sales. Through the websites, customers could order shrimp for delivery anywhere in the United States, and at the time of the interviews both Jacob and Lori were attempting to obtain the certification necessary to ship internationally. By using the internet to find new and lucrative markets for their high-quality catch, as well as taking advantage of shipping and transportation technologies, these local actors had carved out a niche for themselves that enabled them to ride out the waves that threatened to sink the fishing industry for good.

By changing the way they catch and market shrimp, the innovative adapters have significantly modified their operations. And up to that point they experienced relative success as a result. But it is important to recognize that they did not transform their practices completely on their own. Rather, they formed strategic alliances with several prominent marketing and promotion organizations, and thorough these affiliations they were able to make the connections to willing buyers. Two examples of these organizations were the Louisiana Seafood Promotion and Marketing Board (LSPMB) and the White Boot Brigade (WBB), both of which had recently been formed with the purpose of promoting domestic, wild-caught seafood as a higher quality and more sustainable alternative to imported shrimp. In addition to getting the shrimp fishers' product out there in the market, these organizations also helped them with business innovations so they could turn out a higher-quality final product in the first place.

Shrimp fishers who adapted to the decline by changing their practices tended to enjoy a higher level of financial success than those who merely persisted doing things the same way. As a result, innovators generally expressed a higher degree of optimism about their future in the industry. At the time of my fieldwork in 2006 and 2007, they did not report the same levels of stress and depression that persisters often described. Unfortunately, the BP oil spill of 2010 would set the fishing industry as a whole back, especially for adapters who depended upon a consumer base that was willing to pay a little bit more for a better (and safer) product. But the accomplishment of innovative adapters is significant, and although the oil spill has changed the game for fishers, their success in the fight against imports is worth exploring. In doing so, we gain a better understanding of what, exactly, shrimpers are up against in the post-spill, post-imports economy of shrimp fishing. On a deeper level, the case of adaptive innovation brings to light the lengths that social actors go to in order to preserve both their economic livelihoods and deeply meaningful cultural identity.

Struggle as a Catalyst for Change

As the shrimp fishing industry began to collapse around 2001, adapters suffered in the same way as all other fishers. Before the decline, they trawled in the same way that persisters continue today: they went out to catch shrimp for around ten to twelve days at a time and stored their shrimp in their boats' ice holes until it could be unloaded at the docks. They sold their shrimp to the docks where the prices were good and the interactions with shrimp buyers were mostly uneventful and even cordial. When the prices dropped, they were caught off guard, just as all shrimpers were.

Lori was thirty-eight years old when I first spoke with her. She is well known in the community, and her name frequently came up as somebody with whom I should speak, as she was a loud voice among those who were outspoken supporters of the shrimping industry. She was often featured in news stories regarding fishers' responses to the decline and played an active role in the fight against the turtle excluder devices (TEDs). Her roots in the industry were very deep. Her grandparents had been full-time trawlers, but her parents were not; her father had opted to work in the oil industry instead of trawling. Lori's main connection to the industry came primarily from her husband, Kirk, who was a third-generation trawler. They had been married for twenty years and had three sons and one daughter. Lori and Kirk had trawled together before they had children, and continued to do so as their family expanded. Just as with the persisters, their work and family lives were tightly bound together. It is impossible to understand their family dynamics without considering their livelihood as fishers.

We chatted during a very busy time of day for Lori. It was lunchtime, and as we spoke she prepared a meal for her husband and kids. Through interruptions by phone calls and hungry children, she told me what their life was like before the decline. "Every summer we'd trawl as a family. It was nice, because there was no TV."

"We had a TV, Mommy," her youngest daughter chimed in.

Lori clarified. "Well, there's a television, but we got to spend a lot of family time together when we worked on the boat and did our thing. Inside the boat it's like a house. It has everything except a washer and dryer on it, but we just bring our dirty clothes home and wash it. But we'd go as a family, and that is so important."

Lori went on to talk about how before the imports were a problem, shrimp fishing provided a very comfortable living for their family. Their home attested to this. They lived in a fairly large house that faced away from the bayou, where their boat was docked out back. They owned two relatively new trucks and sent all four of their school-age children to private schools. And like so many people in the community, they owned a hunting camp up north where Kirk took his sons every year after the fishing season ended. It was the life they'd always envisioned, and before the collapse it was a lifestyle they took for granted. They did not foresee it changing.

"All of a sudden, we got hit hard in the 2001 season. And we weren't ready for what happened," she told me.

I asked, "So how did you first react?"

"To be honest with you," she replied, "a lot of us panicked. I panicked. We didn't know what to do."

Her first instinct was to turn to the government for help. Because she had been heavily involved in the TEDs fight, she had experience interacting with governmental agencies. During that time, she had regularly attended meetings sponsored by the local shrimp fisher association and had been part of the process of developing strategies for how fishers would respond to the unpopular regulation. She had also traveled back and forth to Washington several times as part of an effort to draw attention to the negative impact TEDs would have on the shrimpers. Through all of this, she had gained both the confidence and skills necessary to be on the front lines of the struggle. But with the TEDs defeat fresh in her mind, and the lack of response from the government that she saw at the outset of the present decline, Lori quickly drew the conclusion that trying to change anything through political channels was likely futile; she lacked faith that political involvement would result in any kind of positive outcomes for fishers. "When the imports hit, with our local government, we were trying to get things done, like where we could get our shrimp out there and make people understand what's going on with the imports. But there was just no help."

Her cynicism toward politics and politicians ran deep. During our conversation, she made numerous references to her distrust. She attributed the lack of responsiveness on the part of political actors to how far removed they were from the everyday life of working people. "To be honest with you," she said, "when it comes to government, I think they're the most pathetic part of America. Because they are no help. They don't live like we live. And I mean like middle-class America. Or even those in poverty. These people have no idea what it's like to live from check to check. Half of them have no idea what it is to run a business. To have these people in our country sickens me, and I mean *sickens* me! And I've been up to DC, and I've been at the local level, too. It's all of them, *all* politicians." For Lori, waiting around for governmental intervention was not an option. So what did they do?

At first their solution was to just work harder. During the first few years following 2001, Lori and Kirk attempted to remain in the industry by doing things as they always had done: by selling their catch to the docks in the same way persisters continue to do. But in doing so they were forced to deal with the docks' low prices, and they suffered in many of the same ways that persisters described. "It was so hard," she said, "because we struggled so much and Kirk took it all so hard. He was miserable. We all were."

Desperate to find a way to remain in the industry but skeptical of using protest, Lori took a proactive role in figuring out their options. "When the industry tanked," she said, "I went out and researched everything. Everything I could." One solution that they came up with was to sell their shrimp along the road, as with a farm stand. This meant that Lori had to leave her post behind the wheel of the boat and take on a new role as chief marketer. "In 2002 when prices were low, we did a lot of roadside sales. A lot." They had success that year with making money while other fishers they knew were forced to settle for the low dockside prices. Once they realized that selling their shrimp themselves gave them a leg up over the others, they decided to go all in with that option. They knew that they could get an even higher price for their shrimp if they increased the quality of their product—and also that this would entail a significant investment in upgrading their technology. "We saved everything that we had and we poured it right back into our business," she told me. "We have a freezer in the back of our house to store our shrimp, and we put a freezer on board our boat to where you can put it in the freezer as it comes in. I can show it to you if you like."

As she talked about freezers, I imagined a couple of chest freezers full of shrimp. But when we walked outside, I was amazed. The freezer was far from an ice chest. It was more like a large, refrigerated warehouse, inside which sat a very large, walk-in freezer that was kept at a temperature of −10 degrees Fahrenheit. Inside the freezer, tens of dozens of boxes of shrimp were stacked and ready for shipment.

Lori was clearly proud to show me around their facility. It was almost brand new, as she and Kirk had only recently completed it. "The dock is new, it's brand new, we just built that," she said, pointing to the modern-looking dock where two boats were unloading. "You see, after Hurricane Katrina we couldn't unload because we didn't have a place to go unload anything. Most of the docks were damaged." Before the storm, their business had really begun to take off, and they had thought about expanding. But when the storm hit, it disrupted normal operations (although not nearly to the extent suffered by neighboring communities that experienced a more direct hit). They saw the slow-down as an opening for growing their business. "Other boats didn't have a place to unload, either," she told me. "So we just put it together as quickly as possible and started unloading for us and other boats, too."

Their processing equipment provided them the capability of selling more shrimp than they themselves were able to produce. When demand outstripped their supply, they purchased shrimp from other shrimp fishers, as was often the case when there was a certain size of shrimp they needed, say, the larger ones. "We do buy shrimp off of other boats. We hand out our cards and tell them this is what we're looking for. So this is what you have to provide. And that's worked for us." And because they knew how frustrating low dockside prices can be for fishers, they always paid more than the docks paid per pound. Although owning and operating a dock and warehouse had greatly reduced their need to rely on the processors, she admitted that there were times when they had more shrimp than they were capable of processing and storing. At those times, they still dealt with dockside dealers. "Yeah, we still rely on the docks sometimes. We still do. We're working on not having to. But for right now, yeah. We have to. It's just, it's not an option, just because we catch a lot of shrimp."

As the industrial crisis hit and worsened, Lori and Kirk adapted in ways that allowed them to remain viable producers. Possessing an on-board freezer resulted in a value-added product for which they were able to net a higher profit, and their mini-processing plant gave them the capability of selling their product on a larger scale. Their decision to transform had paid off.

Other trawlers had also transformed their practices, but on a somewhat smaller scale. Charles was a third-generation trawler in his mid-fifties who had been fishing his entire life. I contacted Charles after several other fishers recommended him as someone I should track down. I found his name in the phone book and gave him a call. He had some free time and invited me over right then, so I jumped in the car and headed down the bayou to his house. "You ever seen that boat called the *Ruby Lynn*? That's my boat. When you see that boat," he told me, "make a right and my house is the one with the freezer on the side."

Charles's wife was preparing dinner when I arrived. Before we had even begun the interview, I was invited to stay and eat with them. I obliged, then began the interview by asking Charles how long he had been a fisher.

"In '77 I built my first boat. I was just a kid," he told me. While he first began fishing on his own in 1977, it turned out that he'd been doing it much longer. His parents had raised him on board their shrimp boat from the time he was a toddler. Like many other trawlers of his generation, he'd been pulled out of school before he could graduate so he could help his parents trawl year-round. "My daddy used to work in the inside waters, me and my dad and my mom. And Dad took me out of school in the ninth grade to help them make a living. I couldn't tell you what year that was. But in 1977 I built my first boat. I was around twenty-one, twenty. And I'd been doing it on my own ever since."

He built his boat with financial help from his parents, and trawled on that same boat until 1999, when he purchased the sixty-foot boat he had now. The boat was named after his youngest daughter, who at the time was sixteen years old. Charles was one of the truly unfortunate fishers who built their boats right before the collapse. Like all of the others, he had no idea that that year would be one of the last prosperous and relatively untroubled years for shrimp fishing. Although he had to go into debt to build the boat, he expected to be able to pay off his expenses in a relatively short amount of time, as he'd always done. "When I built the boat, I wasn't in debt. I had to put everything I had into it to build that boat. I mortgaged my house to build it. And everything happened, when I did this, not long after, a couple of years after, that's when everything went downhill. It's like, man, I've seen bad years when you don't get no price for the shrimp. But I mean, we was able to make ends meet because everything was cheaper. The price of things was getting higher and higher and higher, and the price of shrimp going lower and lower and lower."

Due to his outstanding debt, the shrimp crisis hit Charles particularly hard. In addition to the boat note and remortgaged home, he also ran into a string of expensive mechanical problems in 2003 that kept him from being able to trawl for over a month, including the opening of the May season that year, which is the most lucrative time to trawl. He could not afford to lose that time or the money that he was sinking into repairs. He tried to borrow more money from the bank but was denied. With mounting bills and a family to feed—he had a wife, two daughters, and a three-and-a-half-year-old grandson—he had few options. Charles began to make preparations to leave the industry, even though he did not want to. With great regret, he put his boat up for sale. He became very emotional as he described how he almost lost the boat.

> I was so fed up and disgusted, and I wanted to sell the boat. I had people to come and look at the boat. Me and my wife went and cleaned out the boat, I went and cleaned everything in the engine room, top to bottom. My heart was broken because I didn't want to sell the boat. And uh, [begins to cry] I was really heartbroken because I didn't want to sell the boat. And uh, [long pause] it makes me, anyway, I ended up not selling the boat. [long pause] I don't like to talk about that. It's just hard. We came so close to losing *everything*, that I went to sell what I worked my life for. You know? But uh, we still going, so far.

For Charles, nearly selling the boat was close to hitting rock bottom. He felt shame about his economic vulnerability. When he remarked, "We came so close to losing *everything*, that I went to sell what I worked my life for," there was disbelief in his voice, as if when thinking back, he had a hard time believing that he *almost* sold his boat. As was true of others, his boat was more than just a fishing vessel; it served as a significant part of who he was and the meanings he attached to his life.

I wondered why Charles just didn't go and work in the oil industry as a way to make quick money. He told me that years ago he had obtained a captain's license in case he ever needed money in the off-season. Back then it was purely a precautionary move, and he never wanted or intended to use the license. But one particular year he was pressured by a friend of his who worked in oil to go out and give it a try, just for a few days. Lured by the promise of the extra money, he decided to take his friend up on the suggestion. But after a few days of working as a captain on a supply boat, he'd had enough: he did not like it and did not wish to return. One of his main complaints was that he felt pressured by higher-ups to perform work he found to be much too dangerous.

> You got ten-foot seas and you're risking other people's lives and you gotta do it because someone's telling you that you gotta go do it. I mean, if I see danger, I'm a fisherman, if I see that it's bad and rough, I stop. I'm not gonna put my crew in the danger. I stop. And you know, I got insurance, but hey. If I see danger, I'll stop. . . . But in the years, things changed in the oil field a lot. With the safety and everything. They paying operators now. It's tempting to want to go back and try it and see, you know? . . . Those guys make good money doing it, they got good benefits and insurance and all that. But uh, it's just like, I like to fish, and I like doing what I'm doing. I was born and raised doing it.

Charles was not accustomed to taking orders from other people. Based on all his years of experience behind the wheel of a boat, he trusted his judgment about what is or is not worth the risk. He did not like feeling coerced into making a decision that ran counter to his instincts.

In the end, Charles didn't sell his boat. He simply could not bear the thought of doing so. Instead, he decided that if he was going to make it as a shrimp fisher, he must somehow change what he was doing to adapt to the new realities of fishing, the low dockside prices and high overhead costs. He knew that he needed to find a way to avoid settling for the low prices offered by the docks. If cutting out the middleman was the goal, installing a freezer on board his boat would facilitate this. Freezers are very expensive to install, and Charles already faced a considerable amount of debt. Despite this, he decided to double-down on his place in the industry, invest in the technology, and try making it by selling what he caught. He knew that if he failed to act, he would lose his boat and be forced out of the industry. He recognized that this was his only chance of making it.

> The year I put the freezer in, I almost lost everything I had. I came down to like eight or nine hundred dollars to my name. *Down to my name!* What happened was I put everything I had into the boat when I built it. I put [the money] into the freezer, 'cause I saw what was happening. I saw that's what we'd have to do. Try to go on our own to build it. I said, we gonna lose everything we have if we don't. So I say, what's the difference? I put everything I had, and I borrowed some more money to put in the freezer. If we lose, we lose everything now, or we lose everything later. There's no difference. We might as well try it. So we did, and so far we've been successful with it.

Once the frozen shrimp was unloaded from his boat, Charles had access to several large freezers to store the shrimp. The freezers permitted Charles to completely bypass the processors and sell the shrimp himself.

But while so far he'd been successful with his operation, and had several consistent buyers for his shrimp, as the dockside prices continued to fall, some of his buyers began expressing reluctance to keep paying the dollar or so more per pound that Charles was asking for his product. "Right now," he said, "I don't sell to the factories [processors], I got a freezer boat. I sell a lot to the markets. But it's just getting to the point where the people in the markets are starting to pay like the factories. They check to see what the factory's got. They say, 'But the factories, they only buying it for *this* much.' They only want to give you thirty, forty, fifty cents above what factories want, you know? *And* they want you to deliver it, too! But, with the price of gas and stuff, it's not worth my time."

At the time of the interview, the future remained uncertain, but Charles was determined to make ends meet doing what he felt he was born to do: catch shrimp.

Like other current fishers, those who followed the path of innovation were motivated in large part to preserve the meaningful occupational identities associated with their way of life. They understood their livelihoods as their ultimate calling in life, as physically part of who they were. But there were limits set on how much they were willing to struggle, and Lori and Kirk had discussed the possibilities of having to tie up the boat permanently. Fortunately, they had peace of mind that finding employment would not be difficult. But that didn't mean exit would be easy. Indeed, Lori described how it would be anything but easy. "If worse came to worst and my husband had to do something else, than that would be it. But I know that his heart is not into doing anything else. He would be miserable, and I'm talking *miserable*, doing something else. Because this is what he knows. It is *who he is*." For Lori and Kirk, the boundaries that separate family from work life are nonexistent. To lose one's occupational standing as shrimp fisher is to lose much more than the income. Shrimp fishing serves as the foundation on which family relations are organized. It is rooted in the rich landscape of coastal wetlands and the bayou that is the centerpiece of the community. And it is where understandings of hard work and self-sufficiency, two celebrated cultural values, are forged. As Lori said,

> People need to realize that shrimping and trawling are a way of life, not just a livelihood or a paycheck. This is something that has been handed down from generation to generation and is our tradition and heritage. We have all been raised to live off the land, and we take pride in being self-sufficient and self-motivated. We take pride in seeing our catch and running our vessel and knowing that it is all built with our own hands. Trawling is the heart and soul of our family, where we feel unity and get to be together. What we know is this: we would not want to trade this lifestyle for anything else.

If economic considerations prevailed in decision-making matters, Lori and Kirk would have left when the industry collapsed. Kirk could make a very profitable living working on tugboats or in another oil related industry, and Lori has a degree in business that increases her employment marketability. But so far Kirk and Lori have decided against these options. Instead, they have chosen to stick it out.

While I seek to highlight the role that nonmarket factors play in decision-making processes, I do not intend to overstate their power. As with the persisters and exiters, economic factors weigh into the innovators' choices as well. Those who do not have dependents are given a leg up over others who have more mouths to feed, and those whose boats are paid off have an advantage over those who carry more debt. The larger point is that in order to fully understand the decisions that individuals make, we must look beyond economic factors alone. For example, Charles admitted to being in quite a bit of debt. He built his boat in 1999, was hit by a series of expensive repairs, and then took what little he had and invested it in freezer technology. Some of this debt was offset by his wife, who worked full time at the local hospital. Together they had a teenage daughter at home to support and were also full-time caretakers of their three-and-a-half-year-old grandson (the son of his oldest daughter, who lived in New Orleans).

We might look at his debt and surmise that his investment is too great for him to back out. Or we could point out that his working spouse enables him to continue on as a shrimper. And to some degree, we might be correct. But I argue that economic considerations alone do not explain why folks like Charles have not called it quits. Charles explained how he knew that he could make a considerable amount of money if he left shrimp fishing.

A lot of guys that I went to the school with and guys that, you know, I met when I was on the streets, like in the bar room you know, who I became friends with, they're all running tugboats and they're making tons of money, hell of a lot of money. I have a friend and he told me he's making $500 a day. He told me that they paying $18,000 for the boat that he's on. I said, it makes no sense. The people wonder why we paying so high for fuel. But it makes sense: they pay $18,000 a day for one boat. But I mean, it's happening. Just like [a friend who owns a shrimp dock], I don't see him very often, but I seen him the other day. And he told me that [he knew of a] crew boat that lost a job because of the captain. What happened, he didn't tell me. But the captain made the boat lose the job. One of the crewmen told [his friend], "You know, that's the best thing that ever happened to me." And [his friend] said, "Best thing that ever happened?" And [the crewman] said, "I got a job for another crew boat now, and they pay $1000 a day, which is more than what we was making before." So, I started thinking, you know, when I came back home. That's $30,000 in a month. $365,000 a year *more* that man is making. And he's making it! . . . And other captains are probably making the same thing. . . . But I'm not into that, you know, it's not something I never did care to want to do. I always wanted to fish, and I love it. It's been my livelihood. It's who I am. I *want* to do it.

If Charles were driven purely by the pursuit of economic gain, then surely he would have exited years ago. He acknowledged that he stood to earn a very comfortable living if he exited and put his captain's license to use. He could pay off his debt while also obtaining the benefits that come with waged work, such as pension plans and health insurance. But he had come away from his one experience working the tugs feeling more assured of his place behind the wheel of his shrimp boat. Shrimp fishing is tightly connected to how he understands himself and the world around him.

Out of the three adapters with whom I spoke, Charles had the smallest-scale operation. He sold only the shrimp that his boat produced, so his customer base was limited to what he could produce on his own. Furthermore, he expressed reluctance to use the internet to market his shrimp. He admitted that he knew very little about computers and was even a little intimidated by them. "It takes me forever, I don't like it," he said when I asked if he ever used it to sell his shrimp. He added, "But we do okay without it." He had a loyal customer base that included one of the supermarkets in town and another in a nearby community. If he had anything left over, he had a list of people that he called who would usually buy from him. Having options allowed him to maximize his selling potential; he went through his list until he could find a buyer willing to pay the price that he set. As he put it:

> I'm fortunate enough, I got me two or three customers. They willing to pay. They like the product, and they willing to pay me. But they're not all I have. I have a book full of people. But out of them, there are only three or four that's willing to pay. And I got one of them, her husband is a fisherman. She won't buy nobody's shrimp but mine. She'll buy it if I can provide it, she'll buy it because she rathers my shrimp. I got a couple of customers like that, not a whole bunch, they'll pay. Another guy buys market. And I got one guy, he'd buy everything that I'd catch, except the real small shrimp. But he's one of those that don't wanna pay. If I can't sell to the people that I get a good price for, if I got a bunch left, I dump it on him. I call him, and he'll come and pick it up. I got two of 'em like that, they're both, uh—well, the one pays a little bit more than the other one sometimes. I guess it depends what's going on at the time with them.

Self-marketing resulted in innovators having a higher level of control over the labor process. Because they decided to whom they would sell their product and at what price, they felt as though they had more control over

their lives generally. They did not have to accept prices for their shrimp
that they deemed unsatisfactory. In their internet business, consumers contacted Jacob and Lori directly and typically paid the price that had been
listed on the website. Sometimes they consented to haggle, but they did not
have to. Because Charles, on the other hand, relied solely on face-to-face
marketing, his customer base was built primarily through word of mouth,
with people from as far north as Atlanta, Georgia, finding out about him
through the networks he had already established. "Sometime I hear some
stories of some people who say, 'I wanna buy a lot of shrimp. I'll pay you
this, I'll pay you that.' But you never hear from them again. I get interest
coming, but after that, it's like, okay, well, let's see if we hear back from
them. If it happens it's good, if it doesn't, well then, it's still good. I don't
have a problem with it."

Having a solid customer base gave him the freedom to refuse to sell to
people who he thought low-balled him on price, a luxury noninnovators
do not have. Charles told me a story about one incident where he chose not
to sell to someone who had given him a hard time about his price.

I know one guy I used to sell to outta Lake Charles [a nearby community].
He called me up, he said, "you got some shrimp?" I said, "Yeah." He asked
what I want for them. I told him. He said, "I'm gonna tell you something:
[the local shrimp dealer] is gonna put you out of business." I said, "What
you mean?" He said, "I could buy all you need at [the local shrimp dealer]
for two dollars a pound." I said, "Oh?" I said, "Well, I tell you what. You
get in your truck and you go there. That's all there is to it." I said, "Why are
you telling all of this to me? I ain't got time to play around with you. Either you want the shrimp, or you don't want it. Hey, this is *my* price. You
told *me* you wanted to deal with *me*, that you was gonna give me the price,
now all of a sudden you calling me? I held this shrimp for you. Now you're
telling me you don't want it because you could get it for two dollars a pound
over there? Well, fine." And this was in the wintertime, we was getting
three dollars plus for it. I said, "It's not a problem. There's no problem with
it. But don't call me and ask me to hold you some shrimp again, because I'm
not gonna do it." I said, "You can't find you no shrimp nowhere, and you
call me, I'll sell it to you, but it's not going to be for three dollar and something a pound no more. It's gonna be *more*. You don't need my business?
I don't need yours. It's pretty simple." He used to be a shrimper, and he don't
wanna help out the shrimpers. And he's turning around and selling it for

high dollars. *That* I know as a fact! And it's just like a lot of these markets I know that I sell to. Some of them are willing to pay me, but some don't wanna pay me.

Researchers of work and occupations have long found that greater control and flexibility over the labor process is associated with higher levels of job satisfaction.[3] And although shrimp fishers cited the autonomy and flexibility of their livelihoods as benefits, innovation expands the level of control to one of the few areas where the fishers typically lack it: price control.

The key to be able to sell one's own shrimp is the availability of consumers who are willing to pay. In Charles's case, he has a list of people that he compiled through years of experience. Some of these people he met through word of mouth, through acquaintances, or by going store to store. He built up his customer list chiefly on his own.

The other two innovative adapters had larger, more sophisticated operations. Like Charles, Jacob and Lori invested in freezer technology and did some word-of-mouth and face-to-face promotion of their products. But unlike Charles, they invested more in the sales and marketing aspects of their businesses, most notably through their use of the internet to sell their shrimp. Indeed, the internet was an important component of their success as innovative adapters. Both had fairly sophisticated websites through which they shipped their product nationwide. When I spoke with them, they were both working toward certification so they could ship their products internationally. They both had an Internet presence on the most popular social networking website at the time, Myspace, and each later went on to develop Facebook accounts through which they promote their product and update their customers and "friends" on the latest news related to their businesses.

Both Jacob and Lori were much younger than Charles, by nearly twenty years. As far as education levels go, there was some variation. Lori had taken several courses on marketing at the local community college, but Jacob—like Charles—had dropped out of school by the tenth grade to shrimp full time. Neither Jacob nor Lori had innovated before the decline hit; both decided to change their operations as a direct response to conditions relating to the decline.

Jacob's business was perhaps the most successful of the three. Like Lori, he also produced more shrimp than he was capable of processing himself, so he still did some business with one of the buyers who ran a seafood dock in the community. But unlike Lori, Jacob was fortunate to have a close and trusting relationship with the owner of the dock he sold to. The dock owner paid a little more for shrimp that was of higher quality (which usually meant shrimp that was recently caught but under standards that were not as strictly enforced as with IQF shrimp). As Jacob put it:

> I do, I deal with the dock. I don't deal with the processor. I deal with a dock that's helped me to come where I'm at now. He's worked with me for years, this guy. . . . And, you know, without this guy working with me at the dock, I wouldn't be where I'm at now. But he knows what I'm doing, you know, can ultimately help *his* business also. That's what he's looking for. He pays his fishermen fifty cents over the other docks for some quality shrimp, he freezes them, he has a CO_2 [carbon dioxide] machine, he freezes them. And you know, it's a program where the fisherman has a little more incentive. He has a lot of boats that work for him, it's a pretty good deal that he has going, but it's not of the *best* quality, it's not IQF.

Most shrimp fishers, including Lori, reported having adversarial relationships with dock owners and with processors. Jacob's connection to a dock owner he knew and trusted facilitated his own business.

Partnerships

Another key to success for Jacob and Lori had been their partnerships with industry-related organizations. Several different types of organizations exist that advocate for shrimp fishers' rights and concerns. First, there are the politically motivated organizations such as the Louisiana Shrimp Association (LSA) and Southern Shrimp Alliance (SSA). Both of these organizations originated after the import crisis specifically to fight for and protect fishers' economic rights. The LSA is Louisiana specific, while the SSA includes members for the eight southern coastal states where commercial shrimp fishing is practiced.[4] But despite the goals of these organizations, few shrimp fishers participated directly in them. While most of the fishers were dues-paying members, they generally lacked faith in the organizations' abilities to bring about concrete change.[5] For the most part they believed that the SSA was created to benefit processors, and they thought the LSA was well intentioned but made ineffective by infighting.

Lori was one of the few shrimp fishers to be active in the SSA. She attended their meetings—though not with great regularity at the time of the interview—and on several occasions early on in her membership, she traveled to Washington, DC, to testify on behalf of shrimp fishers and their families against imports. Jacob lumped the LSA and SSA together in his thoughts about political organizations for shrimpers. When I asked him if he was a member in either of the organizations, he responded, "Let me tell you. That's part of our problem right there. Not only LSA, but all these shrimping organizations. They have their dues and there are ways of, well, I was on the board of LSA. And I just got off of it, because there was too much bickering, they spend more time and money on fighting each other than they do on trying to better the industry."

Instead, Jacob preferred to spend his time working with other industry-related organizations, particularly those focused on the promotion and marketing of Louisiana seafood. He viewed these types of groups as being more effective in bringing about positive changes for seafood harvesters. Two organizations with which Jacob and Lori were involved were the Louisiana Seafood Promotion and Marketing Board (LSPMB) and the White Boot Brigade (WBB), the latter organization promoting mainly shrimp and oysters (and named for the iconic white boots that shrimp fishers and oyster harvesters wear). The main function of these organizations is to promote Louisiana seafood products in order to increase national demand. The WBB facilitates direct marketing for local producers who might lack the skills or knowledge needed to get one's product into a specialty or "boutique" market.

Through these promotion-based organizations, Jacob and Lori have gained knowledge about what it takes to be direct marketers, including strategies for harvesting (improving the quality of product), postharvest (storing the product), and with the business end or "point of sale" techniques. These organizations also provided valuable networking opportunities, both through attending meetings and through traveling with them to cities across the country to promote Louisiana seafood. Both Jacob and Lori have gained from these experiences in significant ways. Jacob described why he prefers to spend his time with LSPMB and WBB over the political associations.

I don't try to get too involved in the politics. I try to focus on what I *know* could make a difference. The last year I've been getting more and more involved with the Seafood Promotion Board, with this and that, and you know, doing this "Chefs Afield," which I only got a couple hundred dollars to do. Like the Shell commercial, I mean, I shut my boat down, we was making ten thousand dollars a week when I shut my boat down. We painted it, cleaned it, did all kind of work, and then did the commercial. And I got twenty-two hundred dollars to do it, and it cost me about ten grand. So I didn't get nothing out the deal. But I thought it was something that needed to be done, and I did it. And it came out really good.

Through his partnerships with various marketing and promotion organizations, Jacob and his shrimp have been featured on a local television show (the "Chefs Afield" reference above) and a commercial for Shell Oil. These organizations did not fight through political channels for improvements; rather, they were established to promote domestic seafood products. Innovative adaptation is therefore an additional way that actors can use agency in the face of decline.

While most of Lori's business came from Internet sales with individuals who contacted her through her websites, Jacob dealt primarily with power players at specialty markets such as Whole Foods, Williams-Sonoma, and high-end restaurants in large cities such as San Francisco and New York. He sold his product to consumers through the internet, but he also took a more active role in contacting those who own gourmet markets and restaurants. During one of his promotional trips with the WBB to California, he made contact with a restaurant owner in San Francisco who sampled Jacob's shrimp and later became a regular customer. Jacob illustrated the degree to which his marketing yielded a much higher profit than relying on the docks. "I have this one restaurant that I'm selling shrimp to," he said, as he handed me a pamphlet from the restaurant. "This one right here. We went [to] do a function there at the restaurant, and I was selling those shrimp to them from thirteen to fifteen dollars a pound. And he's turning around and selling it for twenty-four dollars a pound. So this is something that can and will work. If you just make the time, and people who are willing to support what you're trying to do. It can work."

For the size of shrimp that Jacob was selling, most shrimp fishers would receive around two to three dollars a pound from the dock or processor. Jacob was able to receive four to seven times more by selling directly to the restaurant owner. In addition to high-end restaurants, Jacob told me that his shrimp have been featured in the catalog of the popular, high-end retail company Williams-Sonoma. He also informed me that he has sold his product to Google, whose chefs have used it in meals served in the cafeteria at one of its main offices in California. On top of all of those new business opportunities, he continued to supply one of the area's larger local grocery store chains. Clearly he was doing very well, and he knew it. "When I started doing this, I really didn't extend myself. I just made the shrimp to make the customer base happy. That's a job in itself. You know, right now, we're selling probably ten to fifteen thousand pounds a month. Yeah, some months are more some are less, but the average is about ten thousand pounds a month, just selling shrimp."

Jacob's business expanded as a direct result of his networking and promotion efforts, facilitated through his organizational affiliations. But how did he meet the growing demand as only one shrimp fisher operating from one vessel? To meet demand, he began to purchase shrimp from other fishers he knew, then made deals with several others, and he paid a higher price than they would otherwise receive at the dock. He stressed that he wouldn't settle for just any product—it had to meet the rigid demands for quality dictated by IQF standards. And so as his own business has expanded, other shrimp fishers have benefitted from the higher prices he normally pays for shrimp. At the time of the interview, he was doing this on a smaller scale, working with just a few other fishers who produced IQF shrimp. But he saw a possibility for expansion in the future, a move he saw as benefitting the local industry as a whole. He said, "What could be done is that I could buy shrimp from fishermen, you know, done the same way that I do it and produce the same quality and I can pay these fishermen the right way from the start. I could pay them double what the dock's paying them, without any question, and still turn a profit. You know, just starting out, I could see this thing really starting off."

For Jacob, changing to adapt to the new economic realities of shrimp fishing—with dockside prices held low by imports—provided him with the ability to remain in the industry without the same degree of economic struggle experienced by others. Beyond that, he also believed that others stood to gain from his success, and this is what motivated him in part to continue to expand. Jacob and Lori have significantly altered their practices and invested big money in their operations, but theirs is a high level of investment in equipment and business savvy that can be intimidating to some fishers. Many fishers, like Charles and Daniel, dropped out of school at an early age and lacked the confidence in their abilities to navigate the channels that Jacob and Lori had in transforming their businesses. Jacob and Lori were proponents of helping shrimp fishers convert their boats to freezer boats, as they recognized this opportunity for them to both earn a better living and preserve the important cultural identities associated with shrimping.

Innovative adaptation represents a unique form of action, distinct from persisting, using voice, or quitting. By adapting to the decline, Jacob, Lori, and Charles had found a way to remain viable within the industry and maintain their occupational identities. Because adaptive innovation required fishers to be more involved in the marketing aspect of their products, some might argue that adapters had, in a sense, exited from the more traditional way of making a living as a shrimper. Even though these three innovative adapters invested more time in the sales end of their businesses, all continued to be highly involved in the production process. At the time of research, both Charles and Jacob regularly made trips out on their boats, although each had a crew (including a captain) capable of running the boat if they needed to be absent. Lori spent most of her time involved in direct sales, but because of her efforts, Kirk and their oldest son continued to trawl full time.

I wondered if this made a difference to Lori, if she no longer considered herself to be a fisher because she was spending all of her time on the marketing end. When I asked her the question, she furrowed her brow in annoyance, as if this thought had never crossed her mind. "You know," she told me, "I started out as a fisherman, and adapted to become a dock, because I *need* to be a dock, and a retailer, and a wholesaler. I've adapted to all of those other things because if I didn't we were gonna go down hard. But one thing I know for sure is that I'm *still* a fisherman."

"I See a Bright Future in This"

Changing longstanding behaviors of any kind is never an easy matter. With change comes uncertainty and fear (especially fear of failure), and these worries and fears can prevent people from making positive changes, even when their current situation no longer serves them. Changing to adapt to the industrial crisis of shrimping certainly involves uncertainty and risk, principally because of the resources needed to install expensive equipment like freezers. But those who had taken the risks enjoyed considerable success.

Two notable characteristics set innovative adapters apart from non-adapters. First, they have achieved a higher level of profitability. By cutting out the middleman, they were able to both pocket more and reinvest more into their businesses. But the other, more obvious quality that set adapters apart was their optimism regarding the future of the industry, which was evident in how they felt about the possibility of their children carrying on the family legacy of shrimp fishing. Most shrimpers I spoke with typically expressed reluctance regarding their children's futures in the industry. This was especially true for Daniel, who had a five-year-old son at home. When I asked him whether or not he would like to see his son get into the family business, he responded, "My little boy is telling me he wants to work as a trawler. He says, 'Daddy, when I grow up I want to be a deckhand.' But we're trying to discourage him. He *loves* it, though. He loves it. I think I'm gonna try to make him do some rough stuff so he'll want to quit. But I guess my dad did that to me, too, and it didn't work."

Similarly, the persister named J. T. responded in a similar manner when I posed the exact question about his elementary school–aged son. "I'm a third-generation fisherman, my son would be the fourth generation. But it's stopping right here. I can guarantee that. He will be going to college. I'd drop dead tomorrow if he didn't go to college. If he gets a college degree and wants to come back to fish, fine. But, you can't take that degree away from him." J. T.'s. reluctance—and downright refusal—to permit his son to enter the industry without any solid backup plan is indicative of persisters' grim perception of shrimp fishing's future.

On the other hand, the adapters didn't feel this way. Lori had five children and one grandchild, and she expected them to carry on the family tradition. Her seventeen-year-old son already owned his own boat, which he planned to fully operate when he graduated from high school the following year. In addition to her sons being fishers, she hoped that her daughter would one day take over her part as marketing director for the business (a fact that alludes to the gendered nature of the industry). She said, "Well, we have a fourth-generation seventeen-year-old and a fifth generation who is going on two years old. And my little girl wants to be a captain on one of the boats. Will she? I don't know. She said her husband is gonna be her deckhand, and her daddy's gonna be her deckhand. That's her aspiration because she's watched us and seen what we can do. But hopefully she'll take over my part of it." The fifth-generation shrimp fisher she refers to is her grandson, the son of her oldest daughter. Lori's assumption that he will become a trawler demonstrated her belief in the continued viability of their business.

Charles did not have any sons, but he did have the three-and-a-half-year-old grandson for whom he and his wife were full-time caretakers. Charles was open to the idea of his grandson continuing on with fishing, sometimes bringing the boy out on the boat with him on shorter trips. "He likes to come on the boat with me," Charles said. "As far as to say if he'll do it when he's older, I don't know. By the time he'll be that old, maybe I'll still be around. Maybe I'll still be in business, maybe I won't. I hope I am." In order for Charles to answer the question regarding his grandson's future, he had to look into the future about fifteen years. He was already in his mid-fifties, but even so he could envision himself out there on the boat in some capacity as a man pushing seventy. His general positive outlook signaled both his tenacity as a fisher and his optimism regarding the operational changes he'd made to his business. Hopefulness and confidence were two characteristics that were largely absent in persisters' narratives.

Of the three innovators, Jacob was the most vocal in his optimism. He had one son, who was sixteen years old. He described how he often brought his son out on trips with him when the boy was younger. But over the past few years his son had gotten into a bit of trouble, and he'd recently dropped out of high school. "He wants to run the street with his buddies, and you know, hang out, drink, and do bad things that you do when you're a teenager," he told me. "He wants to do all of those things." Although his son had shown little interest in getting into the business, Jacob hoped that in the future, when his son came out of the rebellious teenage years, he would take it up.

When I asked if his son were going to carry on the legacy, he remarked, "I would love it, I really would, because I see a bright future in this. But he's got to want to do it, I can't force him. And will he? I don't know. He knows what it's all about. He could probably run this boat, if he put his head to it. In six months he could be running this boat. But with the opportunities I've had, he'd be foolish not to get into it. By the time he's twenty years old, I could get him making six figures."

Jacob's confidence about his business was obvious, and the extent to which it contrasts with nonadapters' outlooks cannot be overstated. His difference wasn't just noticeable to me. Other fishers recognized that Jacob did things a little differently, and with success, but instead of looking toward him as a model for how to survive, they looked at him with suspicion, illustrating just one of the impediments that served to keep people persisting on the same course even though that course no longer served their needs.

Obstacles to Changing Course

If innovating has led to success, why had so few shrimpers chosen to change their practices in the way that Lori, Jacob, and Charles had? For starters, changing to adapt is expensive, and many are unable—or unwilling—to take on the financial burden of these practices. Installing the proper equipment to produce IQF shrimp can cost upwards of tens of thousands of dollars, and in order to obtain this kind of capital, most fishers would have to go into debt. All of the adapters had to take on a greater debt burden in order to build their businesses. For example, recall Charles's sentiment regarding taking on debt to attempt to remain viable ("I put everything I had, and I borrowed some more money to put in the freezer. If we lose, we lose everything now, or we lose everything later. There's no difference. We might as well try it."). Compare this statement to that made by Daniel, the fourth-generation shrimper, who wanted to discourage his son from getting into the business:

> Yeah, you gotta have at least fifty thousand or so dollars to get set up to do that. I'd rather just keep the money where it's at in my pocket. You know another thing I learned being in this business? I'm never gonna be rich because I'm too scared to borrow. . . . When I owe somebody something, I can't sleep at night. Let's put it this way and all: it's not that I can't sleep, but I might lay down at night and think about it. You know, I don't owe nobody nothing. I bought a truck last month. My other truck broke in half. A tire fell off and all that. Twenty thousand dollars, and I went and paid for it, right there. I don't wanna owe nobody nothing. That's why I'll never be no millionaire, or at least act like a millionaire.

For Daniel, the expense of upgrading on-board technology to produce the higher-quality IQF shrimp is cost prohibitive. As discussed previously, before the collapse shrimp fishers normally earned enough money to pay off their debts in a relatively short amount of time. Historically, fishing enabled people to pay for new trucks or other major purchases in cash. Being indebted to others runs counter to the self-sufficiency ideal of Cajun culture. Many persisters were just unwilling to take financial risks involved with transforming their practices.

Jacob acknowledged the financial barriers to innovating when he described to me why so few have chosen to take the same path he did. He said, "I have fellow fishermen that are ready right now, if they had money to invest in their boats, they would put a freezer on, they would sell me their products. I have fishermen that are really interested in what I'm doing, and you know, what I'm doing is gonna help to make a difference. But it's lack of money, it's what it is." Because Jacob recognized that financial costs are prohibitive for many fishermen who wish to change to adapt, this was one of the main concerns he brought with him to LSPMB and WBB meetings he attended. He hoped that bringing up these issues to organizational actors would eventually result in programs directed toward providing incentives for adopting adaptive techniques. "These fishermen have boat notes, they have operating costs. They need somebody to come and step in and give them matching grants, or something to give them incentive to get, you know, freezers on their boat, and you know, improve quality."

At the same time, however, he explained that financial costs aren't the only impediment to adapting, there are significant social barriers as well. Jacob was one of the first trawlers in the area who had taken the initiative to change the way he caught and marketed his shrimp. And he believed that because he had achieved success as a result of his modifications in operations, he was being treated with jealousy and skepticism, especially because of his involvement with organizations with which local fishers were not familiar.

[Innovative adaptation has] been helping, but there's always people there that knock you down because you're doing something that's different. There's so much jealousy and envy in this industry. When we was putting this refrigeration on and doing all this work, it was like, you know, others said, "well, the Seafood Promotion Board is paying for his freezer." And they said, "LSU [Louisiana State University] was paying for it." It was a bunch of rumors that were going around. And I didn't pay attention, because I knew that in my heart I was the one who's taking all the bills. Retrofitting this boat is probably, just equipment purchases and parts to put it together, it probably cost me around $120,000.

Jacob's partnerships with marketing and promotion-based organizations facilitated his transformation of business practices, and for this he has been subject to suspicion. Recall that generally shrimp fishers' disdain for governmental agencies runs deep, and the LSPMB and WBB often partner or share members with governmental organizations (such as the Department of Wildlife and Fisheries), universities, and seafood wholesalers (including processors). Many shrimp fishers were reluctant to become involved in these organizations because they distrusted such industrial players. Jacob perceived this as small-mindedness, and it frustrated him because he believed so deeply in the changes that he made that were facilitated by his organizational involvement.

In addition to citing noninnovators' skepticism of groups with outside interests, adapters referred to their general fear of change as being an obstacle to transforming their business practices. Shrimp fishers have been using the same techniques to trawl for decades, and for the most part, the majority of them never foresaw the collapse or envisioned a future where modification would be necessary. With change often comes risk and uncertainty, and these could work against people's best interests. In addition to the obvious financial risks, there are practical risks ("what if this doesn't work?") and cultural risks ("how might changing practices impact my everyday life?"). Innovators recognized the risks but transformed despite them.

As Jacob noted, "We are individual fishermen, and we all have the prerogative to go and do whatever we want, like all this shit that I did. You know, I'm doing it because I want to make a difference and change. It's really, I mean, you roll the dice when you do this."

"Do you think other fishers just find it too risky?" I asked.

"Well," he responded, "a lot of people are afraid of change, they don't want the change. But without change, you're not gonna survive."

Lori expressed a very similar sentiment about why so many people had yet to take the steps necessary to adapt to the decline. "They're gonna have to rely on themselves and get themselves out of this fix if they want to survive in this industry," she said. "Nobody wants to change. They don't want to change, they've been doing it this way for ages and ages, and it's hard to change. So I think that's the problem there."

What struck me about Lori's comments was that in reinforcing Jacob's assertion that fear of change serves as a barrier to innovative adaptation, both of them appeared to be drawing a distinction between "us" (the adapters) and "them" (the nonadapters). By noting how "they" have thus far failed to change, she emphasized the initiative that she and Kirk had taken to survive in an industry in which so many others struggle. In a way, she was creating symbolic boundaries that separated her from those others. She was making the judgment that persisters were acting irrationally by not responding to the post-import realities of fishing. There are tensions that arise when boundaries such as these are established, and the tensions are evident in the suspicion and skepticism that Jacob described.

When considering why so few had transformed their practices, it is important to note that these adaptive techniques to remain viable in a declining industry were at the time fairly new. For example, I attended the inaugural meeting of an organization called the Shrimp Task Force. The Shrimp Task Force is a special division of the Louisiana Seafood Promotion and Marketing Board and was organized to focus specifically on Louisiana shrimp. At the meeting—attended by Jacob, Lori, and several processors—the organization's spokespersons outlined as a future goal bringing more shrimp fishers on board with enhancing the quality of their shrimp through IQF certification. They recognized that doing this would require an on-the-ground education effort, and they further recognized that it would be no easy task. But innovators believed that if they were going to survive in the industry, changing practices to produce and sell a value-added product was necessary. Jacob saw plenty of room for everyone within this movement. "I see it as a lot bigger picture. Either you gonna stay the same or you're gonna go farther. That's how I see it. I don't want it just for me. I can't do it just myself. I want to be able to bring these fishermen together and say, 'Let's take pride in what we do. Let's put out a really good, quality product and create a demand.' That's what I'm trying to do with why I changed my boat, is try to create this demand."

This type of optimism regarding the future was simply not reported by the other shrimp fishers I interviewed. Changing to adapt was a very recent phenomenon, still in its infancy at the time. Although it had proven to be an effective way to remain viable in the industry right then, only time will tell how much promise it holds for shrimping's future. After all, the import crisis appears to be around for the long haul, and there are other kinds of challenges shrimpers face, most notably those related to the delicate ecosystem in which they operate.

But shrimpers were used to being challenged. Indeed, they have incorporated the historical legacy of difficulties, setbacks, and losses associated with Cajun ancestry into their identities. Independence, tenacity, and resolve are all highly valued cultural attributes that some drew upon as resources in times of need. For example, Lori discussed how the Cajuns of southern Louisiana are distinctive in their ability to recover from disasters. In the following example, she drew a distinction between Cajuns on the bayou and non-Cajun people from the city of New Orleans. She said, "We are people who live off the land. Our ancestors came down here from Acadia and began living off the land. And we still do it today. Just for instance, New Orleans is a total disaster; those people don't know anything about putting their lives back together. They don't know how to clean up, it seems like it's such a mess. Down on the bayou, people walked right into their homes, started ripping out everything and putting it all back together, because they've done it before. It's been a constant in their life of losing, building, losing, building. Know what I'm saying? But that's the way it goes for us Cajuns. *We* keep going."

Summing It Up

As the shrimp fishing industry began to collapse under the weight of imported shrimp, a handful of individuals took the initiative to change their business practices in order to adapt to industrial restructuring. Instead of being forced to accept the low prices offered at seafood docks, these enterprising individuals transformed their practices to cut out the middleman and sell directly to the consumer for a higher price. In doing so, they upgraded their production capabilities in order to increase the quality and price of their products. They took proactive measures to build a customer base through face-to-face meetings, partnerships with industry-related organization, and/or developing internet businesses through which they promoted and sold their products.

Adaptive innovators' experiences with industrial decline contain important lessons about the importance and function of meanings attached to work. As their livelihoods became more difficult to manage, they neither chose to hold steady like the persisting fishers, nor folded and cashed in their chips in the way that ex-fishers had done. Instead, they went all-in with their businesses and invested more resources in the hope that their gamble would pay off. At the time of our conversations, they had experienced considerable success, evident through their abilities to continue to invest in their businesses and their optimistic outlooks for their futures in fishing. While more economically minded individuals would measure success by looking at their bottom lines, for them success went beyond profit margins. They were motivated to take the risky path in part by the desire to protect their occupational identities as fishers and the way of life it enabled, and they were all lifelong trawlers who were deeply rooted in the industry. The work that they did infused their lives with meaning. Like persisting fishers, they were unwilling to walk away from the work and way of life it permitted. At the same time, they were reluctant to stand by as the industry deteriorated around them.

The case of the Louisiana shrimp fishers also contributes to our knowledge of how local actors are affected by globalization processes. By using the internet to find new and lucrative markets for their high-quality catch, as well as taking advantage of shipping and transportation technologies, these local actors are not only fighting against global forces, they are using them to advance their own agenda. Much of the research on globalization and deindustrialization emphasizes the power that global forces have in sweeping away traditional occupations. After closely examining how local actors actually respond to and at times resist global forces, the effects of globalization are both more evident and complex. Globalization may pose significant challenges to maintaining meaningful occupational identities while at the same time creating new and unexpected opportunities for preserving and extending traditional ways of life.

5

DOCKED

The Uncertain Futures of Shrimp Fishers in the Post-BP Oil Spill Era

As we sat in the kitchen of his air-conditioned boat, Jacob brought out some photos from the past. Many of the pictures depicted his boat after he pulled an exceptionally large haul, the kind worth preserving in a photo for the ages. In some photos, Jacob stood surrounded by deep piles of shrimp that spread out across the deck of his boat, completely covering it. In others, hulking nets sagged under the weight of thousands of pounds of shrimp as he looked on proudly. In most of the photos that included him—photos exemplifying some of his most proud moments as a fisher—his smile was as wide as the one he wore as he handed them to me. But as he came upon one particular photo, his smile was replaced with a sullen look. "This here," he said, pointing to the photo, of a busy road lined with storefronts, "this community was the heart of the fishing industry in the past. We used to have twenty seafood docks. We had three banks here, a couple of grocery stores. Now there's only three processors left, no banks, and no grocery stores. Back in the seventies and eighties this town used to be really bustling. Not now."

Shrimp fishing in America is currently in a state of decline. What could once be counted on for providing the "honest living" that so many fishers value is barely viable. And while most who are unfamiliar with the industry or the region would probably assume that oil or powerful storms or some combination thereof is what sent the industry reeling, the key factor driving this decline is something much less dramatic but perhaps more devastating: globalization and the rise of imported shrimp. Over the past decade, the shrimp fishing industry has undergone significant restructuring in order to accommodate the recurring tidal wave of imported product. Consumers certainly benefit from the lower cost of shrimp, but domestic producers like Jacob are not so fortunate. The so-called pink tsunami has left low dockside prices in its wake. To make matters worse for fishers, the steep and sudden escalation of fuel prices has pushed up overhead costs associated with fishing: ice, food and supplies, and repairs. Shrimp fishers are used to contending with hurricanes, but from now on the impact of every storm will be magnified by the industrial crisis caused by imports.

Shrimp fishers are hardly unique in their struggle to remain competitive in a market being taken over by cheaper imports. Deindustrialization is a longstanding process that has crippled the U.S. manufacturing sector and left behind millions of unemployed workers. Some choose to abandon their communities in search of other jobs, while those who stay behind endure the struggle to make ends meet as their overall quality of life declines. But shrimp fishers are fortunate to live in a region rich with oil and the many jobs it creates. Unlike laid-off factory and mill workers in the rust belt, they do not have to worry about how they will make ends meet. They live right down the road from one of Louisiana's busiest sea ports, so they are spared the experience of filling out an application for a job at Wal-Mart. Instead they can take skilled jobs as welders, mechanics, and boat captains. Shrimp fishers have the skills needed to perform these tasks, and the jobs pay accordingly. So while shrimpers aren't unique in their struggles, what makes them distinctive in a community where viable employment prospects abound is how they stand to experience deindustrialization. We might assume that they would follow the natural paths to prosperity, jump from their sinking boats into the well-built lifeboat waiting nearby. We might even assume that they would come out ahead. They'd probably have a "better" job that pays more for doing less (shrimp fishing is very hard on the body), one that has benefits and maybe some paid time off for them to go hunting in the late autumn months. And we might assume that the community would not undergo much change, as oil had long ago been incorporated into the community's landscape.

And we would be wrong.

I was stunned to find that, instead of doing these things, many shrimp fishers had refused to leave, even though they knew that they would likely make better money if they took another job. These persisting shrimpers indicated time and again that they knew they could make better money if they left the industry and that they had the skills and credentials—like captain's licenses—required to perform the skilled jobs. And while some had working spouses and fewer dependents—economic factors that make it easier to stick it out—not all of them had these kinds of advantages.

While some chose to stick it out, others did leave the industry for other jobs. When I spoke with ex-fishers, I was surprised and moved to hear how painful the decision-making process was for them, especially with regard to selling their boats. These men were all working in and around the oil industry, many were tug or supply boat captains, others repaired equipment, and a few others worked in the retail of offshore equipment. They had fared well financially in the transition, but some of them described the suffering they endured as a result of losing cherished occupational identities. I also encountered a small group of fishers who refused to exit but who were also motivated to find a way to remain profitable in an industry taken over by imports. These intrepid few invested serious time and money into changing their practices to adapt to the economic restructuring. By selling their product directly to the consumer, they were able to cut out the middleman and increase their profits. Yet they also spoke at length about the importance of maintaining valuable occupational identities associated with shrimp fishing.

The stories shared with me by current and former shrimp fishers move us toward an understating of people's choices in situations where they're confronted by occupational decline in a rapidly changing world. From their struggles and triumphs we gain an appreciation for the centrality of culturally based considerations to choices that relate to economic well-being. Persisting fishers were not merely loyal to their work, it was bound tightly to their overall identities. To leave behind a way of life that one views as a cultural calling removes an integral part of one's identity. To leave fishing, then, would require a high level of identity work, and many persisters were unwilling to undergo this process. Their experiences draw attention to the significance of work to the construction and maintenance of identity, and the way that it is coupled with other important facets of the self. In shrimp fishers' cases—as in other family-based, extractive businesses like farming—work life overlaps significantly with family life, and each is given meaning by the rich landscape that provides the backdrop against which people live, work, and play. The experience of persisting shrimp fishers emphasizes the value of work that goes well beyond monetary reward. We should consider these types of consequences for workers and perhaps think a little harder as a society about how to nurture meaningful identities in place, even in declining industries.

Even if we do consider nonmaterial consequences of industrial decline, identity loss is still going to occur. A rich history of important research on globalization, economic restructuring, and occupational decline (and rise) have documented the negative impacts of these economic processes for people and communities. Most of this research focuses on the more quantifiable outcomes of these processes: income loss, declining rates of physical and mental health, divorce rates, and crime statistics, to name a few. These consequences are significant, but the case of exiters draws attention to other losses experienced as a result of industrial decline. The availability of replacement income opportunities serves as a saving grace for those who have been forced out of the shrimp fishing industry, sparing them the totality of the deindustrializing experience suffered by steelworkers in Youngstown or auto workers in Detroit. The changes experienced by many ex-fishers are less perceptible, and if we didn't take the time to talk to these people, we might never know the extent to which their losses have been difficult. Their loss of occupational identities—some that have been forged over generations and shaped out of the rich coastal environment where they continue to live—was considerable and should not be dismissed.

Finally, I encountered a small group of fishers who have responded to economic restructuring by changing their practices to adapt. As the industrial crisis worsened, they figured out a way to stay in the industry while also remaining profitable, doing so in large part by drawing upon such cultural resources as tenacity, resolve, and the desire to continue to live off the land that in itself is an important cultural symbol. If shrimp fishers are to survive and thrive in a market driven by imports, innovative adaptation might be the only option they have. While this option may not always be available to workers facing layoffs or plant closings, I argue that adaptive innovation in place is an important form of agency in many organizational settings, and one we need to recognize.

Although the journey we have taken in this book has been led by shrimp fishers, the implications of their experiences go far beyond the bayou. Their stories of perseverance, loss, and possibility demonstrate the centrality of work in how people both construct and express their identities. The meanings people attach to work are complex and at times even contradictory. For example, shrimpers touted the independence and flexibility that trawling provides, at the same time acknowledging the grueling nature of the job and the many disappointments that accompany it. Even in types of jobs that we might perceive to be the most oppressive, deskilled, physically demanding, or demeaning—working in slaughter house, steel mill, or even fast-food restaurant—workers often find ways to derive a sense of pride or worth in their work. Take, for example, the arduous nature of working in a steel mill. In their study on work and memory in postindustrial Youngstown, Sherry Lee Linkon and John Russo note that "in Youngstown, where the shared work of steelmaking was so central, ideas about the relationship between work and place helped to form the community's identity and gave individuals a sense of themselves. . . . Work might represent virtue, pride, and a sense of belonging to a significant project that was much larger than the individual, but it might also mean danger and hard physical labor."[1] Work confers status and self-esteem, which is why some psychologists have equated the experience of job loss with the trauma of divorce or a close family member's death, when major issues—from financial panic to a sinking sense of self-worth and depression—can arise.[2]

The experience of job loss can be so crushing because the significance of work extends far beyond the paycheck and even beyond the point of production. Workplaces have distinct cultures that both shape and are shaped by those who labor in them. The "sense of belonging" mentioned in the above quote can deeply shape our experiences both on and off the job. To illustrate the degree to which work can influence our nonwork experiences, I once again return to steelworkers in Youngstown. In his study of the endurance of a working-class consciousness, the sociologist Robert Bruno interviewed retired steelworkers on what their working lives were like. Their stories emphasized the centrality of the mill in structuring almost every facet of their everyday lives. As Bruno put it, "When they spoke of their friends, they cited other workers. When asked about their economic conditions, they noted their meager earnings and irregular work. On the many occasions I asked about socializing, they took me to clubs, picnics, and parks where there were other workers. Neighbors who also happened to earn their living at a mill shared their unfenced yards, gardens they tended, homes they painted, roofs they attached, and lawnmowers they repaired."[3] Economic dislocation is not only disruptive to matters of finance, it also disrupts longstanding social relationships that are sites of interaction where meanings are formulated.

Like the fishers who have struggled with what it means to lose—or to be on the brink of losing—a culturally valuable livelihood, communities also grapple with issues of identity, sometimes years or decades after an industry collapses. The import crisis has surely left its mark on Bayou Crevette. Fewer shrimp boats travel up and down the bayou, shrimp-related businesses have begun to close their doors for good, and more and more people now get their shrimp at the Wal-Mart instead of from neighbors or family. As difficult or bumpy a process it might be to move on, people and communities eventually adjust to changes. Almost a decade after the pink tsunami crashed ashore on the Louisiana Gulf coast where shrimpers have trawled for generations, people had begun to settle into the new realities of economic change. While they might not be fond of how the landscape had changed to reflect new economic realities, people had begun to adjust to the diminished role of shrimp fishing in the town. Yet there is an old saying that often rings quite true: "The only thing constant in life is change." Soon their lives and the community would once again be forever changed, this time by an extraordinary disaster: the *Deepwater Horizon* oil spill.

The Oil Spill

When the *Deepwater Horizon* oil rig exploded on April 20, 2010, it claimed the lives of eleven crewmen. Their deaths were overshadowed by the vastness of the devastation that continued to worsen in the days and months that oil flowed freely into the Gulf of Mexico. For the friends and families of those victims, there is no hope that their lives will one day return to normal; they lack the luxury of hopeful optimism for restoration that many people continue to hold.

Just how bad has the BP oil spill been for those who rely on the Gulf to earn a living? The frustratingly simple answer is that it is much too soon to know. The short-term impacts of the spill have been relatively easy to identify. Oil-covered birds and sea turtles washed up on shore, some of them dead, most of them dying. The U.S. Fish and Wildlife Service reported that over eight thousand birds, sea turtles, and marine animals died as a result of the spill.[4] Dead and dying deep-sea corals have been discovered seven miles from the *Deepwater Horizon* oil well.[5] Tar balls washed ashore where many people recreate, and even today some delicate marshes remain filled with sludge. Although these initial signs are far from positive, the long-term impacts will be much harder to pinpoint. Scientists are monitoring the region closely, but it will be years—or decades—before we know just how devastating the oil's impact will be on fish and wildlife populations. Marine and wetland ecosystems are incredibly fragile and depend upon a delicately balanced food web, and the oil spill has surely thrown it out of balance, the extent of which won't be known for some time. It took four years after the *Exxon Valdez* disaster for the herring population to collapse as a result of contamination, and over twenty years after that tragedy, many species of fish and wildlife have yet to recover. In addition, certain human services—recreation, commercial fishing, and tourism—remain impaired.

I returned to the bayou for a brief visit in November of 2010, and during that time I chatted with several shrimp fishers—including Jacob and Lori. At that time they all reported that they were caught up in an agonizing game of wait-and-see, but right then they had plans on sticking with shrimping. Some talked about how shrimp in some parts of the Gulf might be ruined, but they stated that the Gulf was big. "We'll be able to go west to get some shrimp, I think. I hope. The shrimp that's coming back now looks okay," Daniel told me. Despite the horrific images that were shown nightly in news reports, shrimp fishers remained surprisingly optimistic about the industry's ability to recover. Yet nobody could say for certain what the final verdict would be.

The spill has certainly called into question shrimp fishers' abilities to continue to earn a living catching shrimp. It served as an especially hard blow to those who changed their practices to adapt, as the oil spill may have seriously weakened the promise of innovation as a solution to the import problem. To best understand why the spill is especially devastating for innovators, we must think about the process of how the food that we eat gets to our table, and how we—as consumers—decide what lands on our plates.

Food Systems and Shrimp Production: Saltwater Feedlots and Free-Range Shrimp

The term *food system* is used to describe all of the processes involved with feeding a population, from growing and harvesting to marketing and consumption. Most of the food we eat today—grains, meat, poultry, dairy, fish, and so on—is produced using the methods of industrialized agriculture, commonly known as the *conventional food system.*[6] A conventional food system functions on the principle of economies of scale, which refers to reductions in cost that come about as a result of the expansion of operations. While lower costs and greater food variety can be beneficial for consumers, the industrialized agricultural practices used to produce most of the food we eat are associated with a host of ecological, health, and social problems.[7]

One particularly problematic outcome of industrialized farming is the high rate of energy consumption required to maintain operations. Fossil fuels are necessary not only to operate machinery and maintain basic farm operations but to manufacture the chemical fertilizers that are used in large-scale farming, as well as to process, package, and transport the food. As such, industrialized farms are a leading source of air and water pollution. In addition to the emission of greenhouse gases, farm runoff that consists of fertilizers, heavy metals from fertilizers and other sources, and manure contaminate water supplies. And it's not just local water supplies that are being contaminated. Runoff from farms all over the nation's heartland (where the concentration of farms is high) spills into the Mississippi River and eventually makes it down to the Gulf of Mexico. As a result, there is currently a dead zone in the Gulf that in 2006 was the size of New Jersey.[8] Still other problems related to industrialized farming include a low-paid workforce with few workplace protections.

The turn toward industrialized agriculture in the postwar period increased American consumers' appetite for grain-fed livestock such as beef, chicken, and pork. And as our appetite for meat has continued to intensify, we have not only been feeding ourselves more meat and dairy, we have also been feeding the beast that has become industrialized agriculture. To meet the growing demand for meat, grain, and dairy products, agribusiness has become much more highly intensive. The numbers of animals that now live on "farms" have become so concentrated that a new term has been developed to distinguish these farms from traditional ones: *concentrated animal feeding operations*, or CAFOs.

As I described in greater detail in chapter 1, the rise and growth of intensive aquaculture parallels the growth of industrialized agriculture. To meet increased consumer demand, foreign producers turned to more intensive means of growing shrimp in ponds. What were once small-scale operations have grown to resemble CAFOs and have been referred to by some as "saltwater feedlots."[9] These large-scale operations are subject to many of the same problems as CAFOs, including disease outbreaks, overcrowding, and pollution. The chemicals used to control these problems often leach into the shrimp and are ingested by the humans and animals that eat them.

As more and more people have become aware of the problems of industrialized agriculture, interest in alternative food systems has grown. An alternative food system, also referred to as *alternative food network*, refers to methods of production that lie outside of the conventional system to include local, organic, and/or cooperative food systems. As a direct response to the rise of agribusinesses—with their high yields and low prices—some smaller-scale farmers developed other, more sustainable ways of both producing and marketing their products.[10] Some turned to organic methods of production, others began to market their products directly to the public through roadside stands, U-pick businesses, and Community Supported Agriculture (CSA) arrangements, and still others have combined organic farming practices with direct marketing to the public.[11] One primary advantage, according to the scholars Wendy Parkins and Geoffrey Craig, is that alternative food networks often have qualities that agribusinesses simply cannot effectively exploit: "Here there is a valuing of local food production because of its contribution to the local economy and a regional food culture, the ecological benefits associated with short supply chains and particular production methods, and the possibility of reestablishing direct connections between producers and consumers that yield relations of trust, social regard and pleasure."[12]

Alternative food systems offer a way for some farmers to remain viable in a market where government subsidies keep prices for grain and livestock artificially low and thus privilege large-scale agribusinesses. The success and continued growth and influence of alternative food systems depend upon a solid base of consumers who are willing to participate. The more that consumers learn about the problems associated with industrialized agriculture, the more willing they have been to seek out alternatives. Over the past decade, shopping has become much more tightly linked to social and environmental causes. The growth and wild success of chain grocery stores like Whole Foods attests to the willingness of consumers to pay more for what they *perceive* to be a more just and/or sustainable product.[13]

The three adaptive innovators that I spoke with all relied on a willing base of consumers to pay more for a value-added product. Part of the added value of their shrimp is the higher-quality product that IQF techniques yield, but there is also value in the local-ness of their product. Their success can be understood by examining how they have participated in alternative food networks. With the help of organizations such as the White Boot Brigade and the Louisiana Seafood Promotion and Marketing Board, the innovators have found new markets for their shrimp that go beyond the docks of the seafood sheds and processors. Jacob, for example, regularly sold his shrimp to several high-end restaurants in San Francisco and Chicago, where he received as much as fifteen dollars a pound for his shrimp. In 2007 Lori was attempting to get the proper certification to ship her shrimp internationally because she said that several restaurant owners around Europe were interested in purchasing her product. Supermarkets around town and in New Orleans regularly purchased adapters' products, advertising it as a local product and charging a higher price for it. While most buyers would not likely purchase the shrimp if they did not think it was high quality, both the shrimp fishers and the purchasers exploited the cultural significance and short-supply-chain quality of the shrimp. In sum, local "wild caught" shrimp are a value-added product that can be sold at higher cost.

In addition to using the cultural and local significance of their shrimp, innovative adapters—and the organizations they partner with—actively worked to position Gulf shrimp as a healthier alternative to farm-raised imported shrimp. They have begun to use the moniker "free range" to describe their product as a way to extract a higher price. Whether wild-caught shrimp are "free range" in the way that chickens or pigs might be (that is, given the proper space to roam in a natural environment) is up for debate. Slow Food USA, an organization founded to promote and preserve local cuisine, has recently promoted U.S. Gulf shrimp in their catalog as free range: "The wild gulf coast shrimp are wild-caught—or free-range—from the Gulf Coast of the US, where they naturally exist."[14] It appears as if consumers, at least at the time, are willing to buy the moniker.

For all of the talk about the wild-caught, "free range" character of shrimp, it would be careless and dishonest not to recognize the negative environmental impacts associated with bottom trawling for shrimp. In this sense, shrimp fishers diverge from alternative food network counterparts like organic and sustainable farmers. One of the biggest ecological problems associated with trawling is the bycatch produced when nontarget marine species are ensnared within the nets as they are dragged across the ocean floor. Indeed, bycatch rates are in some cases alarmingly high: it is estimated that in the United States the bycatch-to-catch ratio ranges from 3:1 up to 15:1.[15] The federal mandates requiring the use of turtle excluder devices (TEDs) and bycatch reduction devices (BRDs) are the results of pressure exerted by environmental groups—along with the commercial and sport fishing lobbies—to protect aquatic life incidentally trapped, and often killed, in trawl nets.

The negative environmental impacts of trawling have not been lost on the innovators, who recognized that bycatch issues jeopardized their chances of selling their product as a more sustainable alternative to imported shrimp. Lori and Jacob both recognized the ecological problems associated with trawling, and as a result, both claimed to be actively engaged in finding ways to reduce their impact on the environment. They wanted their consumers and potential consumers to know that they were aware of the issues. Lori included the following statement in the promotional materials distributed by her family's company, including on their website:

> We believe that it is extremely important to maintain the balance of the Gulf of Mexico where we shrimp. Our goal is to make sure there is a future for the generations to come to partake in the shrimping industry. We have

taught our children the importance of preserving our way of life and the gulf. Our children have attended and still attend meetings in which much of the environmental and shrimping sectors have to reach some kind of compromise on what is to take place in our future. We do much of this work by allowing observers aboard our vessel from the National Marine Fisheries Service and The Gulf and Atlantic Fisheries Foundation. . . . We feel it's important to teach the younger generation how to work with the different agencies within our realm.

Lori's willingness to partner with federal agencies is quite a departure from shrimp fishers' historic aversion to the same organizations during the TEDs debacle, as described in chapter 2. Her new-found willingness to comply was a testament to the degree of changes that fishers needed to make in order to remain viable. While Lori and her family heeded the importance of preserving valuable ecosystems and species, they also recognized that their ability to market themselves through alternative food networks requires that they conform to the core principles out of which these food systems have developed.

It is easy to see how the BP oil spill might jeopardize the ability of all fishers to continue to make a living. If Gulf seafood is proven to be unsafe—or if there is serious doubt raised about its quality—many more Gulf Coast shrimp fishers will certainly be out of work. At the time of this writing, the Food and Drug Administration—the agency responsible for ensuring the food safety—has found Gulf shrimp to be safe for consumption. In March of 2011 the FDA reported that "the results of the tests, all publicly available, should help Americans buy Gulf seafood with confidence: the seafood has consistently tested 100 to 1000 times lower than the safety thresholds established by the FDA for the residues of oil contamination."[16] However, other scientists have argued that the FDA's methods of testing significantly underestimate the risk from seafood contaminants among sensitive Gulf Coast seafood populations.[17] Even if Gulf seafood is safe, the public's perception of seafood quality has been brought into question. If there is no demand for Gulf shrimp, shrimp fishers will find fewer and fewer outlets for their product. Moreover, if the innovative fishers are to be successful participants in an alternative food system, there must be a base of consumers willing and eager to purchase their higher-priced product.

Are there enough consumers out there who are willing and able to purchase wild-caught Louisiana shrimp if it means paying a higher price? Before the BP oil spill tragedy, Jacob and Lori seemed to think so. However, since then the future is not so certain. In November of 2010 Lori reported that her internet business had dried up completely, and that they had returned to the docks for selling their shrimp for the time being. A year later her internet business had returned somewhat, but it was still slow and they still relied on the docks more than they liked to. Jacob reported that although his business had slowed a little, he still sold his shrimp to Whole Foods, at the farmer's markets, and to the specialty restaurants in San Francisco and Chicago. (Anecdotally, one of the upscale restaurants in my community in the Pacific Northwest recently had a "Gulf Seafood Celebration" featuring dishes made with food from the Gulf, including shrimp. It was billed as a way to show solidarity with the fishers who were recently affected by the oil spill and cited the FDA's endorsement of the safety of Gulf seafood, and it was fairly well attended.) Although it is early on in the recovery process, at the time of this writing Lori and Jacob were continuing to earn a living as shrimp fishers—just as their parents and grandparents had done.

While the oil spill undoubtedly serves as an additional blow to the industry, it has not affected *how* shrimpers arrive at the fundamental decisions that they make in response to change. As I show time and again throughout this book, they go through a careful calculation of nonmaterial costs and benefits as they grapple to figure out what their next move will be. Remaining in the industry permits them to carry on family traditions and thus fulfills their perceived Cajun cultural purpose. To be sure, there are real material costs involved with the maintenance of this identity. Imported shrimp have pushed dockside prices perilously low and made fishing for them a much more uncertain and difficult way to earn a living. Conversely, leaving the industry, for whatever the reason, comes with the high cost of losing meaningful cultural identities so cherished by the fishers, even as they enjoy the economic benefits of working at a better-paying job. Furthermore, innovating to adapt to the new economic realities of fishing remains a risky endeavor where the economic payoff is unknown but where valuable occupational identities are maintained, at least for the time being. To put it another way, no matter the impetus for change, the outcomes remain the same: quitting is heartbreak, persisting is toil, and innovation is risky and unpredictable.

METHODOLOGICAL APPENDIX

The primary goal of this study was to reveal how local actors respond when their livelihoods and cultural identities come under siege by globalization processes. The principal method I used for this sociological analysis was the ethnographic interview. Ethnography is the systematic and immersive study of human cultures. Ethnographic interviews consist primarily of in-depth, unstructured, and semiformal conversations. This interviewing technique departs from a more "traditional" interview in that researchers typically immerse themselves in the life world of the research subject in order to best attain a deep understanding of the nuances and complexities that characterize human culture and societies. While other types of interviewing tend to be comprised of a more rigidly structured, formal interview schedule with a predetermined list of questions, ethnographic interviews more resemble a conversation, where questions and responses flow naturally as both the interviewer and respondent see fit. Although ethnographic interviewers ultimately guide the conversation, they must be willing (and able) to deviate from the order and content of their original interview questionnaire as the conversation unfolds.

Ethnographic interviews served my purposes for several reasons. Although my primary research objective was to uncover local actors' responses to globalization processes, this was far from my only objective. If that were the case, then I might have saved myself the time, money, and frustrations that are inherent in field research and instead mailed closed-end surveys to all current and ex-shrimp fishers that required them to mark the box that best indicated their future plans and outlooks. The survey method is common to sociological analysis because it can provide a bird's-eye view of social phenomena, allowing us to see how large populations of individuals generally act or feel at a given point in time. However, a mailed-out survey would have been woefully inadequate for my empirical interests.

In addition to focusing on responses, I also sought to uncover the cultural meanings and significance that shrimp fishers attach to their occupation. Such an understanding is essential for fully comprehending the outcomes of occupational decline. Why do some remain in the declining occupation, but other exit? What motivates some to change? Ethnographic analysis takes as a starting point the notion that what people do conveys much about the meanings they attach to various facets of their social worlds. But examining actions is not always adequate, as behaviors are not always accurate reflections of how one really thinks. Ethnographic interviews provide a forum for individuals to articulate how they make sense of the world around them, and how they negotiate the complexity of the social world.

To put it simply, the goal of ethnographic interviews is to get people to talk about what they know, and to discover how that knowledge affects behavior. Ethnographic interviews seek to uncover *tacit* knowledge in addition to the *explicit* knowledge that more traditional interviews or questionnaires can reveal. But tacit knowledge is not easily revealed and is likely drawn out only after a rapport has been established between researcher and research participant. My previous year-long experience with living and working in Bayou Crevette provided me with a foundation upon which rapport could be more easily built. To be sure, I do not claim that by living in the community for a year before my actual fieldwork instantly bestowed on me an insider status that other researchers lacking my experience would be denied. But my previous experience would prove to be advantageous in a variety of ways.

Over the course of that year, I became familiar with many of the cultural norms and customs that make up the community. As part of the training we received with AmeriCorps, we attended a variety of workshops and cultural events designed to provide members with an understanding of not only the community's natural environment but also its rich cultural heritage. Many of these training sessions were held in the various cultural centers that were located in the town or surrounding communities. Others were held on the campus of the community college that was about forty-five minutes outside of the town. We also attended a host of cultural events, such as Cajun dances and food celebrations held periodically throughout the year. Taken together, these experiences facilitated an appreciation for the community's unique and rich cultural qualities.

Perhaps the best training we received was not any kind of formal training or workshop at all. Rather, working alongside a variety of community members—from educators to oil workers to those sentenced to perform community service—provided valuable opportunities to gain insight into the everyday lives of the inhabitants in Bayou Crevette. The environmental nonprofit that I worked for was the only one of its kind in the community. As such, it attracted many community members who desired to volunteer for the projects that the organization hosted, such as beach cleanings and marsh grass plantings. Several of these individuals were high-ranking members of the community, serving on the parish council or school board, and whose connections would later prove to be immensely useful in helping me to find and build rapport with research participants.

During the five years separating my AmeriCorps and fieldwork experiences, I revisited the bayou three times. And although both visits were for a relatively short time (a week or less), they were instrumental to the development of this research project. It was during these trips back that I learned about the sudden and unexpected downturn the shrimp fishing industry had taken. If I had not gone back to the bayou, at some point I surely would have read about the decline in the newspaper or heard a story about it on the national news. But hearing firsthand about the deterioration of the industry as it was happening was a much more poignant and accurate way to reach an understanding of just how painful the collapse of the industry was for Louisiana shrimpers and the larger community. These short visits back to the bayou also helped to keep fresh my connections to the community and several of its key members.

In 2006 I decided to pursue my interest in the collapse of the shrimp fishing industry for my dissertation research. I wanted to understand exactly how the decline had impacted shrimpers and the community, how the fishers were making sense of the decline, and what their plans were for a future that might very well exclude the industry. To answer these questions, I knew I had to return to the bayou. Part of the reason why I needed to return was logistic. Although I had a few connections to shrimpers, most of the connections I had were with nonshrimping members of the community. These individuals would be instrumental in helping me find current and former fishers who were willing to participate in my study, many of whom would help me in turn to further grow the "snowball" sample upon which this study was based.

There were other, more pressing reasons why I knew that I had to go back to the bayou and live. I needed to reimmerse myself in the community in order to get a better-developed sense of what it was going through, and how it had changed since I had lived there five years before. An ethnographic approach requires that researchers step out of their familiar surroundings and into the life worlds of those who they seek to better understand. Ethnographers strive to understand humans in their fullest possible contexts, and this includes the places where they live and the spaces they regularly inhabit. I simply could not have attained the same level of detail from the respondents (and from the field notes that I took) if I had conducted interviews by phone or through a written questionnaire. I needed to be there.

Because I was a graduate student who earned a living working for the university during the academic calendar year, my opportunity to travel to the bayou was limited to summer quarters. Thus, most of the ethnographic research used in this project was collected during the summers of 2006 and 2007. Each summer I spent around eight weeks in the field. I stayed in the spare bedroom of two generous individuals—a married couple named June and Herbert—whom I had met during my AmeriCorps days. June and Herbert, well known people in the community, were in their seventies. One of their five children was a member of the parish school board, another one ran the local civic center where most of the cultural and community events in the town were held, and still another was a tugboat captain. Each of these individuals lived within walking distance of June and Herbert, and would often pop in to see how I was doing or invite me to have dinner with them.

My connection to June, Herbert, and their family was beneficial for several reasons. First, because they were a well-regarded family in the community, my affiliation helped with building trust and rapport with shrimp fishers and other individuals who otherwise did not know me. But of equal importance was the feedback I received from them through the daily conversations we had at the beginning and end of each day. Most of my days began with sharing breakfast with June and Herbert, when I would talk about my strategy and what I hoped to accomplish for the day. Most nights, before bed, we'd sit around the same table with a glass of wine (or two), and I would fill them in on what I'd done, whom I'd talked with, and how I felt about what I had learned that day. They were patient and gracious listeners, but they were not shy when they disagreed with something I said or thought I was being incomplete with my views on a particular issue. Sometimes they challenged my assumptions or ideas, while other times they added insight to the questions or problems that I would raise. It was through this experience that many of my ideas began to solidify and take shape, so with them I was always sure to have a pen and paper nearby so I could document their suggestions and insights.

My previous experience living in the town, and my affiliations with a well-regarded family and nonprofit organization, proved quite useful in helping me to find willing interview participants. And because it was not easy to locate participants (especially former shrimpers), I needed all the help I could get. In 2006 I focused my attention on finding current shrimp fishers. This was my first stab at collecting data for my dissertation, and at that time I was unaware of how important ex-shrimpers would be to the final project. Current shrimp fishers are a visible presence in the town: their boats are docked along the bayou, and they can often be found working on their boats, getting them ready for the next trip out.

When I returned to Ohio that fall, I struggled to make sense of what I had found that summer: despite the deterioration and ensuing hardships, most shrimp fishers were adamant about remaining in the industry, even though they had other, better employment alternatives. This flew in the face of economic rationality; what could explain this? During this time, I was preparing for my upcoming comprehensive examinations for my graduate program. My academic adviser, Steve Lopez, worked closely with me to construct a reading list directed toward my dissertation questions, and it was at that time that I became familiar with Hirschman's theory of exit, voice, and loyalty. I found that many shrimpers were not exiting as Hirschman predicted. But what about those who did exit? Why did they decide to leave, while others chose to stay? And what could this tell us about the nature of occupational decline?

To answer these questions, I needed to return to the bayou to track down ex-shrimpers. And so this became the major goal of my 2007 fieldwork. But finding ex-shrimpers was a difficult task. I spent a great deal more time beating the streets and trying to compile a list of potential interview participants. Because many ex-shrimpers go into the tugboat or oil industries, I visited businesses there and talked to whoever was willing. Another tactic I used was writing down phone numbers on the boats that were up for sale. And I followed up with current fishers I'd spoken with the year before, many of whom provided me with relevant names I later looked up in the phone book.

During both years, to get a more complete sense of the current state of the shrimping industry and community, and to find participants, I also took part in many aspects of daily life. I attended numerous events—local festivals and dances, seafood boils, shrimping-related community meetings. By the end of the second summer, I had conducted fifty tape-recorded, in-depth interviews with nineteen current shrimpers, seventeen former shrimpers, and fourteen individuals connected to the shrimp industry, at net shops, seafood docks, and tugboat companies.

While community members here generally have a reputation for being friendly, hospitable, and quite open, many shrimp fishers also have a high degree of distrust for researchers, a sentiment that I develop more fully in chapter 2. But I learned that soon after I identified myself as "one of the AmeriCorps kids" who was now back in the community and living with June and Herbert, initial misgivings and skepticism seemed to dissipate: "You're not from the government, are you?" often quickly turned to "Oh, you know Herbert! He's a good guy, and has a beautiful boat." And while I cannot be fully certain that all of these individuals fully trusted me—or trusted me at all—upon learning about my history with the community, many invited me on board their boats or into their houses (and often extended an invitation to dinner). Interviews lasted anywhere from between thirty minutes to three hours long. The number of individuals who provided me with contact information so I could follow up with them in the future is also indicative of some level of trust.

One of the core standards of ethnographic interviewing is to eventually achieve a sense of empirical saturation, or the point when participants are offering similar or consistent responses to the same question—and when a researcher can feel more confident that it is time to leave the field. By the end of the second summer of fieldwork, I had reached this point of saturation.

After I left the field in 2007, I had over 150 hours of audio files that needed to be transcribed. My first instinct was to find out how much it was going to cost me to have them transcribed professionally. But Steve had other ideas: he thought it would be better if I transcribed all of the interviews myself. Farming them out, he argued, would impede my ability to be fully immersed in the data and to recognize the subtleties and nuance that characterize ethnographic interviews. Much as I was resistant to the prospect of transcribing all of the interviews myself, I could not disagree with these assertions. I got to work transcribing right away, and I did so for months and months.

While I transcribed, I kept a journal in which I recorded my thoughts and observations as they unfolded. These field notes were immensely useful for both advancing my theoretical objectives and for the coding that I did later on. After all of the interviews were transcribed, my coding scheme was fairly straightforward, if not archaic. I used the highlight function in the Microsoft Word program to color-code themes that emerged in each interview. I pored over the transcripts time and again, and eventually I recognized the patterns that characterize my data.

Ethnographic interviewing, supplemented by a little fieldwork provided me with the valuable opportunity to gain insight into how shrimp fishers thought or felt about the decline of the industry, and the subsequent decisions that they have made as a result. However, relying mostly on ethnographic interviewing for data collection surely has its limitations. Regretfully, one important facet of shrimpers' lives that I did not participate in during my fieldwork was going out on a shrimp boat to experience the fishing process firsthand.

There are both practical and cultural reasons for this. Practically, my propensity toward seasickness prevented the few shrimp fishers who offered to take me out on the boat from actually following through. "Do you get seasick?" was the question that without fail followed the offers. Shrimp fishing is an incredibly expensive endeavor, especially after fuel prices went through the roof around 2005. I feared that once I would get out there, I would become too sick to make it worthwhile, therefore forcing the fisher to waste fuel to take me back to land. Being someone who becomes seasick from the gentle movement of a porch swing, I did not want to take that risk.

Culturally, many shrimp fishers expressed reservations about taking an unfamiliar woman out on the boat. Some shrimpers told me that they would take me out with them but their wives might become upset or think it was strange. Bayou Crevette is a relatively small community, where most of the people know (or know of) each other. And like many small, rural communities, gossip is a pastime. Many shrimpers expressed the desire to keep their names off the gossip circuit, fearing that by taking an unknown woman out on an hours-long fishing trip, they would be opening themselves up to it. But by not going out on a boat to experience the process of shrimp fishing, I surely missed out on a valuable opportunity to gain a deeper understanding of the process of shrimping. However, the ethnographic interviews I conducted with the shrimp fishers and members of their families served my overall research purposes well.

Only a short time after I was finished collecting data for this project, the history of shrimp fishing in Louisiana took yet another dramatic turn. The BP oil spill has certainly affected the working lives of shrimp fishers, but it is too soon yet to say how. Roughly six months after the spill, I returned to the bayou for a few days to reconnect with some of those who contributed to this project most significantly. All those I spoke with felt it was too soon to say how much or how little they stand to be affected by this terrible tragedy. Most fishers were still grappling with what had happened to not only their livelihoods but also to their communities and recreational areas. They remained cautiously optimistic that the gulf would recover. My research in this region and on this culturally rich livelihood is ongoing, and I aim to continue to trace these life histories—anchored firmly in family, community, and environmental structures—well into the post–BP oil spill era.

NOTES

1. Setting Sail

1. Elizabeth LaFleur, Diane Yeates, and Angelina Aysen, "Estimating the Economic Impact of the Wild Shrimp, *Paneaus* sp., Fishery: A Study of Terrebonne Parish, Louisiana," *Marine Fisheries Review* (Winter 2000): 28–42.

2. Michael G. Haby, "Status of the World and U.S. Shrimp Markets." Document prepared for the Louisiana Sea Grant Program 2003, http://www.seagrantfish.lsu.edu/pdfs/TAAWild Shrimp_1.pdf.

3. In 2001 shrimp surpassed canned tuna as the most popular seafood product in the United States. By 1996 Americans were eating around 4.4 pounds per person, or 1.3 billion pounds total, annually. See Taras Grescoe, *Bottomfeeder: How to Eat Ethically in a World of Vanishing Seafood* (New York: Bloomsbury, USA, 2008), p. 150.

4. Brian Marks, "Effects of Economic Restructuring on Household Commodity Production in the Louisiana Shrimp Fishery" (MS thesis, Department of Geography and Regional Development, University of Arizona, 2005).

5. For more on the early history of Louisiana shrimp fishing, see Laura Landry, "Shrimping in Louisiana: Overview of a Tradition," originally published in 2003 in *Louisiana's Living Traditions: Articles and Essays,* an online journal of the Louisiana Folklife Division of the Louisiana Department of Culture, Recreation and Tourism. Accessed at http://www.louisianafolklife.org/LT/Articles_Essays/creole_art_shrimping_overv.html.

6. Colin Clark, *The Conditions of Economic Progress* (London: Macmillan, 1957); Daniel Bell, *The Coming of Post-Industrial Society: A Venture in Social Forecasting* (New York: Basic Books, 1973).

7. For a more recent discussion of the deindustrialization debates, see Christopher Kollmeyer, "Explaining Deindustrialization: How Affluence, Productivity Growth, and Globalization Diminish Manufacturing Employment," *American Journal of Sociology* 114, no. 6 (2009): 1644–74; and also David Brady, Jason Beckfield, and Wei Zhao, "The Consequences of Economic Globalization for Affluent Democracies, "*Annual Review of Sociology* 33 (2007): 313–34. See also Barry Bluestone and Bennet Harrison, *The Deindustrialization of America* (New York: Basic Books, 1982).

8. Brady, Beckfield, and Zhao, "Consequences of Economic Globalization," 316.

9. Some economists have claimed that globalization has had little influence on the weakening of the manufacturing sector in affluent democracies. For more on this, see Mathias Dewatripont, André Sapir, and Khalid Sekkat, *Trade and Jobs in Europe. Much Ado About Nothing?* (New York: Oxford University Press, 1999). But others provide empirical support for globalization's influence on deindustrialization of manufacturing. See Arthur Alderson, "Globalization and Deindustrialization: Direct Investment and the Decline of Manufacturing Employment in 17 OECD Nations," *Journal of World-Systems Research* 3 (1997): 1–34; and also David Brady and Ryan Denniston, "Economic Globalization, Industrialization and Deindustrialization in Affluent Democracies," *Social Forces* 85 (2006): 297–329.

10. For a more detailed description of economic restricting in the farming industry, see Linda Lobao, *Locality and Inequality: Farm and Industry Structure and Socioeconomic Conditions* (Albany: State University of New York Press, 1990); see also Katherine Meyer and Linda Lobao, "Economic Hardship, Religion, and Mental Health during the Midwestern Farm Crisis," *Journal of Rural Studies* 19, no. 2 (2003): 139–55.

11. Roger Friedland and A. F. Robertson, *Beyond the Marketplace: Rethinking Economy and Society* (New York: Aldine de Gruyter, 1990), p. 25.

12. See Saskia Sassen, *The Global City: New York, London, Tokyo*, 2nd ed. (Princeton, NJ: Princeton University Press, 2001); also Manuel Castells, *The Rise of the Network Society,* 2nd ed. (Oxford: Blackwell Publishing, 2000); and Robert Reich, *The Work of Nations: Preparing Ourselves for 21st Century Capitalism* (New York: Vintage Books, 1992).

13. Meyer and Lobao, "Economic Hardship, Religion, and Mental Health during the Midwestern Farm Crisis"; also Vicki Smith, *Crossing the Great Divide: Worker Risk and Opportunity in the New Economy* (Ithaca, NY: Cornell University/ILR Press, 2002); also Richard Longworth, *Caught in the Middle: America's Heartland in the Age of Globalism* (New York: Bloomsbury Publishing, 2007).

14. See Mauro F. Guillen, "Is Globalization Civilizing, Destructive or Feeble? A Critique of Five Key Debates in the Science Literature," *Annual Review of Sociology* 27 (2001): 235–60.

15. Marks, "Effects of Economic Restructuring."

16. Landry, "Shrimping in Louisiana."

17. T. Becnel, "A History of the Louisiana Shrimp Fishing Industry 1867–1961" (MS thesis, Department of History, Louisiana State University, 1962).

18. Marks, "Effects of Economic Restructuring," p. 39.

19. Ibid.

20. The boundaries separating the four sectors are not always rigidly defined. For example, a single unit may perform only one function (e.g., a shrimper who does not possess the capability to process or retail shrimp) or multiple functions (e.g., a shrimper who catches, processes, and sells shrimp directly to the consumer).

21. LaFleur, Yeates, and Aysen, "Estimating the Economic Impact of the Wild Shrimp, *Paneaus* sp., Fishery."

22. "Louisiana Shrimp and Shrimping," Louisiana Department of Wildlife and Fisheries, accessed June 23, 2009, http://www.wlf.state.la.us/apps/netgear/index.asp?cn=lawlf&pid=689.

23. "The Louisiana Shrimp Industry: A Preliminary Analysis of the Industry's Sectors," Louisiana Department of Wildlife and Fisheries, accessed June 23 2009, http://www.wlf.state.la.us/pdfs/education/La.%20Shrimp%20Industry.pdf.

24. LaFleur, Yeates, and Aysen, "Estimating the Economic Impact of the Wild Shrimp, *Paneaus* sp., Fishery," p. 39.

25. Indicates shrimp size. In this instance, it would take roughly thirty-six to forty shrimp to make up one pound of shrimp.

26. "NMFS New Orleans Market Shrimp Statistics for May and November 2001 and 2004," National Marine Fisheries Service, accessed June 26, 2009, http://www.seafood.com.

27. Louisiana's shrimp prices are typically lower than other states' because state regulations permit shrimp fishers in Louisiana to catch a higher quantity of smaller shrimp than is permitted in other states.

28. Shrimp imports have made up a sizable share of the domestic market since demand increased in the postwar era.

29. Marks, "Effects of Economic Restructuring."

30. Haby, "Status of the World and U.S. Shrimp Markets."

31. Ben Belton and David Little, "The Development of Aquaculture in Central Thailand." *Journal of Agrarian Change* 8, no. 1 (2008): 123–43.

32. Michael Pollan, *The Omnivore's Dilemma* (New York: Penguin Press, 2006), p. 52.

33. Marks, "Effects of Economic Restructuring."

34. Belton and Little, "Development of Aquaculture in Central Thailand."

35. For a more detailed explanation of the problems associated with industrialized shrimp farming, see Grescoe, *Bottomfeeder,* pp. 147–74.

36. Ibid.; see also American Society for Microbiology, "Globalization Impacts Food Safety Standards in the United States," *Infectious Disease News*, July 1, 2008, accessed June 29, 2009, http://www.infectiousdiseasenews.com/article/37077.aspx.

37. Chloramphenicol is a "drug of last resort" used to treat meningitis and typhoid in humans. It has been found to cause aplastic anemia, a condition in which bone marrow stops producing red and white blood cells and platelets, which carry oxygen in the blood. See R. Wallerstein et al., "Statewide Study of Chloramphenicol Therapy and Fatal Aplastic Anemia," *Journal of the American Medical Association* 208 (1969): 2045.

38. "Import Alert: Government Fails Consumers, Falls Short on Seafood Inspections," Food and Water Watch, 2007, accessed January 13, 2012, http://www.foodandwaterwatch.org/reports/import-alert.

39. Katrin Holmström et al., "Antibiotic use in shrimp farming and implications for environmental impacts and human health," *International Journal of Food Science and Technology* 38 (2003): 255–66.

40. Roy Lewis et al., *Thematic Review on Coastal Wetland Habitats and Shrimp Aquaculture,* World Bank/NACA/WWF/FAO Consortium Program on Shrimp Farming and the Environment, 2003, http://library.enaca.org/Shrimp/Case/Thematic/FinalMangrove.pdf.

41. I. Valiela, J. L. Bowen, and J. K. York, "Mangrove Forests: One of the World's Threatened Major Tropical Environments." *BioScience* 51, no. 10 (2001): 807–15.

42. Jack Rudloe and Anne Rudloe, *Shrimp: The Endless Quest for Pink Gold* (Upper Saddle River, NJ: FT Press, 2010), p. 215.

43. For a more detailed discussion of the conflicts over land rights, see Susan C. Stonich and Peter Vandergeest, "Violence, Environment, and Industrial Shrimp Farming," in *Violent Environments,* ed. Nancy Peluso and Michael Watts (Ithaca, NY: Cornell University Press, 2001), pp. 261–86; see also P. Siregar, "Indonesia: Mounting Tensions over Industrial Shrimp Farming," *World Rainforest Movement Bulletin* 51 (2001), http://www.wrm.org.uy/bulletin/51/Indonesia.html.

44. Haby, "Status of the World and U.S. Shrimp Markets."

45. Belton and Little, "Development of Aquaculture in Central Thailand."

46. Jim Carrier, "All You Can Eat: A Journey through a Seafood Fantasy," *Orion Magazine Online,* 2009, http://www.orionmagazine.org/index.php/articles/article/4395.

47. For more on the process of plant closings and its impacts on employees, see Louise Moser Illes, *Sizing Down: Chronicle of a Plant Closing* (Ithaca, NY: Cornell University Press, 2001).

48. Paul Amato and Brett Beattie. "Does the Unemployment Rate Affect the Divorce Rate? An Analysis of State Data 1960–2005," *Social Science Research* 40 (2011): 705–15.

49. Tami Friedman,"A Trail of Ghost Towns across our Land: The Decline of Manufacturing in Yonkers, New York," in *Beyond the Ruins: The Meanings of Deindustrialization*, ed. Jefferson Cowie and Joseph Heathcott (Ithaca, NY: Cornell University Press, 2003), pp. 19–43.

50. For further discussion, see Jefferson Cowie and Joseph Heathcott, "The Meanings of Deindustrialization," in *Beyond the Ruins*, pp. 1–18.

51. While the oil industry supplies a number of jobs, it is necessary to point out that the industry is characterized by a history of volatility, given to booms and busts. In the 1980s the surplus of crude oil depressed prices and resulted in a bust cycle. As a result, many were put out of work and the industry was restructured to accommodate the changes. The surplus was largely as a result of the energy crisis of the 1970s, when the scarcity of oil supplies slowed economic activities in industrial countries and led to energy conservation practices brought about by high prices (see Jad Mouawad, "Oil Prices Pass Record Set in '80s, but Then Recede," *New York Times*, March 8, 2008). Shrimp fishers recognized the volatility of the oil industry but generally viewed the jobs associated with oil to be viable employment opportunities.

52. See the appendix for further discussion of the methods.

53. For an overview of the various ways that the exit, voice, and loyalty thesis has been used and modified by researchers in various disciplines, see Keith Dowding et al., "Exit, Voice, and Loyalty: Analytic and Empirical Developments," *European Journal of Political Research* 37 (2000): 469–95.

54. Hirschman's Exit, Voice, and Loyalty thesis has been used to predict employee behavior in a variety of workplace settings. See Dan Farrell, "Exit, Voice, Loyalty, and Neglect as Responses to Job Dissatisfaction: A Multidimensional Scaling Study," *Academy of Management Journal* 26 (1983): 596–607; also Caryl E. Rusbult et al., "Impact of Exchange Variables on Exit, Voice, Loyalty, and Neglect: An Integrative Model of Responses to Declining Job Satisfaction," *Academy of Management Journal* 31 (1988): 599–627; Michael J. Withey and William H. Cooper, also "Predicting Exit, Voice, Loyalty, and Neglect," *Administrative Science Quarterly* 34 (1989): 521–39. For an ethnographic analysis, see Elizabeth A. Hoffman, "Exit and Voice: Organizational Loyalty and Dispute Resolution Strategies," *Social Forces* 84, no. 4 (2006): 2313–30.

55. It is important to note that there has been a small degree of voice activity associated with the declining industry. For example, several shrimp-related organizations have developed as a response to the flood of foreign shrimp into the U.S. market. These organizations—led by the Southern Shrimp Alliance (SSA)—have engaged in a series of legal battles to impose tariffs on foreign shrimp that they claim are dumped onto U.S. shores. Many of the shrimpers I spoke with were dues-paying members of this organization but had not actively participated in the organization's activities. Most were very disgruntled with the organizations in general and lacked faith in their ability to bring about significant change. Those who paid dues did so mostly out of obligation or for purely symbolic reasons, and some admitted that they'd likely stop paying dues in the near future. The main problem shrimpers had with these organizations was the political infighting and bickering that took place at the meetings. But they were also skeptical of their power to reverse the decline. What could be done to save the industry, they asked me, except maybe fight for the imposition of tariffs, from which they could collect a little money? I was told by many trawlers

that they did not want any kind of government subsidy or ""handout," that they just wanted to earn an "honest living" on their own, as they had always done. Accepting "handouts" or "charity" was contradictory to the self-sufficiency norm that characterized Cajun cultural identity. But the prospect of making even just a little money was enough to continue paying their dues to the organizations fighting for subsidies.

Although it might be tempting to classify this activity as voice, to do so would be a mistake. At the time, organizations like the SSA were not fighting to decrease the amount of shrimp that came into this country, nor were they fighting to increase dockside prices that had dropped as a result of cheaper imports. Imports are the chief problem for domestic producers, and while imposing tariffs might result in a little extra money in the pockets of fishers, tariff monies do not come close to replacing income lost due to depressed dockside prices. Gulf Coast shrimpers are well aware that they lack the capability to meet the expanding demand for shrimp in this country. Working at full capacity, domestic shrimpers only supply around 10 percent of the nation's shrimp supply. They recognize the importance of imports. Those shrimpers who pay dues to the SSA or the Louisiana Shrimp Association, another organization founded in response to the import crisis, were primarily involved because of the hope of receiving compensation collected from the tariff money.

56. Jacques Henry and Carl Bankston III, *Blue Collar Bayou: Louisiana Cajuns in the New Economy of Ethnicity* (Westport, CT: Praeger Publishers, 2002).

57. Carl Bankston III and Jacques Henry, "Endogamy among Louisiana Cajuns: A Social Class Explanation," *Social Forces* 77, no. 4 (1999): 1317–38.

58. Through studying a variety of workplaces—from meteorology to kitchen work—Gary Alan Fine has written extensively on how workplaces function as arenas where individuals' senses of self are constructed, both individually and collectively. See Gary Alan Fine, *Kitchens: The Culture of Restaurant Work* (Berkeley: University of California Press, 1996). Other researchers have specified how worker socialization is often spatially defined, as in occupations that are limited to specific locales (mining, fishing, and farming). See, for example, Forrest Deseran and Carl M. Riden, "Troubled Water or Business as Usual: Ethnicity, Social Capital, and Community in the Louisiana Oyster Fishery," in *Communities of Work: Rural Restructuring in Local and Global* Contexts, ed. William K. Falk et. al (Athens: Ohio University Press, 2003), pp. 131–55; and Charles Vaught and David L. Smith, "Incorporation and Mechanical Solidarity in an Underground Coal Mine," *Work and Occupations* 7, no. 2 (May 1980): 159–87.

59. Anthony V. Margavio and Craig J. Forsyth, with Shirley Laska and James Mason, *Caught in the Net: The Conflict between Shrimpers and Conservationists* (College Station: Texas A&M University Press, 1996), p. 16.

60. Shrimp fishing is an extractive industry dependent upon the health of southern Louisiana's rich and unique ecosystem. The millions of acres of coastal marsh that border the entire southern region of the state serves as a nursery for many varieties of young fish and shellfish, including shrimp. The environment is what enables fishers to earn a living, but it also structures their leisure activities (hunting for ducks, deer, alligator, and nutria and also fishing). The existence of coastal marshes is essential for the continuation of harvesting wild shrimp, but it is highly vulnerable and presently imperiled by a host of threats. While the extent to which the coast was damaged by the recent oil spill is currently unknown, the coast faces another threat that is better understood but less recognized: coastal erosion. Due primarily to the permanent levying of the Mississippi in the 1930s that cut off the vital supply of sediment that built the delta upon which much of Louisiana sits, it is estimated that between twenty-five and thirty-five square miles of coastline are lost every year. Since the 1930s, around one million acres of wetlands have disappeared. The marshes not only provide fishers with the bounty of their catch, but they also serve as an important natural barrier to potential flooding by powerful storms. And so it is easy to see how environmental challenges pose a threat to the continuation of livelihood.

2. Identity

1. See Margavio et al., *Caught in the Net.*
2. Ibid.
3. In Florida, TEDs regulations were passed in 1988. Florida's waters are more turtle rich, and therefore there was less opposition from trawlers in these areas.
4. See "Kemp Ridley's Sea Turtle" (factsheet posted on the website for the U.S. Fish and Wildlife Service), accessed January 20, 2012, http://www.fws.gov/northflorida/SeaTurtles/Turtle %20Factsheets/PDF/Kemps-Ridley-Sea-Turtle.pdf.
5. Marks, "Effects of Economic Restructuring," p. 15.
6. Ronald Kline, *Consumers in the Country: Technology and Social Change in Rural America* (Baltimore: Johns Hopkins University Press, 2002).
7. Harry Targ et al., *Plant Closings: International Context and Social Costs* (Piscataway, NJ: Aldine Transactions, 1988).
8. See Henry and Bankston, *Blue Collar Bayou.*
9. Forrest Deseran and Carl M. Riden,"Troubled Water or Business as Usual: Ethnicity, Social Capital, and Community in the Louisiana Oyster Fishery," in *Communities of Work: Rural Restructuring in Local and Global Contexts*, ed. William K. Falk et al. (Athens: Ohio University Press, 2003), pp. 131–55.
10. Robert Lee Maril, *The Bay Shrimpers of Texas: Rural Fishermen in a Global Economy* (Lawrence: University of Kansas Press, 1995).
11. In their comparison of Texas and Louisiana shrimp fishers, Anthony Margavio and Craig Forsyth found that among Texas shrimpers, trawling with kin was uncommon. Louisiana, on the other hand, reported high rates of trawling with kin. See Margavio et al., *Caught in the Net.*
12. This is consistent with previous research that finds the tendency for Louisiana shrimpers to be slightly older than fishers in Texas and Alabama. For more, see Margavio et al., *Caught in the Net.*
13. Jacques Henry and Carl Bankston III, *Blue Collar Bayou: Louisiana Cajuns in the New Economy of Ethnicity* (Westport, CT: Praeger Publishers, 2002).
14. Toby A. Ten Eyck, "Situating Food: Economic and Cultural Aspects of Cajun Foodways," *Rural Sociology* 66 (2001): 227–43.
15. See Thomas Greider and Lorainne Garkovich, "Landscapes: The Social Construction of Nature and the Environment," *Rural Sociology,* 59, no. 1 (1994): 1–24.
16. Margavio et al., *Caught in the* Net, p. 16.
17. The economic restructuring is reflected in the U.S. Census data. In 1930 those employed in agriculture, forestry, or fishing comprised 38 percent of the total workforce (the largest occupational category). By 1950 this number had dropped to 18.3 percent and to 7.8 percent in 1960. What these numbers obscure, however, is the number of people continuing to shrimp on a part-time basis. See Henry and Bankston, *Blue Collar Bayou.*
18. Margavio et al., *Caught in the Net*, p. 27.

3. Loss

1. Phyllis Moen and Elaine Wethington, "The Concept of Family Adaptive Strategies," *Annual Review of Sociology* 18 (1992): 233–51; Louise Lamphere, *From Working Daughters to Working Mothers: Immigrant Women in a New England Industrial Community* (Ithaca, NY: Cornell University Press, 1987).
2. Ruth Milkman, *Farewell to the Factory: Auto Workers in the Late Twentieth Century* (Berkeley: University of California Press, 1997).

3. Margaret Nelson and Joan Smith, *Working Hard and Making Do: Surviving Small Town America* (Berkeley: University of California Press, 1999).

4. Innovation

1. This statement describes what fishing was like before the Deepwater Horizon Oil spill that occurred in April of 2010.

2. Margaret Condrasky, Ferdinand Viuya, and David Howell, "Measuring Product Difference By Sensory Analysis: The Case of Imported and U.S. Domestic Shrimp," *Foodservice Research International* 1, no. 16 (2005): 69–85.

3. See Randy Hodson, *Dignity at Work* (New York: Cambridge University Press, 2001).

4. These states are Alabama, Florida, Georgia, Louisiana, Mississippi, North Carolina, South Carolina, and Texas.

5. Of the two organizations, the SSA has been more politically successful in its accomplishments than the LSA. The SSA was instrumental in the legislative process that led to the 2005 imposition of antidumping duties on imported shrimp from Brazil, China, Ecuador, India, and Thailand. As of 2010, the duties resulted in about $186 million being made available to the domestic industry. However, most of that tariff money went into the hands of shrimp purchasers and processors (who are also members of the SSA), and shrimp fishers themselves did not benefit much. The SSA recognized this as problematic and issued a statement about it on its website that said, "The $186 million in collected antidumping duties that has been distributed to the domestic industry has overwhelmingly benefited shrimp purchasers and not fishermen. Thus, despite the influx of substantial funds into the hands of purchasers of shrimp, what shrimpers receive for their catch has continued to deteriorate" [SSA website, accessed October 20, 2011]. Inequalities like this was cited as the reason shrimp fishers put little faith in the SSA's ability to improve industrial conditions for them (recall that the relationship between fishers and purchaser has been rife with conflict and tensions). Shrimp fishers generally perceived organizations like the SSA and LSA as designed to benefit those with more power in the industry.

5. Docked

1. Sherry Lee Linkon and John Russo, *Steeltown USA: Work and Memory in Youngstown* (Lawrence: University of Kansas Press, 2002), pp. 67–68.

2. See S. V. Kasl and S. Cobb, "Some Mental Health Consequences of Plant Closing and Job Loss," in L. A. Ferman and J. P. Gordus, eds., *Mental Health and the Economy* (Kalamazoo, MI: W. E. Upjohn Institute, 1979), pp. 255–99 ; see also Terry Buss, *Shutdown at Youngstown* (Albany: State University of New York Press, 1983).

3. Robert Bruno, *Steelworker Alley: How Class Works in Youngstown* (Ithaca, NY: Cornell University/ILR Press, 1999), p. 17.

4. "Deepwater Horizon Response Consolidated Fish and Wildlife Collection Report: November 2, 2010." Posted on the website of the U.S. Fish and Wildlife Service, accessed November 14, 2011.

5. John Collins Rudloff, "Dead Coral Found Near Site of Spill with Oil Main Suspect," *New York Times*, November 6, 2010, p. A10.

6. See Wendy Parkins and Geoffrey Craig, "Culture and the Politics of Alternative Food Networks," *Food, Culture and Society* 12, no. 1 (2009): 77–103.

7. For more on the problems associated with intensive agricultural practices, see Pollan, *Omnivore's Dilemma*; see also Eric Schlosser, *Fast Food Nation: The Dark Side of the All American Meal* (New York: Harper Perennial Publishing, 2005); and Marion Nestle, *Food Politics: How the Food*

Industry Influences Nutrition and Health, rev. and expanded ed. (Berkeley: University of California Press, 2007).

8. Pollan, *Omnivore's Dilemma.*

9. Jim Carrier, "All You Can Eat: A Journey through a Seafood Fantasy," *Orion Magazine Online,* 2009, http://www.orionmagazine.org/index.php/articles/article/4395.

10. Susan Andreatta, "Marketing Strategies and Challenges of Small-Scale Organic Producers in Central North Carolina," *Culture and Agriculture* 22, no. 3 (2000): 40–50.

11. In a CSA, a farmer is prepaid in the winter or spring months for food that the consumer will later receive when the produce comes into season. For more on CSAs, see Thomas A. Lyson and Amy Guptill, "Commodity Agriculture, Civic Agriculture and the Future of U.S. Farming," *Rural Sociology* 69, no. 3 (2004): 370–85.

12. Parkins and Craig, "Culture and the Politics of Alternative Food Networks," p. 79.

13. Participants in this movement are not comprised solely of better-educated and more affluent individuals (although organic local produce remains a luxury that many can't afford). Recent research has shown that lower-income and more economically vulnerable households also recognize the benefits of participating in alternative food networks. See Susan Andreatta, Misty Rhyne, and Nicole Dery, "Lessons Learned from Advocating CSAs for Low-Income and Food Insecure Households," *Southern Rural Sociology* 23, no. 1 (2008): 116–48.

14. "Wild Gulf Coast Shrimp," in Slow Food USA's *Ark of Taste Catalog,* accessed July 7, 2009, http://www.slowfoodusa.org/index.php/programs/ark_product_detail/wild_gulf_coast_shrimp.

15. Martin Hall, D. L. Alverson, and K. I. Metuzals, "By-catch: Problems and Solutions," *Marine Pollution Bulletin* 41 (2000): 204–19.

16. This quote appeared in an op-ed entitled "Consumers Can Be Confident in the Safety of Gulf Seafood" that was written by Eric Schwaab (assistant administrator for NOAA's Fisheries Service), Donald Kraemer (deputy director, FDA's Center for Food Safety and Applied Nutrition), and Dr. Jimmy Guidry (Louisiana State health officer, Louisiana Department of Health and Hospitals). It appeared in numerous newspapers in early March 2011, and as of January 2012 it remained posted on the website of the U.S. Food and Drug Administration,http://www.fda.gov/Food/FoodSafety/Product-SpecificInformation/Seafood/ucm251969.htm.

17. Miriam Rotkin-Ellman, Karen K. Wong, and Gina M. Solomon, "Seafood Contamination after the BP Gulf Oil Spill and Risks to Vulnerable Populations: A Critique of the FDA Risk Assessment," *Environmental Health Perspectives,* posted on October 11, 2011, http://dx.doi.org/10.1289/ehp.1103695.

BIBLIOGRAPHY

Alderson, Arthur S. 1997. "Globalization and Deindustrialization: Direct Investment and the Decline of Manufacturing Employment in 17 OECD Nations." *Journal of World-Systems Research* 3:1–34.

Alderson, Arthur S., and Francois Nielson. 2002. "Globalization and the Great U-Turn: Income Inequality Trends in 16 OECD Countries." *American Journal of Sociology* 107, no. 5: 1244–99.

Amato, Paul R., and Brett Beattie. 2011. "Does the Unemployment Rate Affect the Divorce Rate? An Analysis of State Data 1960–2005." *Social Science Research* 40:705–15.

American Society for Microbiology. 2008. "Globalization impacts food safety standards in the United States." *Infectious Disease News*. July 1. http://www.infectiousdisease news.com/article/37077.aspx. Accessed June 29, 2009.

Ancelet, Barry Jean, Jay Edwards, and Glen Pitre. 1991. *Cajun Country*. Jackson: University Press of Mississippi.

Andreatta, Susan. 2000. "Marketing Strategies and Challenges of Small-Scale Organic Producers in Central North Carolina." *Culture and Agriculture* 22, no. 3: 40–50.

Andreatta, Susan, Misty Rhyne, and Nicole Dery. 2008. "Lessons Learned from Advocating CSAs for Low-Income and Food Insecure Households." *Southern Rural Sociology* 23, no. 1: 116–48.

Bankston III, Carl L., and Jacques Henry. 1999. "Endogamy among Louisiana Cajuns: A Social Class Explanation." *Social Forces* 77, no. 4: 1317–38.

Baron, James N., and Michael T. Hannon. 1994. "The Impact of Economics on Con-temporary Sociology." *Journal of Economic Literature* 22:1111–46.

Becnel, T. 1962. "A History of the Louisiana Shrimp Fishing Industry 1867–1961." MS thesis, Department of History, Louisiana State University.

Bell, Daniel. 1973. *The Coming of Post-Industrial Society: A Venture in Social Forecasting.* New York: Basic Books.

Belton, Ben, and David Little. 2008. "The Development of Aquaculture in Central Thailand." *Journal of Agrarian Change* 8, no. 1: 123–43.

Bluestone, Barry, and Bennett Harrison. 1982. *The Deindustrialization of America.* New York: Basic Books.

Brady, David, Jason Beckfield, and Wei Zhao. 2007. "The Consequences of Economic Globalization for Affluent Democracies."*Annual Review of Sociology* 33:313–34.

Brady, David, and Ryan Denniston. 2006. Economic Globalization, Industrialization and Deindustrialization in Affluent Democracies. *Social Forces* 85:297–329.

Brady, David, and Michael Wallace. 2000. "Spatialization, Foreign Direct Investment andLabor Outcomes in the American States, 1976–1996." *Social Forces* 79:67–100.

Bruno, Robert. 1999. *Steelworker Alley: How Class Works in Youngstown.* Ithaca, NY: Cornell University/ILR Press.

Burawoy, Michael. 1979. *Manufacturing Consent.* Chicago: University of Chicago Press.

Buss, Terry F. 1983. *Shutdown at Youngstown.* Albany: State University of New York Press.

Carrier, Jim. 2009. "All You Can Eat: A Journey through a Seafood Fantasy." *Orion Magazine Online.* http://www.orionmagazine.org/index.php/articles/article/4395.

Castells, Manuel. 2000. *The Rise of the Network Society.* 2nd ed. Oxford: Blackwell Publishing.

Clark, Colin. 1957. *The Conditions of Economic Progress.* London: Macmillan.

Condrasky, Margaret, Ferdinand Viuya, and David Howell. 2005. "Measuring Product Difference by Sensory Analysis: The Case of Imported and U.S. Domestic Shrimp." *Foodservice Research International* 1, no. 16: 69–85.

Cowie, Jefferson, and Joseph Heathcott. 2003. "The Meanings of Deindustrialization." In *Beyond the Ruins: The Meanings of Deindustrialization*, ed. Jefferson Cowie and Joseph Heathcott, pp. 1–18. Ithaca, NY: Cornell University Press.

Dandaneau, Stephen 1996. *A Town Abandoned: Flint, Michigan, Confronts Deindustrial-ization.* Albany: State University of New York Press.

DeLind, Laura. 1999. "Close Encounters with a CSA: The Reflections of a Bruised and Somewhat Wiser Anthropologist." *Agriculture and Human Values* 16:3–9.

DeSantis, John. 2003. "Processors Have Tradition, Legacy." *Houma Courier,* January 29.

Deseran, Forrest, and Carl M. Riden. 2003. "Troubled Water or Business as Usual: Eth-nicity, Social Capital, and Community in the Louisiana Oyster Fishery." In *Commu-nities of Work: Rural Restructuring in Local and Global Contexts*, ed. William K. Falk, Michael D. Schulman, and Ann R. Tickamyer, pp. 131–55. Athens: Ohio Univer-sity Press.

Dewatripont, Mathias, André Sapir, and Khalid Sekkat. 1999. *Trade and Jobs in Europe. Much Ado about Nothing?* New York: Oxford University Press.

Diop, Hamady. 1999. "Impact of Shrimp Imports on the United States' Southeastern Shrimp Processing Industry and Processed Shrimp Market." PhD diss., Department of Agricultural Economics, Louisiana State University.

Dollar, David, and Aart Kraay. 2002. "Spreading the Wealth." *Foreign Affairs* 81, no. 1: 120–33.

Dowding, Keith, Peter John, Thanos Mergoupis, and Mark Van Vugt. 2000. "Exit, Voice, and Loyalty: Analytic and Empirical Developments." *European Journal of Political Research* 37:469–95.

Dudley, Katherine. 1994. *The End of the Line: Lost Jobs, New Lives in Postindustrial America*. Chicago: University of Chicago Press.

Farrell, Dan. 1983. "Exit, Voice, Loyalty, and Neglect as Responses to Job Dissatisfaction: A Multidimensional Scaling Study." *Academy of Management Journal* 26:596–607.

Fine, Gary Alan. 1996. *Kitchens: The Culture of Restaurant Work*. Berkeley: University of California Press.

Food and Water Watch. 2007. "Import Alert: Government Fails Consumers, Falls Short on Seafood Inspections." http://www.foodandwaterwatch.org/reports/import-alert. Accessed January 13, 2012.

Friedland, Roger, and A. F. Robertson. 1990. *Beyond the Marketplace: Rethinking Economy and Society*. New York: Aldine de Gruyter.

Friedman, Tami. 2003. "A Trail of Ghost Towns across our Land: The Decline of Manufacturing in Yonkers, New York." In *Beyond the Ruins: The Meanings of Deindustrialization*, ed. Jefferson Cowie and Joseph Heathcott, pp. 19–43. Ithaca, NY: Cornell University Press.

Garkovich, Lorainne, Janet L. Bokemeier, and Barbara Foote. 1995. *Harvest of Hope: Family Farming/Farming Families,* Lexington: University of Kentucky Press.

Greider, Thomas, and Lorainne Garkovich. 1994. "Landscapes: The Social Construction of Nature and the Environment." *Rural Sociology* 59, no. 1: 1–24.

Grescoe, Taras. 2008. *Bottomfeeder: How to Eat Ethically in a World of Vanishing Seafood*. New York: Bloomsbury, USA.

Guillen, Mauro F. 2001. "Is Globalization Civilizing, Destructive or Feeble? A Critique of Five Key Debates in the Science Literature." *Annual Review of Sociology* 27:235–60.

Haby, Michael G., Nathaniel M. Rickard, and Lawrence L. Falconer. 2010. "Documentation to Support a Regional Petition from Shrimp Producers in the Gulf and South Atlantic States for Certification to Participate in the Trade Adjustment Assistance for Farmers Program Offered by the U.S.Department of Agriculture," document prepared for the Foreign Agricultural Service, U.S. Department of Agriculture, by extension specialists in the department of Agricultural Economics, Texas AgriLife Extension Service, Sea Grant College Program, The Texas A&M University System, April 12.

Hall, Martin A., D. L. Alverson, K. I. Metuzals. 2000. "By-catch: Problems and Solutions." *Marine Pollution Bulletin* 41:204–19.

Hareven, Tamara K. 1982. *Family Time and Industrial Time*. New York: Cambridge University Press.

Hein, Steven. 1995. "Skimmers: Their Development and Use in Coastal Louisiana." *Marine Fisheries Review* 57, no. 1: 17–24.

Henry, Jacques, and Carl Bankston III. 2002. *Blue Collar Bayou: Louisiana Cajuns in the New Economy of Ethnicity*. Westport, CT: Praeger Publishers.

Hironimus-Wendt, Robert J., and Fred Spannaus. 2007. "The Social Costs of Worker Displacement." *Social Policy* 37, no. 3/4, 83–89.

Hirschman, Albert O. 1970. *Exit, Voice, and Loyalty*. Cambridge, MA: Harvard University Press.

Hodson, Randy. 2001. *Dignity at Work*. New York: Cambridge University Press.

Hoffman, Elizabeth A. 2006. "Exit and Voice: Organizational Loyalty and Dispute Resolution Strategies." *Social Forces* 84, no. 4: 2313–30.

Holmström, Katrin, Sara Graslund, Ann Wahlstrom, Somlak Poungshompoo, Bengt-Erik Bengtsson, and Nils Kautsky. 2003. "Antibiotic use in shrimp farming and implications for environmental impacts and human health." *International Journal of Food Science and Technology* 38:255–66.

Illes, Louise Moser. 1996. *Sizing Down: Chronicle of a Plant Closing*. Ithaca, NY: Cornell University Press.

Jackson-Smith, Douglas B. 1999. "Understanding the Microdynamics of Farm Structural Change: Entry, Exit, and Restructuring among Wisconsin Family fFrmers in the 1980s." *Rural Sociology* 64, no. 1: 66–91.

Kline, Ronald. 2002. *Consumers in the Country: Technology and Social Change in Rural America*. Baltimore: Johns Hopkins University Press.

Kollmeyer, Christopher. 2009. "Explaining Deindustrialization: How Affluence, Productivity Growth, and Globalization Diminish Manufacturing Employment." *American Journal of Sociology* 114, no. 6: 1644–74.

LaFleur, Elizabeth, Diane Yeates, and Angelina Aysen. 2000. "Estimating the Economic Impact of the Wild Shrimp, *Paneaus* sp., Fishery: A Study of Terrebonne Parish, Louisiana." *Marine Fisheries Review* (Winter): 28–42.

Lamont, Michele. 2000. *The Dignity of Working Men: Morality and Boundaries of Race, Class and Immigration*. Cambridge, MA: Harvard University Press.

Lamphere, Louise. 1987. *From Working Daughters to Working Mothers: Immigrant Women in a New England IndustrialCcommunity*. Ithaca, NY: Cornell University Press.

Landry, Laura. 1990. "Shrimping in Louisiana: Overview of a Tradition." http://www.louisianafolklife.org/LT/Articles_Essays/creole_art_shrimping_overv.html. Accessed June 17, 2009.

Lewis, Roy R., Michael J. Philipps, Barry Clough, and Donald Macintosh. 2003. *Thematic Review on Coastal Wetland Habitats and Shrimp Aquaculture*. World Bank/NACA/WWF/FAO Consortium Program on Shrimp Farming and the Environment. URL: http://library.enaca.org/Shrimp/Case/Thematic/FinalMangrove.pdf.

Lieber, James B. *Friendly Takeover: How an Employee Buyout Saved a Steel Town*. New York: Viking Press, 1995.

Light, Donald W. 2003. "No Exit and the Organization of Voice: Market Boundaries and Social Movements in Health Care." Paper presented at the annual meeting of the American Sociological Association, Atlanta Hilton Hotel, Atlanta, GA, August 16.

Linkon, Sherry Lee, and John Russo. 2002. *Steeltown USA: Work and Memory in Youngstown.* Lawrence: University of Kansas Press.

Lobao, Linda. 1990. *Locality and Inequality: Farm and Industry Structure and Socioeconomic Conditions.* Albany: State University of New York Press.

Labao, Linda, and Kay Meyer. 2000. "Institutional Sources of Marginality: Midwestern Family Farming in a Period of Economic Decline." *Research in the Sociology of Work* 9:23–49.

Longworth, Richard. 2007. *Caught in the Middle: America's Heartland in the Age of Globalism.* New York: Bloomsbury Publishing.

Louisiana Department of Wildlife and Fisheries. 2000a. "Louisiana shrimp and shrimping." www.wlf.state.la.us/apps/netgear/index.asp?cn=lawlf&pid=689. Accessed June 23, 2009.

———. 2000b. "The Louisiana Shrimp Industry: A Preliminary Analysis of the Industry's Sectors." http://www.wlf.state.la.us/pdfs/education/La.%20Shrimp%20Industry.pdf. Accessed June 23, 2009.

Lynd, Staughton. 1987. "The Genesis of the Idea of a Community Right to Industrial Property in Youngstown and Pittsburgh, 1977–1987." *The Journal of American History* 74, no. 3: 926–58.

———. 1982. *The Fight against Shutdowns: Youngstown's Steel Mill Closings.* San Pedro, CA: Singlejack Publications.

Lyson, Thomas A., and Amy Guptill. 2004. "Commodity Agriculture, Civic Agriculture and the Future of U.S. Farming." *Rural Sociology* 69, no. 3: 370–85.

Margavio, Anthony V., and Craig J. Forsyth, with Shirley Laska and James Mason. 1996. *Caught in the Net: The Conflict between Shrimpers and Conservationists.* College Station: Texas A&M University Press.

Maril, Robert Lee. 1995. *The Bay Shrimpers of Texas: Rural Fishermen in a Global Economy.* Lawrence: University of Kansas Press.

Marks, Brian. 2005. "Effects of Economic Restructuring on Household Commodity Production in the Louisiana Shrimp Fishery." MS thesis, Department of Geography and Regional Development, University of Arizona.

Marks, S.A. 1991. *Southern Hunting in Black and White: Nature, History, and Ritual in a Carolina Community.* Princeton, NJ: Princeton University Press.

McDonald, Donna. 1990. "Shrimpers Arrested for Non-Compliance as Efforts to Enforce TED Regulations Intensify." *Marine Turtle Newsletter* 51:10–12.

Meyer, Katherine, and Linda Lobao. 2003. "Economic Hardship, Religion, and Mental Health during the Midwestern Farm Crisis." *Journal of Rural Studies* 19, no. 2: 139–55.

Milkman, Ruth. 1997. *Farewell to the Factory: Auto Workers in the Late Twentieth Century.* Berkeley: University of California Press.

Moen, Phyllis, and Elaine Wethington. 1992. "The Concept of Family Adaptive Strategies." *Annual Review of Sociology* 18:233–51.

Moore, Robert M., III. 2001. *The Hidden America: Social Problems in Rural America for the Twenty-first Century.* Cranbury, NJ: Associated University Presses.

Motkin-Ellman, Miriam, Karen K. Wong, and Gina M. Solomon. 2011. "Seafood Contamination after the BP Gulf Oil Spill and Risks to Vulnerable Populations:

A Critique of the FDA Risk Assessment." Environmental Health Perspectives. http://dx.doi.org/10.1289/ehp.1103695. Accessed November 15, 2011.

Mouawad, Jad. 2008. "Oil Prices Pass Record Set in '80s, but Then Recede." *New York Times* March 8, 2008.

Munton, Anthony G., and Michael A. West. 1995. "Innovations and personal change: patterns of adjustment to relocation." *Journal of Organizational Behavior* 16:363–75.

National Marine Fisheries Service. 2004. "NMFS New Orleans Market Shrimp Statistics for May and November 2001 and 2004." http://www.seafood.com. Accessed June 26, 2009.

Naus, Fons, Ad van Iterson, and Robert Roe. 2007. "Organizational Cynicism: Extending the Exit, Voice, Loyalty, and Neglect Model of Employees' Responses to Adverse Conditions in the Workplace." *Human Relations* 65, no. 5: 683–718.

Nelson, Margaret K., and Joan Smith. 1999. *Working Hard and Making Do: Surviving Small Town America.* Berkeley: University of California Press.

Nestle, Marion. 2007. *Food Politics: How the Food Industry Influences Nutrition and Health.* Rev. and expanded ed. Berkeley: University of California Press.

Parkins, Wendy, and Geoffrey Craig. 2009. "Culture and the Politics of Alternative Food Networks." *Food, Culture and Society* 12, no. 1: 77–103.

Perucci, Carolyn C., Robert Perucci, Dena B. Targ, and Harry R. Targ. 1988. *Plant Closings: International Context and Social Costs.* Hawthorne, NY: Adeline de Gruyer.

Pollan, Michael. 2006. *The Omnivore's Dilemma.* New York: Penguin Press.

Reich, Robert. 1992. *The Work of Nations: Preparing Ourselves for 21st Century Capitalism.* New York: Vintage Books.

Rotkin-Ellman, Miriam, Karen K. Wong, and Gina M. Solomon. 2011. "Seafood Contamination after the BP Gulf Oil Spill and Risks to Vulnerable Populations: A Critique of the FDA Risk Assessment." *Environmental Health Perspectives.* Posted on October 11, 2011. http://dx.doi.org/10.1289/ehp.1103695.

Rudloe, Jack, and Anne Rudloe. 2010. *Shrimp: The Endless Quest for Pink Gold.* Upper Saddle Brook, NJ: FT Press.

Rudloff, John Collins. 2010. "Dead Coral Found Near Site of Spill with Oil Main Suspect." *New York Times,* November 6, 2010, p. A10.

Rusbult, Caryl E., Dan Farrell, Glen Rogers, and Arch G. Mainous III. 1988. "Impact of Exchange Variables on Exit, Voice, Loyalty, and Neglect: An Integrative Model of Responses to Declining Job Satisfaction." *Academy of Management Journal* 31:599–627.

Sassen, Saskia. 2001. *The Global City: New York, London, Tokyo.* 2nd ed. Princeton, NJ: Princeton University Press.

Schlosser, Eric. 2005. *Fast Food Nation: The Dark Side of the All American Meal.* New York: Harper Perennial Publishing.

Schofer, Evan and Francisco J. Granados. 2006. "Environmentalism, Globalization and National Economies, 1980–2000." *Social Forces* 85, no. 2: 966–91.

Schwaab, Eric, Donald Kraemer, and Dr. Jimmy Guidry. 2011. "Consumers Can Be Confident in the Safety of Gulf Seafood." Op-ed published on Food and Drug Administration website. http://www.fda.gov/Food/FoodSafety/Product-SpecificInformation/Seafood/ucm251969.htm.

Sherman, Jennifer. 2006. "Coping With Rural Poverty: Economic Survival and Moral Capital in Rural America." *Social Forces* 85:892–913.

Siregar, P. 2001. Indonesia: Mounting Tensions over Industrial Shrimp Farming. *World Rainforest Movement Bulletin* 51. http://www.wrm.org.uy/bulletin/51/Indonesia. html.

Slow Food USA. 2009. "Wild Gulf Coast Shrimp." *Ark of Taste Catalog.* http://www. slowfoodusa.org/index.php/programs/ark_product_detail/wild_gulf_coast_ shrimp. Accessed July 7, 2009.

Smith, Vicki. .2002. *Crossing the Great Divide: Worker Risk and Opportunity in the New Economy.* Ithaca, NY: Cornell University/ILR Press.

Stonich, Susan C., and Peter Vandergeest. 2001. "Violence, Environment, and Industrial Shrimp Farming," In *Violent Environments*, ed. Nancy Peluso and Michael Watts, pp. 261–86. Ithaca, NY: Cornell University Press.

Targ, Harry, Dena Targ, Robert Perrucci, and Carolyn Perrucci. 1988. *Plant Closings: International Context and Social Costs.* Piscataway, NJ: Aldine Transactions.

Ten Eyck, Toby A. 2001. "Situating Food: Economic and Cultural Aspects of Cajun Foodways." *Rural Sociology* 66:227–43.

Tilley, Louisa A, and Joan W. Scott. 1987. *Women, Work and Family.* New York: Routledge Press.

United States Government Accounting Office. 2009. "Seafood Fraud: FDA Changes and Better Collaboration between Key Federal Agencies Could Improve Detection and Prevention." GAO 09–258. http://www.gao.gov/htext/d09258.html. Accessed June 23, 2009.

U.S. Fish and Wildlife Service. "Kemp Ridley's Sea Turtle." http://www.fws.gov/ northflorida/SeaTurtles/Turtle%20Factsheets/kemps-ridley-sea-turtle.htm. Accessed January 20, 2012.

———. "Deepwater Horizon Response Consolidated Fish and Wildlife Collection Report: November 2, 2010." http://www.restorethegulf.gov/sites/default/ files/documents/pdf/Consolidated%20Wildlife%20Table%20110210.pdf. Accessed November 14, 2011.

Valiela, I., J. L. Bowen, and J. K. York. 2001. "Mangrove Forests: One of the World's Threatened Major Tropical Environments." *BioScience* 51, no. 10: 807–15.

Vaught, Charles, and David L. Smith. 1980. "Incorporation and Mechanical Solidarity in an Underground Coal Mine." *Work and Occupations* 7, no. 2: 159–87.

Wallerstein, R., P. Condit. C. Kasper, J. Brown, F. Morrison F. 1969. "Statewide Study of Chloramphenicol \Ttherapy and Fatal Aplastic Anemia." *Journal of the American Medical Association* 208:2045.

West, M. A., N. Nicholson, and A. Rees, (1987). "Transitions into Newly Created Jobs." *Journal of Occupational Psychology* 60:97–113.

Withey, Michael J., and William H. Cooper. 1989. "Predicting Exit, Voice, Loyalty, and Neglect." *Administrative Science Quarterly* 34:521–39.

Wolf, Martin. 2004. *Why Globalization Works.* New Haven, CT: Yale University Press.

Wood, Adrian. 1994. *North-South Trade, Employment and Inequality.* Oxford: Clarendon Press.

Index

Numbers in *italics* refer to figures.

fiscal caution, 13
industrial decline, responses to, 31–33
    (*see also* adaptive innovators;
    exiters; persisters)
innovative adaptation, obstacles to,
    137–40
physical demands on, 44, 62
TEDs, protests and complaints
    against, 46–48, 49–51, 53
tensions with processors, 113
turtle planting sabotage, claims of,
    51–53
work ethic, 85–87
shrimp fishing
environmental impact of bottom
    trawling, 153
family affair, 74–75, 170n11
shrimp imports, 21, 26–27, *27,* 167n28
antidumping duties imposed on,
    171n5
See also farm-raised shrimp
shrimp industry, Louisiana, 11, 155,
    167n27
BP oil spill, threat of, 1–2, 116–17,
    148–50, 154–55, 164
coastal erosion, danger of, 169n60
cultural identity, shaping of, 73–74
decline of, 6–8, *22,* 22–23, 93–94,
    143–44
economic importance, 21–22, 73
owner-operatorship, rise of, 18
price fluctuations, 18–19
structure of, 12–13, 19, *20,* 21–22,
    166n20
technological advances, 17 (*see also*
    on-board freezer technology)
See also dockside dealers; import cri-
    sis; processors; shrimp fishers
shrimp industry, U.S.
farm-raised versus wild-harvested,
    27, *27*
imports, 21, 26–27, *27,* 167n28
shrimp market, U.S. , *26,* 26–27
shrimp processors. *See* processors
Shrimp Task Force, 140
skimmer net, 17

Slow Food USA, 153
southern Louisiana, 37, 164
contribution of fishing industry to the
    landscape, 81–82
cultural identity, 83
oil industry and, 30, 83–84
rich natural environment, 38–39, 73,
    80, 169n60
Southern Shrimp Alliance (SSA),
    130–31, 168–69n55, 171n5
steel industry, U.S.
collapse of, 8
sense of belonging among workers,
    147–48
suicide, 66–67
survey method, 158

TEDs (turtle excluder devices), 153, 170n3
shrimp fishers' protests and com-
    plaints against, 46–48, 49–51, 53
Terrebonne Parish, 22
Texas, 170n11
Thailand, 8, 25, 27, *27,* 171n5
trawling, environmental impact of, 153
turtle excluder devices, 153, 170n3. *See*
    TEDs

U.S. Fish and Wildlife Service, 51, 149

Vietnam, 8, 27, *27*
voice, 34

White Boot Brigade (WBB), 116,
    131–32, 152
Whole Foods Markets, 115, 152, 155
wild-harvested shrimp, *27, 27,* 152–53
Williams-Sonoma, 132
work
as expression of identity, 147
multidimensionality of, 15
workforce, U.S.
economic restructuring of, 170n17

Youngstown, Ohio, 8–9, 28, 147

Zhao, Wei, 14